Miles Away: Adventures In Tourism

Contents

Introduction	4
Chapter One: London, England, U.K. – September 1983	7
Chapter Two: England, Scotland, and Wales, U.K and Republic of Ireland – July and August 1984	25
Chapter Three: Kenya and The Netherlands – September 1988	41
Chapter Four: Iceland – July 1989	58
Chapter Five: Morocco – October 1990	68
Chapter Six: Vietnam – February and March 1999	80
Chapter Seven: Ecuador/Galapagos Islands and Peru – October 2001	103
Chapter Eight: Costa Rica – April 2002	123

Chapter Nine: Argentina and Antarctica – November and
                    December 2003   141

Chapter Ten: China – June 2005   160

Chapter Eleven: Turkey – June 2006   189

Chapter Twelve: Indonesia – April and May 2019   210

Postscript   249

Post-Postscript   251

There and Back Again (Flight Routing)   252

How Many Miles Away?
(Distances from Albany, New York)   255

Introduction

Library and bookstore shelves are filled with the memoirs and adventures of men and women who refer to themselves as *travelers*. Some are swashbuckling, machete-wielding bushwhackers, hacking through the Amazon or the Congo. Some have immersed themselves in exotic cultures, becoming honorary tribe members. Some have climbed to heights, or descended to depths, or crossed broad widths. Some have tangled with bandits, corrupt police, child soldiers, wild animals. They have slept on floors, ridden atop dangerously overcrowded buses, eaten eyeballs and tentacles, escaped from foreign jails, contracted exotic diseases. They have been away from home for months or years at a time. The ones who make it home alive write books.

This is not one of those books.

Those intrepid travelers often express a chauvinistic disdain for *tourists*. To them the tourist is a cheater, a fraud, a dilettante. The tourist is just a gawker, an interloper, skimming the surface of a place without getting to know or understand it, Coke or Budweiser firmly in hand as they complain about how spicy the food is and how dirty the children are.

But I would suggest that there are actually two main types of tourist. The first bunch is exactly as just described – middle or upper class dullards with a little too much time and money on their hands who just have to "do" Paris before they die (and, of course, buy an Arc de Triomphe refrigerator magnet before they leave).

But the second group consists of people who have a genuine interest in the people and places they visit and who show a great deal of respect for differences they encounter, for unusual foods and strange customs. What they lack is the willingness to risk their lives, the vigor to climb a mountain, or simply the financial resources or the time away from family, friends, home, and job that would be required for longer, fuller explorations.

So, in writing this book, I would like to represent this second type of tourist. Yes, I like to have the way smoothed for me a bit, the language barriers bridged for me. I like comfy beds and swimming pools and air conditioning. I like vehicles with good shock absorbers. But I'm also genuinely interested in getting to know the places I visit, as well as can be done in a short space of time.

The type-one tourists can keep their refrigerator magnets. The travelers can keep their machetes. What follows is an account of *my* adventures, such as they have been.

Travel is the stuff of memories but memories become fuzzier with the passage of time. My travels span nearly forty years and the longer ago the trip was, the less sharply detailed it now is in my mind. Notes and photographs can only jog my memory just so much. After that, I have just my impressionistic sense of the places I've been. Therefore, as you read through these chapters, you will notice them becoming a bit more detailed, trip after trip. That is simply a reflection of time and distance.

If I can bring my view of the world into *your* world, I have done my job here. If you are inspired to follow in any of my footsteps, so much the better. Bon voyage and happy travels to you!

CHAPTER ONE: LONDON, ENGLAND, U.K. – SEPTEMBER 1983

Maybe I was feeling a little suggestible. After all, I was more than a little drunk. But it suddenly sounded like a very good idea. London. For a week. Yeah! Why not? I'd start looking into it in the morning, if I wasn't hungover.

I had just attended a retirement party for my boss where I'd had the poor judgment to get drunk but the good sense to call for a ride home before it went too far. My mother had come to pick me up and for some reason had spent the entire ride home talking me into using some of my meager income to do some traveling. Yes, I had said with alcohol-fueled enthusiasm, I had long been wanting to visit London. My mother thought this an excellent choice, Travel 101 for beginners, a destination safe, not too far away, not too expensive, and English-speaking. By the time my buzz wore off I had Plans (always to be capitalized), or at least I planned to have Plans.

As I have come to realize, travel isn't just about hopping in the car, or a train, or a boat, or a bus, or an airplane. It isn't just about poking around ancient ruins, wandering down narrow alleys in historic cities, watching the wildlife, taking in the scenery, and floating in tropical swimming pools under palm-laced skies. It isn't just about ballooning and rafting and snorkeling in shark-infested waters. It isn't just about exotic cultures, foreign languages, strange currency, and unfamiliar food. No, travel is also about the research, the planning, and, above all else, the anticipation. Travel is about putting together and executing the Plans. And at twenty-five, and on a bank clerk's salary, I could just barely afford the most meager of Plans.

Not long after that fateful evening, I found myself walking into the Liberty Travel office on the second floor of a local mall. I told them what I was looking for and that it needed to be cheap. A little while later, and an affordable $574 poorer, I walked out with my very first set of honest-to-goodness travel Plans. I had booked a charter flight operated by Arrow Airlines, which would gain some unwanted notoriety two years later when another of its charter flights crashed in Newfoundland while bringing US troops home for the Christmas holidays. I had bought a round-trip seat on the airport bus connecting Albany to New York City's airports. And I had booked eight bargain-basement nights at the very British-sounding Pembridge Square Hotel. I didn't intend to spend much time in my room.

Eight nights is not a long trip and so I had just a small suitcase and a carry-on bag with me when I arrived at JFK for my overnight flight to London. Arrow Airlines was a small operation running mostly charter flights like the one I was booked on, so they had no permanent counter location at JFK. After a bit of confused searching I was able to check in for the flight, only to be informed that our departure would be delayed by three hours. Seems they were having a problem closing one of the doors. My fellow passengers and I were invited to wait in Arrow's luxurious lounge, which meant sitting on the floor of a little-trafficked hallway, leaning against the white walls, until an Arrow representative eventually appeared to tell us exactly what the hell was going on. They had managed to solve their door problem (a little Super Glue here, a paper clip there, a twisted wire coat hanger to hold it all together, I assumed) and we would be boarding soon. Although I had flown once or twice as a baby, this would be my first real flight experience and I'd already been a bit apprehensive. Realizing that a door opening in mid-flight might not be such a good thing, but having an already-paid-for $25-a-night room waiting for me in London, I accepted my fate and shuffled my way forward to my almost certain doom aboard Arrow Airlines.

After taking my seat, settling in, and surveying my surroundings, I was pleased to note a Catholic priest in a seat nearby. As we were about to ascend to high places, I figured it couldn't hurt to have a neighbor with a hotline to even higher places. I leaned my head back and wondered what takeoff would be like.

Taxiing to the runway was like riding on a slow, wobbly bus. But once we reached the head of the runway I knew the time had come to experience my first takeoff. The engines started to whine, higher and higher, and then we began to roll, picking up speed and then more speed. The ground began rushing by outside, faster and faster, the plane rumbling and bouncing slightly. The bouncing stopped, the rumbling faded and we were airborne.

It seemed to take forever to gain altitude. I would come to realize that that is always my reaction - "Why is it taking so long to gain altitude?" - and not a fault with the airplane. As we rose above New York City I could see other planes zigzagging below us and hoped that the air traffic controllers had gotten enough sleep. But soon we were out over the dark

Atlantic, the lights of the city fading away.

      I couldn't sleep. Half an hour after leaving New York we'd landed in Boston for a refueling stop. The needle must have been pushing "E" all the way. I'd felt like running into the terminal for a can of soda and a bag of chips, maybe a lottery ticket. But I was soon experiencing my second takeoff and we were out over the ocean again, next stop (with luck) London. But I couldn't sleep.

      I had heard all about jet lag and how important it was to try to sleep on the flight. But even though it was after midnight in whatever time zone I called home, and there was nothing but darkness to see out the window, and sitting on the plane was less interesting than sitting in the departure lounge had been, I still couldn't sleep. It wasn't apprehension keeping me awake. It was just the novelty of it all. Plus, in just a few hours I would be in London. London! And then there would be work to do.

      The plane touched down mid-morning at Gatwick, London's lesser airport (think LaGuardia vs. JFK). While Heathrow was receiving the major airlines and the rich and famous spilling from their first-class sections, my charter flight was only good enough to merit a landing at Gatwick, an hour-long train ride to London's south.

      With the ink still wet on my passport's first official stamp, I followed the signs to the ticket window and bought a seat on the next train into London. As the train made its way north I gazed out the window, waiting for my first real glimpse of one of the world's great cities. We were rattling along through the southern outskirts, past a semi-industrial landscape of scrap metal yards, crumbling concrete, and crappy cinder block houses with clothes drying on fraying lines, a little taste of the Bronx in England. It went on for miles but eventually, before

London had even really come into view, the train plunged underground and we crossed beneath the Thames and into the heart of London, beating somewhere above us.

The train finally emerged like some sort of tunneling rodent into the depths of Victoria Station and I, suitcase and carry-on in hand, walked up and out through a huge arched opening onto a life-sized movie set called London.

At least it seemed like a movie set. Everything looked stern and ancient, brooding gray stone buildings facing the station, the massive Westminster Cathedral just up the street to my left, red double-decker London buses driving past, movie-set extras playing ordinary Brits walking by in all directions. I confess that I was a bit overwhelmed. I wasn't in Kansas anymore, Toto. As relatively safe and easy a first destination as London was, it was still very much *somewhere else* and even had quite a bit of the some*when* else to it. Of course, some of that was just big city shock, something I might have felt a bit of in Manhattan as well. But once the initial shock wore off I was eager to explore. There was just one small detail to sort out first – I had no idea where I was going.

The only address I had for my hotel was 25 Pembridge Square, London. I had been unable to locate any such place on any of my maps. So I turned my back on the movie going on outside and went back into Victoria Station in search of an information counter.

Victoria Station is one of London's busiest travel hubs, a constant coming and going of thousands of people intent on reaching their destinations, and so, of course, has the most well-informed information desk in all of London. And, of course, they also had no idea where Pembridge Square might be.

Alan didn't have a clue so he called Betty over and the two of them searched their maps in vain until Graham wandered past and was roped into the search party. Just when all seemed lost, Colin vaguely remembered where the city of

London may have misplaced this rather forgotten square. It turned out not to be all that far from Victoria Station, although considerably more of a walk than I cared for with two fully-laden bags, plus the two other bags forming beneath my eyes from lack of sleep. I was provided with the name of the Underground stop where I should get off and a set of directions from there to Pembridge Square. There was just one more thing I needed before I set off.

I knew I would be traveling all over the city for the next eight days and I wanted to get a pre-paid travel pass, which would be good on all the trains and buses. Colin, Betty, and the gang heaved a collective sigh of relief at this softball question and told me exactly what to do and where to go. Their instructions seemed a strange mix of screwball comedy and spy thriller but I was determined to follow them and get this mission done, the sooner to be able to collapse on my $25-dollar-a-night bed at the good old Pembridge Square Hotel. And so I set off for my first appearance in the movie called London.

My first task was to have my picture taken at one of the photo booths in the station. With knees wedged against baggage I fed a pound note (I had changed some dollars into pounds before leaving Albany, a hassle I have forgone on all subsequent travels) into the machine and soon had a set of four droopy-eyed pictures of myself in hand. My instructions had me next leave the station through that huge archway, turn right, and make my way up the street, with another right turn, then a left, and so on, twisting through the neighborhood directly behind the station, until I came to a firehouse with four firetrucks occupying four bays. I was to walk past the firetruck on the extreme right-hand side and then enter, walking alongside the last truck until I came to a door in the right rear corner of the firehouse. I was to go through that door and then up a flight of stairs leading to a formidable-looking wooden double door. And there, through those doors, hidden away in the upper floor of an ordinary fire station, was the Issuer of Transit Passes, an elderly, bespectacled man behind a forbidding counter, a veritable Wizard of all things transit-related, the Pope of Passes, the Dean of Double-Deckers, Lord of the Underground. This huge room full of benches and tables was nearly empty and my footsteps echoed as I approached the inner sanctum of his domain, the Counter of Doom. He checked my paperwork severely, examined my photo suspiciously, held my pound notes up to the thin light leaking through the room's small, grimy window and then, with a flourish of gluing and stamping, with just a little throat-clearing to express his disapproval, approved my petition to suffer my presence on his trains and buses for the next week. I was good to go.

I backed away from the counter, backed away all the way to the door, then bolted for the stairs back down to the firehouse, brushed past the firetrucks, and never looked back as I tried to remember how to twist my way back to Victoria Station.

All I had to do was get off at the Bayswater station and follow the directions to the hotel. That seemed simple enough. Getting to Bayswater was a breeze. The London Underground was a wonderful maze of crisscrossing lines and little stations, with bigger, busier stations where more than one line intersected, all the different color-coded lines represented in the delightful spaghetti-tangle of the London Underground Map. To some the Map was a confusing jumble of green and yellow and brown and orange (plus gray, black, red, light and dark blue) lines. To me it looked the way my car's engine must look to my mechanic – it was perfectly clear to me how it all fit together. The subway trains came and left frequently and were by far the easiest and fastest way to get around the city. By contrast, the buses were crowded and confusing and I could never find a good reason to hop aboard one, as I never had a clue where they were going.

It was 1983 and punk fashion was still in

style, with many purple, red, blue, or green Mohawks enlivening the subway platforms and cars. I didn't need to stalk through the African bush to observe exotic plumage, it was right here in front of me, leaning, smoking, pacing, checking the arrival time on the electronic board mounted overhead.

So I took the Circle Line from Victoria to Bayswater, going underground amid the imposing edifices surrounding Victoria Station and popping up again minutes (and centuries) later on the hip strip called Queensway.

Queensway was what the guidebooks like to call "trendy". In other words, it was swarming with people under the age of forty. There were restaurants, pubs, shops. In the evening there was nightlife. At a small grocery store on Queensway I would often purchase food for another budget-saving dinner in my hotel room. But checking things out would have to wait – I was still lugging two bags with me and I needed to stop and check my directions. It seemed simple enough – exiting the Bayswater station I was to turn left on Queensway, then left again onto Moscow Road, then straight on to Pembridge Square. Half an hour later I turned a corner to find myself back on Moscow Road. My bags were like two elephants strapped to my hands. I knew I'd find Pembridge Square if I kept walking in ever-widening circles. It was past noon and I just wanted to arrive, take a deep breath, and go out exploring without the cinder blocks dangling from my hands. Mercifully, it wasn't raining, but in London that can change quickly. And then, suddenly, there it was – Pembridge Square!

After checking in and finally being able to set my bags down and rest for a moment, it was time to take stock of my surroundings. First, my $25 a night room: bed, chair, toilet, sink, telephone, window. A radio built into the bed's headboard had a knob that could be turned to one of four settings: BBCs 1, 2, 3, and 4. There was a shower room down the hall. If I wanted to watch TV I could go down to the ground-floor parlor and park myself in a stiff-backed chair and watch whatever Nigel and Harriet (or whatever their names were) were watching. Next to that was the dining room where each morning I would be served a continental breakfast (thimbleful of sour orange juice, stale roll with butter) if I felt like choking it down.

I spread my London map out on the bed and mentally sectioned it into eight pieces, one piece for each day I would be there. One of the pieces was a side-visit to nearby Greenwich. I wasn't quite sure of the distance involved, but it seemed the London Underground would get me close enough to hike the rest of the way. I set it aside for day eight and began concentrating on London itself.

There were a handful of places I knew I wanted to visit – the Tower of London, Buckingham Palace (for the changing of the guard), Abbey Road Studios, Whitechapel, Westminster Abbey, Trafalgar Square, the British Museum. Each would be the centerpiece of my sightseeing for that day. Logistics completed, and half a day shot already, I grabbed my camera and my umbrella and headed back to the Bayswater station. Now unburdened by baggage, transit pass in hand, and with a better understanding of where I was, I was free to stroll, wander, and generally poke around.

The first thing I noticed was that my hotel was in a neighborhood of small, tidy houses, mostly white with picket fences and flower boxes, a modest and quiet neighborhood of umbrella-toting folks going about their quite proper English lives – I imagined tea kettles and biscuit tins and umbrella stands in every home. Just a few blocks away, down in the Bayswater tube station, the proper English mixed with the improper – Sid Vicious lookalikes and giggling schoolgirls – as well as plenty of tourists, maps and guidebooks splayed in their hands, some with puzzled looks on their faces. They were speaking French, German, Swedish, a dozen other languages. I couldn't understand a single word but I knew exactly what they were saying, pointing at their maps - "We're right *here*, right? If we get off at this station, *here*, we can transfer to this red line going east. That should get us to St. Paul's." "Are you *sure*?" "No, but I *think* that's right."

Wind signaled the train's arrival, the train pushing a plug of air ahead of it through the tunnel. I got on and headed back to Victoria Station.

Turning left out of Victoria Station, I walked up the road a short distance until I came to Westminster Cathedral. I had read that the cathedral had a 200-foot tower that could be visited. A bird's eye view of London seemed like the perfect way to begin my explorations.

There was a creaky old elevator to the top of the tower, and a creaky old man operating it. It was just the two of us as we ascended within the brick tower and the old man informed me that my timing couldn't have been better. Apparently, he was the one and only Keeper of the Tower and had been taking people up in his elevator every day, without fail, for the past thirty-two years (or was it thirty-six? thirty-one? does it matter?). But yesterday he had not felt well enough to fulfill his duties and so the tower had been closed.

London's skyline has changed a bit since then but at the time it was not particularly impressive. Most of the city having been built centuries before, the only buildings reaching higher than their surroundings were the various famous old cathedrals, abbeys, and towers. There wasn't much of the modern steel-and-glass architecture. And so I mainly found myself looking down on rooftops from my 200-foot perch, surveying a 360 degree panorama of the city as it sprawled away to the horizon. After a few minutes I asked to go back down. The nearby Westminster Abbey was my next destination.

Any decent London guidebook can describe the places I visited better than I can, so I offer here a few of my own personal thoughts and highlights:

In St. James' Park there is a small lake full of various birds. From the middle of the bridge across the lake there are wonderful views of Buckingham Palace in one direction and the Horse Guards in the other direction. I could have rested there for hours.

Seeing the Rosetta Stone at the British Museum. Over the years since, my memory has transformed the Rosetta Stone into a fat cube, which it is not (it's a foot thick and mostly flat). But I swear I remember everything else *perfectly*. Uh-huh. (To be fair, the Rosetta Stone *has* changed since I viewed it – in 1999 it was cleaned, removing chalk and wax that had been added to make it more legible and to protect it from the elements.)

Watching people being attacked by pigeons. This is great fun. Trafalgar Square is teeming with pigeons and there are vendors there who will sell you cups of pigeon treats so you can feed the birds. Don't fall into this trap. As soon as the treats are purchased, the well-intentioned victim is immediately swarmed by dozens of unruly pigeons. If you've ever seen Alfred Hitchcock's *The Birds* you get the picture.

Walking across the crosswalk near Abbey Road Studios, recreating the iconic Beatles album cover (if the Beatles had been a one man band).

Learning that having a little bird drop a dripping white gift onto your shoulder is a great way to get a little extra elbow room while watching the changing of the guard at Buckingham Palace.

Fish and chips. Greasy as hell but I had to

have it once while in London.

Bringing an umbrella with me as I left the hotel on a sunny morning. I would almost always need it by noon.

The Underground. The *Tube*. I fell in love with subway travel on this trip and have sought out the subway experience anywhere I can ever since. Who knew Pittsburgh has a subway?

Trying to find Oscar Wilde's house in Chelsea, the rain sweeping across the Thames and into my face the whole time, forcing me to give up on my umbrella lest it be shredded.

More fish and chips. Okay, okay, I had it twice.

Eric The Australian

One day about halfway into the trip I was minding my own business, perusing my map while wandering along in some neighborhood I can no longer recall, when I heard someone call out to me.
"Hey, mate!"
I turned to see a man crossing the street toward me. He was thirty-five-ish and wrapped in a rumpled brown coat, ruddy face peeking out from a wild tangle of hair. He thrust one hand at me from within his coat's wrinkled sleeve.
"How are ya, name's Eric", he said, shaking my hand before I could even react.
"You know if there are any pubs 'round here?"

It was just past noon and so, of course, time to nip into the nearest tavern for a leisurely pint. Sounded like a good idea to me, too.

I assured him that, in spite of the fact that I didn't even know the name of the neighborhood we were standing in, it would be easy as steak and kidney pie to find someplace suitable. London abounds with local drinking spots with names like *The Crow's Bladder* or *The Old Fox and Bucket*. Surely there must be one around the next corner, no matter what direction we chose. And there was.

We settled in amongst the lunchtime crowd at *The Queen's Rump* (or was it *The Iron Pudding*?), setting ourselves and our pints of Guinness down at a table. I soon knew all about Eric the Australian and what he was doing in this part of the world.

According to him, he was a buyer and seller of diamonds, shuttling back and forth between Brussels, London, and Amsterdam. I should go with him to Amsterdam for a quick day trip, he was saying. We'd take a morning train, spend the afternoon in Amsterdam, and be back in London in time for a late dinner. All on him, of course, he told me, removing an unruly wad of pounds and guilders from a pants pocket (the Euro wouldn't come into existence until 2002). He was loud and chatty, bordering on obnoxious, a self-contained whirlwind, jumping from subject to subject like an acrobat.

Eric was curious about all aspects of politics in the USA and we were soon discussing the current president, Ronald Reagan. Before long we had moved on to Jimmy Carter, Gerald Ford's pratfalls, Edmund Muskie's tears, and Richard Nixon. When had Nixon first won national office, he wondered aloud, and we discussed the possibilities.

"It had to have been after the end of World War Two", I surmised, "but before he ran for vice president in 1952. So it must have been '46, '48, or '50. Congressman, I'd guess".

Eric was keen to gamble on it.

"Tell you what. Twenty pounds. You pick two of those years and I'll take whatever's left over".

The bet seemed overly generous but Eric could barely contain his enthusiasm for it and his pockets could barely contain all of his crumpled money. I chose '48 and '50, leaving him with 1946. Glasses empty, we set off in search of a library (as people did in those pre-internet times).

Libraries are almost as numerous as pubs in London so we were soon searching the shelves for a reference book that would settle the bet. Any encyclopedia would have a section on Nixon, so we pulled down the "N" volume of one of them and flipped it open, twenty pounds hanging in the balance.

It turned out that Nixon had been elected to the House in 1946. Ouch. I handed Eric twenty pounds to crumple up. I would have to stop at the little grocery store on Queensway before returning to the hotel. With a twenty pound hole blown in my limited budget, dinner would be a little bit of ham, a little bit of cheese, a couple of crusty rolls, and a can of something to wash it down. And the same thing again tomorrow, and tomorrow again.

It figures the guy with all the money also has all the luck, I mused as Eric and I walked toward the nearest tube station. Or was it luck? I began to feel a little paranoid. Was this some sort of scam? Diamond dealer my ass! Did Eric have different versions of different encyclopedias scattered around London, giving him whatever answer he might need to any question? Or was I just stupid and unlucky? I'll never be sure, but 1946 *was* the right answer anyway, as I later confirmed for myself.

Parting ways at the tube station, Eric suggested I meet him out for a drink that night. He jotted down my hotel phone number and said he'd call around eight.

Figuring I'd probably never see Eric the

Australian again, I enjoyed my ham and cheese sandwiches in my room while serenaded by BBC4. Eight o'clock came. The phone rang. It was Eric.

He told me he was at a place near Piccadilly Circus called *The Tavern* or *The Pub* or *The Tavern Pub* or something like that, I couldn't miss it, and that he was sitting with a couple of girls he'd chatted up. "So get on over here, mate, let's get the party started!"

An hour later I got off the tube at the Piccadilly station. Five major roads converge at Piccadilly, forming a massive traffic circle that is the "circus". Which way to go? The majority of lights and people seemed to be gathered on the other side of the circus from me, so I made my way across and wandered into neighboring Soho, toward the theater district. I asked a policeman I came across if he knew of anywhere nearby named *The Tavern* or *The Pub*. He had no idea. I kept walking.

A scenario like this would never occur these days. We'd just whip out our phones and triangulate. Actually, that's a lie. Anyone who knows me knows I still don't own a cellphone. I kept going. Maybe there was something around the next corner. There was.

The *St. James Tavern* loomed just ahead. That must be it! I opened the door and stepped inside.

Despite the flow of people outside, there wasn't much going on at The *St. James*. I surveyed the room. No Eric. I ordered a beer at the bar and sat down to consider my options. One beer later I decided to just continue up the road. If I found Eric, so be it. If not, I might as well make the most of things and have a look around this busy area.

Mr. and Mrs. Tourist Couple have probably read that they must visit Piccadilly at night, and bring the kids. Well, yes and no.

As I wandered through Soho toward Leicester Square and the theater district I passed through an area dominated by X-rated theaters, strip clubs, and many, many clip joints. If you don't know what a clip joint is, let me explain it. A clip joint is like a spider's web for men looking for "action", whether that action be prostitution, naked women, or something hovering somewhere between. All you have to do is step inside, pay a modest entry fee, and go down the stairs. In that basement you will find empty tables and an empty stage. But not to worry, it's just a little slow tonight and the show will begin shortly. A scantily-clad waitress approaches and you, of course, order a drink. She brings your drink and sits with you while you wait for the show to begin. She's chatty, friendly, a little touchy-feely. She excuses herself and soon returns with the bill for your drink – a modest price for the drink plus a jaw-dropping charge for whatever they feel like calling it - "entertainment services", "hostess fee", and the like. The bill can run to a hundred dollars or more. You suddenly realize you've been had, there is no "show" and no other customers. You refuse to pay, they insist, you sputter and fume and head for the stairs back up. There is a man at the top of the stairs with a cricket bat or an iron pipe or something equally threatening. You must pay before leaving. In these days of the cell phone I suppose you might try calling the police. In 1983 you just paid.

There were dozens of these places strung out along the tangle of streets, like spiders who all built their webs on the same chain-link fence. And here were tourist couples with kids in tow walking past them like they were at Disneyland. I'd have loved to hear some of the questions the kids might ask back at the hotel. "Mommy, what's a live sex show?" "Daddy, what's a peep show?"

But don't let me confuse you – most of these rip-off joints have been closed in recent years and London these days has a slew of hair salons called The Clip Joint. So don't be afraid to have your hair cut while in London. The hairdresser probably won't be wielding an iron pipe.

The Soho scene grew stale quickly and I eventually gave up and took the tube back to my hotel. I never did find Eric or hear from him again.

The last day of the trip arrived – time to see if I'd judged my map correctly and I could reach Greenwich. According to the map, I could take the underground to its most extreme southeastern station, New Cross, and then walk from there, although exactly how far was a little unclear, maybe two miles, maybe four. It would be a full day undertaking.

The train came up out of the ground well before reaching New Cross and bumped along the rest of the way as a regular train. London was thinning out to almost nothing here and when I finally reached the New Cross station it felt like a frontier outpost, the end of the line, the edge of the world. But a road ran in front of it and I turned left and started walking.

About halfway, as it turned out, to Greenwich I stopped for lunch at a Wimpy's, England's answer to McDonald's. But unlike the uniformity of the latter franchise, every Wimpy's I had walked into so far had been different. One had been the old familiar paper-hats-and-stainless-steel-counter burger joint like McDonald's. One had been a sit-down restaurant with waitresses and menus. The one on the road to Greenwich was like a 1950s diner, with a linoleum counter and an actual blender for making milk shakes. I wouldn't have been surprised to see Fonzie walk in and punch the jukebox. The menu was the same at each, but the execution of it was completely different. Fueled up, I continued on my way.

Greenwich turned out to be no more than two miles or so from New Cross so I had plenty of time and energy left to look around. Near the Royal Observatory there is a line on the ground that one can stand on. It is the Prime Meridian, the line that divides East from West (or the line that joins them together, depending on your perspective). I stood with one foot in the Western Hemisphere and one foot in the Eastern Hemisphere and pointed the camera at my feet.

Down by the Thames sat two famous sailing ships, the 19th century clipper ship *Cutty Sark* and one of 20th century fame, the relatively tiny *Gipsy Moth IV*.

The *Cutty Sark* was one of the last great sailing ships and is an English icon, though most Americans are probably more familiar with it as a brand of booze. Built in 1869 for the cost of approximately twenty thousand dollars, it had been sitting on display at the docks in Greenwich since 1954. In 2007 it was extensively damaged by fire. Since then at least sixty million dollars has been spent restoring this twenty thousand dollar ship.

The little *Gipsy Moth IV* had famously been sailed solo around the world in 1966-67 by Sir Francis Chichester. It is no longer on display in Greenwich. Having been restored to seaworthiness, it travels here and there once again.

I walked back to New Cross and sat on the platform waiting for another train to reach this last outpost, where it would turn around and take me back, station by station, link by link, until I stepped out again into the late afternoon air of Queensway. I bought dinner at the little grocery and walked slowly back to the hotel.

My travels were just about at an end for now but, like the *Gipsy Moth IV*, I, too, would continue to test my own seaworthiness in travels here and there time and again. In fact, I'd be back in London in less than a year.

CHAPTER TWO: ENGLAND, SCOTLAND, AND WALES, U.K. AND REPUBLIC OF IRELAND – JULY AND AUGUST 1984

The seed of my next trip was planted at the end of my first. Arrow Airlines had overbooked my return flight to New York by a significant margin and I was bumped from not only the flight but the airport as well. I was to be bused ninety minutes to Heathrow where I would board a proper scheduled flight on a proper airline (British Airways) with unbroken doors and a real check-in counter. I would have a row of seats to myself to stretch out in for the long flight home. I had won the overbook lottery.

On the bus ride to Heathrow the seed was planted and began to take root. All around London there had been signs warning supposedly baffled pedestrians from far-off lands to LOOK LEFT before crossing the street, basically telling them that here in jolly old England they would have to do everything backwards to avoid becoming road kill. That had really been my only experience of the drive-on-the-left oddness. I hadn't set foot in a cab or a bus during my stay. The bus ride to Heathrow gave me my first taste of being part of that mirror-image traffic. And I realized that there was much more to England than just London. There was backwards traffic all over the country and I intended to follow those roads in the near future.

And when, a few months later, I began to fall in love with Irish folk music, the next Plan began to take shape.

So here I was arriving in London again, this time on a real airline, TWA, and at a real airport, Heathrow. I had booked myself on a tour of England, Scotland, Wales, and Ireland. I had two days in London for some sights I missed the first time around and almost two weeks for the rest of the trip.

I was staying at the Kennedy Hotel, a rather decrepit place with creaky, uneven floors in the hallways and not an ounce of charm, set in a neighborhood of construction projects and chain-link fences near Euston Station. It was unusually hot for London, even in late July.

I made my way first to Victoria Station to see if I still remembered how to get to that old firehouse with the upstairs transit office. The Pope of Passes was still there, scowling as I presented all the required items for a three-day travel card, the shortest one available.

And so I went here and there in this now-familiar city, much of the novelty now worn off. I spent two days as a newly world-weary traveler. Ho-hum. London *again*. At least the scaffolding that had covered Big Ben last year had been removed. I couldn't wait to hop aboard the big tour bus and hit the road.

I briefly searched Piccadilly in daylight to see if I could locate the mysterious *Tavern Pub*. A little way beyond the *St. James Tavern* I came upon the *Lyric Pub*. Putting two and two together and dividing by Eric the Australian's hyperactive babble, I surmised that Eric had been waiting at the *Lyric* that night months past. Mystery solved to my satisfaction, I treated myself to a pint at the *Lyric* and a return visit to Trafalgar Square to watch the pigeons swarm the unsuspecting tourists. It really is great fun.

The time came to leave London behind and begin a meandering path that would eventually take us north to Scotland. I had booked myself on a big-bus tour and climbed up into the air-conditioned forty-seater, taking my assigned place. We were headed first to Windsor, then to Salisbury, Stonehenge, Bath, and finally to Bristol to spend the night. There was a strange and wonderful encounter waiting for me in Bristol that evening. I'll tell you about it later.

Twice in my life I have been underwhelmed by the size of something famous. The second time was when I saw the Liberty Bell in Philadelphia. If there hadn't been a small crowd gathered around it I would have walked right by this pipsqueak of a bell. I had always imagined it as being quite large, certainly towering over me, not something that would comfortably fit in my living room – "Hey, excuse me, please don't put your feet up on the Bell" – although I'm not sure if my living room floor could support its one-ton weight.

The first time was when I got my first glimpse of Stonehenge. As we crested a small rise in the road it suddenly came into view, sitting all by itself on an otherwise mostly empty plain, surrounded by grazing cows and low hills. But it was a miniature of the Stonehenge in my mind's eye. Of course, it was a bit bigger when I was standing right next to it, and I know those stones were very heavy, but I walked all the way around it in a couple of minutes, checking it out from every angle, and, well, it's just not that *big*.

But what Stonehenge *is* is *old*. Even by English standards – Windsor Castle is almost a thousand years old – Stonehenge is ancient, somewhere between four and five thousand years old. But, really, it doesn't look a day over a century. Those stones haven't started to sag at all.

One castle, one cathedral, and some old Roman baths later we pulled into the parking lot of our hotel on the far fringes of Bristol. There was a message waiting for me, as I knew there would be.

Let me start the story where it really begins – the end of World War Two. Still barely a teenager, my mother had become pen pals with a Scottish girl named Joan. They had maintained their correspondence over the decades, beginning with letters as girls and eventually graduating to Christmas presents for the whole family as they had both married and had children. My mother had moved from place to place in the United States while Joan had moved from country to country, finally ending up in Wales. Occasional phone calls eventually helped supplement their postal interactions. And yet, though by 1984 they had been friends from afar for almost forty years, they had never met. Joan and her husband, Ian, had a son attending college in Bristol at that time and decided to do the next best thing – they would come to Bristol to visit their son, but mostly to meet *me*.

They would be coming to the hotel after I had had my dinner and they would take me out for drinks and conversation. It would be the first meeting between the two families. I think I was a little nervous about it as I pushed my Yorkshire pudding around my plate.

I met them in the hotel's comfortable lobby – Ian a tall, distinguished, silver-haired ex-military man, tall and straight, Joan a small and stylish woman who I could easily think of as "Aunt Joan". They decided to take me to a famous pub in Bristol, a bit of a drive from the hotel, which was so far out of town that I almost couldn't say that I was staying "in Bristol".

The pub turned out to be the *Llandoger Trow*. Built in 1664, it is believed to be the place where Daniel Defoe interviewed Alexander Selkirk. Selkirk was a Scotsman and naval officer who was marooned on an island off the coast of Chile in the early 1700s, surviving there for over four years before being rescued. His story, as told to Defoe, became the basis for Defoe's novel *Robinson Crusoe*, one of the first, perhaps the very first, novel ever written. The place reeked of history, and ale.

The *Llandoger Trow* was dark and woody, so very, very woody. I could easily imagine Defoe and Selkirk hunched over one of the rough-hewn tables, faces flickering in the light of an oil lamp as old Alex described living off wild goats and turnips.

In the semi-darkness we drank dark ale and made what conversation we could, strangers as we were. I was barely older than the son they had also come to visit. We spoke of current events and about where my tour had been so far, and where it would be taking me next, which was north to Joan and Ian's native Scotland. It was all quite pleasant, if a trifle awkward at first, and the pub around me was like a time capsule. Those same wooden beams had looked down upon Defoe and Selkirk. All that had changed since then was the calendar.

Well, okay, there had been one other major change at the *Llandoger Trow* in all those years. Almost half of it had been destroyed by German bombs in World War Two. But the rest had survived intact. And pints of Guinness had not been available when the *Llandoger Trow* first opened its doors. It would be another 115 years before Guinness even existed. The place was *old*.

But I had started something that wouldn't be stopped. It would be far less than 115 years before our two families met again. Within the next few years my parents would meet Ian and Joan more than once. Better late than never. I like to think I got the ball rolling on that. I doubt my mother ever dreamed that encouraging me to travel would lead where it did.

Leaving Bristol behind, we drove on winding roads through a rolling countryside of bungalows and flower boxes, and villages of stone houses and thatched roofs, the absolute Heartland of Quaintness, much like visiting Tolkien's Shire – I half-expected to see hobbits hanging out their laundry – until we reached Stratford-on-Avon, birthplace of William Shakespeare. The house where he was born still stands, his wealthy family's large home. Standing in the room in which he was born in 1564, I couldn't help thinking that the only thing separating us was the slow passage of time, that the gradual accumulation of seconds, minutes, and hours, if replayed as a movie in fast forward, would show a blur of people entering and leaving this room, ending with my arrival. Although the exact dates of his birth and death are subject to dispute, he is believed to have died on his 52nd birthday, April 23, 1616. Must have been one hell of a birthday party.

From Stratford we continued on to Coventry, the legendary home of Lady Godiva.

Coventry's most striking feature was its two cathedrals, the old one and, right next door, the new one. The old one was almost entirely destroyed by German bombs in 1940, only one wall, one tower and one spire remaining intact, a bombed-out shell. The new cathedral is a controversially modernist Rubik's cube of abstract sculpture and stained glass, a Museum of Modern Art in the form of a church. I liked it a lot. But that evening we gathered in the ruins of the old cathedral for some appropriately old entertainment. We had come to see a Mystery play.

Mystery plays were originally performed during the Middle Ages to tell certain biblical stories to the common people. Local craft guilds were each responsible for various aspects of the productions, which typically were acted out on wagons, which could then be moved to another location for the next performance, sort of an early version of a bookmobile.

Now the old cathedral ruins were the performance space, with three stages having been erected, front, center, and right. When the action was up on one or more of the stages, the audience watched from the ground below. When the action shifted to the ground level, the audience sat on the stages. Tonight we were being treated to the story of Jesus, from birth to death and beyond. With the cast and the audience regularly changing places, one occasionally had to be careful not to bump into Jesus or throw an elbow at Mary. I have to say, the medieval mosh pit vibe really brought the Bible to life as never before.

With the play being performed at night in the eerie ruins, with the bright new cathedral towering above, the setting was the perfect embodiment of a resurrection story. The Romans and the Germans may come and go, but life goes on much as before.

We continued north until we reached York, and a brand new ruin.

Actually, York Minster, one of the most massive cathedrals in England, was more of an ongoing ruin. Originally constructed in the 7th century, it had a long history of ruination. Fires (at least five of them), marauding Danes, crumbling stonework, and civil wars had reduced all or part of the cathedral to rubble again and again. Less than a month before we arrived a lightning strike had set fire to a portion of the roof, which then collapsed into the cathedral's interior. With the cleanup partially completed, we walked past stacks of charred timbers as we admired what was left.

We arrived at our hotel in nearby Harrogate in time for dinner and a bit of relaxation in my room watching TV, or so I had expected. I turned on the television and stretched out on the bed. Within a minute the TV's volume had done a Spinal

Tap and gone to eleven. It was deafening. I tried to turn the volume down without success. There seemed to be two options: "ear-splitting" and "off". I called the front desk. After trying and failing to do anything about the TV, the man that had been sent to take care of it asked if I'd like a replacement. When I said yes, his sigh of resignation was almost as loud as the TV had been. Acting very put-upon, he eventually dragged another set into my room and turned it on. Satisfied that the problem had been solved, he left to attend to his other important business, which, I imagined, involved putting his feet up and taking a nap.

Of course, this was far from the worst hotel I've stayed at. That distinction might belong to the Pocono View Inn, which, mercifully, was destroyed by a fire a couple of years after my brother and I had the misfortune of staying there. The gaping pothole that greeted us at the entrance was a foretaste of the swimming pool, which was another gaping hole in the ground. Neither would contain water unless it rained. On the ground floor, near our room, was a defunct nightclub. Pressing our noses to the window we could make out stacks of dusty tables and chairs inside. After checking us in to our room, we never saw the proprietor, or any other employee, again for the rest of our stay. The room was disgusting, the air conditioner rattled and leaked, and the best place to be was outside. The only thing the Inn had going for it, the only truth behind any of its advertising, was that it did indeed have a spectacular view of the Poconos. Pennsylvania is one of those states with legal fireworks, with multiple opportunities to purchase them available within yards of crossing the state line. It was mid-July and my view at dusk of the rolling Poconos was punctuated here and there by showers of exploding lights of many colors, but mostly red, white, and blue, leftovers from the Fourth. The sky around there wouldn't be lit up again so brightly until the Pocono View Inn burned to the ground. USA! USA!

Continuing on our way, we drove ever further north, approaching the Scottish border. The increasingly rugged hills and valleys were stitched together by a seemingly endless maze of low stone walls, crisscrossing the fields and going up and down the ever-steepening hills, dividing the land into manageable pieces. It was August and the heather was in bloom, painting the landscape with a purple tinge.

We arrived in Edinburgh in the late afternoon. The hotel sat near the bottom of Calton Hill, so I decided to take a hike up it and get a good overview of the city as the afternoon faded into dusk.

Calton Hill looms more than 300 feet above Edinburgh and contains a truly odd mixture of functional buildings, tombs, and monuments, including a half-finished replica of the Parthenon and several other distinctly Greek-style structures. It was a wonderful place to just sit and let Edinburgh's natural gloominess wash over me. The city is *dark*, its three main colors being regular gray, dark gray, and extra-dark gray. The older part of the city sits above the newer, which sprawls out along the coast, like an elderly grandfather watching over ill-behaved children. Oil tankers and other ships slid silently in and out of Edinburgh's port on the Firth of Forth. I sat until the dusk became the same color as the city, then made my way back down to the hotel.

I was in Scotland, but thank god I wasn't staying at a place called the Scottish Inn.

Once, while on a baseball road trip with my brother, we needed a place to stay after attending a game in Philadelphia and before a Yankees game in New York. My brother had booked us for a night at a Scottish Inn in Paterson, New Jersey, the perfect marriage of hotel and city. Paterson is a museum of urban blight, the boarded-up windows helping to prop up the crumbling buildings. And the Scottish Inn was the cheapest place to stay and deservedly so, sitting right in the middle of Paterson's worst neighborhood. We noticed the high concrete walls topped with barbed wire before we had even entered the office. We woke the clerk, who was napping behind bullet-proof glass, and he handed us the key with a shrug that said "it's your funeral". The only thing missing was a chalk outline of the most recent victim scratched out in the parking lot. Before we went to sleep we had fun guessing what various crimes might have been committed in our very room, and how many people might have died there.

The next morning we were off to Edinburgh Castle, to tour the place and, as the grand finale, to view the Scottish crown jewels. The Scottish crown jewels consist of a crown, a sceptre, and a sword, with the crown perched on its own regally puffy pillow. I'm sure it's all worth a small fortune but I kept wondering where they were keeping the rest of it. At the Tower of London I had seen England's crown jewels, a whopping 140-piece collection of eye-popping dazzle including plates, trumpets, crowns, sceptres, swords, robes, rings, orbs, a spoon, and a walking stick, most of it encrusted with as many jewels as could be inlaid, inset, or simply glued on. But arrayed before me at Edinburgh Castle was a poor man's fortune, a pauper's treasure. It was time to return to England, where jewels fall from the sky like rain.

We re-entered England on the west side and made our way south through the rainy Lake District before spending the night in Chester. After dozing off in my room and missing dinner at the hotel, I took a walk around Chester, looking for something to eat. I found a place called American Burger where I had the best cheeseburger I've ever had outside of the USA. Two spiky-haired girls hurled expletives at me from across the street as I sat on a bench and ate. That summed up Chester –

full of Tudor charm and two-tone hair. I finished up and hurried back to the hotel before they could cross the street and kick me with their pointy boots.

The next day we made a quick dash across the northern part of Wales, reaching Carnarvon on the west coast by lunchtime. I had my usual low-budget lunch – I found a small grocery store where I bought a roll, some pre-packaged ham and cheese, and a can of soda. In those bygone days of removable pop-tops, I used the razor sharp tab from the soda can to slice open the plastic packaging of the ham and cheese. Pleased with my ingenuity, I ate my lunch and then wandered around until it was time to continue on to Holyhead and catch the ferry to Ireland.

From the ferry's passenger deck I watched Wales recede until it was gone. It would be a couple of hours before Ireland came into view and I realized that I had never before been out of sight of land while on a ship. While not exactly the wide-open ocean, the Irish Sea was big enough to span the distance from horizon to horizon. I was glad that Ireland wasn't too far away. The ocean tends to give me the creeps.

All over the world vacationers flock to white sand beaches, surf, swim, snorkel, and scuba dive in aquamarine waters, splash in shallow tide pools under azure skies, and frolic in foamy surf. I prefer the hotel swimming pool. Although I have on occasion ventured into the ocean, I view it with great trepidation. To me it's just a huge fish bowl stocked with stingers, suckers, tentacles, and teeth. When I visit the zoo I don't get in the enclosures with the animals. So I prefer not to enter the ocean's vast aquarium, with its sharks, jellyfish, eels, sea snakes, urchins, barracudas, stonefish, and saltwater crocodiles. Even the beach is creepy, with its crabs, sand fleas, seaweed, and random bits and pieces of dead sea creatures.

Before I could start fantasizing about sea

monsters, Dublin came into view. The ferry pulled into its slip and began disgorging cars and trucks from its bowels. I stepped off and walked to our waiting tour bus and got on. As I sat on the bus waiting to make the drive to our Dublin hotel it dawned on me that, though I had just entered another country, I hadn't passed through any sort of customs checkpoint or had my passport checked and stamped. Nothing. No one. Not even a "welcome to Ireland". This sort of "free border" is now the norm across Europe, but it remains the only time I've ever just strolled into a country unchallenged. It actually felt a little disconcerting, like I was a spy sneaking in.

My first impression of Dublin was that it would be an easy city to get lost in, as there were few tall buildings to use as landmarks. This would turn out to be prescient, as we shall soon see.

Taking a double-decker city bus into the heart of Dublin to visit O'Connell Street, the city's main tourist magnet, I got my second impression of Dublin – a poor city struggling to get by. Half of the bus's seats were just bare metal frames with the cushions missing. This was third-world Europe. As I traveled around Ireland, most of it looked much the same to me, like a quaint village that had received a fresh coat of white paint a century ago and no further upkeep since then.

The bus let me off near O'Connell Street, which turned out to have been just a few yards off to my right. But I turned left and began looking for telltale street signs as I walked. Half an hour later I began to realize that I had no idea where O'Connell Street was hiding itself and no idea where I was at all. As mentioned before, there were no structures looming above the horizon by which to orient myself. Everything looked the same in all directions. And I couldn't simply turn around and go back. I had taken too many twists and turns to know which direction was "back". I was wandering in a quiet residential neighborhood. There was a woman walking toward me, sixty-ish, carrying a small bag of groceries. I stopped and asked her how to get to O'Connell Street. The reputation the Irish have for friendliness is well-deserved. She considered my question, then let out the friendliest burst of laughter you can imagine.

"Oh", she guffawed with a delightful Irish accent, "you're *miles* away!"

Well, she may have found my situation just a little more hilarious than I did, but I chuckled along with her at my own terrible sense of direction. And at least "miles" turned out to be only two, and not five.

By the time I finally got back to the bus stop near O'Connell Street it was time to take the bus back to the hotel for dinner. I never did see O'Connell Street.

The monastic ruins at Glendalough, with their weird round towers with conical caps, looked to be some of the sturdiest and well-built structures in the whole country. This was third-world Europe, where the old ruins will stand for millennia while everything newer falls into disrepair.

But Ireland was ferociously green, the people were chatty, and Irish folk music could be heard coming from radios here and there. That was enough for me.

Arriving in Cork in the mid-afternoon, I had time to walk around and do some shopping, looking specifically to buy myself an Aran sweater or two. The Aran sweater is also known as the Irish fishermen's sweater, a heavy, intricately woven piece of clothing that is as warm as any high-tech winter coat I've ever owned. It's like woolen Kevlar. Although the traditional Aran sweater is usually an off-white color, I went *way* off-white, choosing a blue one and a green one. Thirty-five years later they still look almost as good as new.

On my way back to the hotel, walking alongside the River Lee, which cuts through the city, I was noticing a rather pungent stench in the air. I eventually realized that it was wafting up from the river itself and just hanging in the still air like London fog. It would be a good night to sleep with the windows closed.

      Not far from Cork stands Blarney Castle, built in the mid-1400s. And up at the top of the castle is the Blarney Stone. Kissing the Blarney Stone has become an almost mandatory activity for tourists visiting Ireland, endowing the kissers with the "gift of gab", like they don't talk enough already. I have heard that long lines to kiss the Stone usually form early and continue throughout the day. But my tour group was there before anyone else had arrived and we had it all to ourselves.

      Kissing the Blarney Stone is not as easy as just smooching some random rock. Built right in to the battlements at the top of the ninety foot high castle, the stone is part of a wall extending out from the castle that provides a gap, a hole through which all sorts of nasty things could be dropped on anyone intent on invading the place. A widely-spaced iron grate now spans the gap. In order to kiss the Stone one must lie on their back and reach out for the iron handrails that have been installed on either side of the Stone. Head thrown back, one must reach their mouth toward the Stone and give it a peck while hanging upside down over that daunting gap, with a view of green Irish grass ninety feet below. A helping hand is almost a necessity to get back up.

      The Stone itself is as smooth as glass, worn down from years of lip-induced erosion and sponge baths. As the first people there that morning, we were able to answer the age-old question "do they ever wash that thing?". A young boy and girl with a bucket and a rag gave the Stone a good wipe-down before the day's geological orgy began.

      After kissing the Stone I remained atop the castle, partly to watch other people struggle with the gymnastics and partly to take in the magnificent view of the Irish countryside.

As I stood there gazing and snapping a few photos, I rested my hand for a moment on the top of the castle wall and came away with a palmful of fresh bird droppings. This was a pretty good signal that it was time to twist my way down the narrow stairways and leave the castle. I had come for the gift of gab, not this other "gift". Besides, the best part of the day was still to come.

Running a circuit around the Iveragh Peninsula in southwestern Ireland, the Ring of Kerry is a 100-plus mile long road featuring some of the country's most spectacular scenery. Tour buses travel around it only counterclockwise, like disconnected train cars, as there isn't enough room for two buses to pass each other on the narrow road. Ocean views vie with the mountains and lakes of the Ring's interior for attention as the road winds through a few small towns along the route, with names like Sneem, Ballinskelligs, and Killorglin. A cottony layer of clouds sat perched on the mountains that afternoon, shrouding their tops. A pint of ale in Waterford provided all the fuel needed to complete the circuit before stopping for the night in Killarney, where it had begun raining gently.

And that was it. We passed through Limerick on the way to Shannon Airport, a quick peek at a place that became a word, like China. Ironically, because very little rhymes with it, Limerick is rarely used as a place name in limericks. Here is my feeble attempt to right that injustice:

> There once was a young man from Lim'rick
> Whose diet would sometimes make *him* sick
> To toughen him up
> He drank sand from a cup
> While training to win the Olympics

Okay, let's see *you* do better.

Aer Lingus whisked me back home, where I

arrived the same afternoon, thanks to the magic of time zones, and perhaps leprechauns.

CHAPTER THREE: KENYA AND THE NETHERLANDS – SEPTEMBER 1988

Oh, wow, I'm surrounded by Africa! That's what I was thinking as I searched the darkness around me. There could be *anything* out there!

The flight into Nairobi had landed after dark and I was now standing in an airport parking lot, looking out into the murky night, half-expecting a lion to come roaring out of the darkness, or an elephant.

There wasn't much to see as our minibus rolled through the darkened streets, past closed businesses, on our way to the Hotel Intercontinental. There wasn't much else to do than check in to my room and get some sleep, but I stood out in front of the hotel for a while, breathing African air, even if it was polluted by Nairobi traffic, and listening to African sounds, even if those were just the honking of car horns. This was my first time journeying outside of the First World. This was *Africa*   !
I couldn't wait to explore Nairobi in the morning. I went inside and went to bed.

We had arrived late on a Saturday night, and this would prove to be not such a good thing, as I later found out. It was Sunday morning and after changing some money at the hotel's front desk I returned to my room to find a man cleaning it. He asked me a question, but I couldn't understand what he was saying, so he repeated himself. I still couldn't understand him. I just wasn't comprehending his Kenyan-accented English, wondering what language he might be speaking, and he quickly jumped to the conclusion that I must not be an English-speaker at all. There we were, utterly failing to understand each other in a common language. But as I adjusted to his accent, the communication barrier fell away.

Kenyan English is salted with a variety of Swahili terms, but chief among them is "Jambo!", the ubiquitous East African greeting. So when the cleaning man had prefaced his question to me with "Jambo!", I was already off on the wrong foot, comprehension-wise. But he had simply been saying, "Hello, how are you?". With that sorted out, I was now ready to go out exploring, eager to put my new linguistic skills to the test.

Not far from the hotel I began walking up Kenyatta Avenue, taking in the palm trees and the tropical sunshine. A man approached me on the street.

"Hello, my friend!"

He was laden with items to sell, batiks folded over one arm and rolls of what looked like plastic wire in his free hand. The rolls of wire were elephant-hair bracelets, I found out later. He started naming prices.

By the time we reached the end of the block we had been joined by two more men.

"Hello, my friend!"

"Hello, my friend!"

My first day in town and look at all the friends I suddenly had!

By the end of the second block my stubborn refusals had sent two of the men off in search of softer targets, but my best and original friend was still with me. By the end of the third block we had negotiated a price.

I still had no idea what the rolls of wire were. After some spirited haggling we had settled on a price for one of his batiks. But now I was looking for an even better deal.

"How much for two?" I asked. There would be a discount, of course.

"How much for three?"

With three batiks rolled up and stuffed in a plastic bag I continued on my way, fending off the other sellers by waving the bag at them, telling them I already had what I came for and they needn't waste their time. A few blocks later I turned a corner and met The Teacher.

"Hello, my friend!" I was the most popular man in Nairobi on that warm Sunday morning.

The Teacher was a tall, respectable-looking Kenyan gentleman of about fifty. Would I perhaps have some time to discuss education in America with him? He was curious about our methods and materials. I wasn't a teacher but I had gone to school, so maybe I could answer some of his questions. A little further down the street he opened a door and led me inside. It was a juice bar, a counter up front and a couple of tables with chairs off to the side. There was no one else in the place. The Teacher bought us each a glass of passion fruit juice and we settled down at one of the tables. Within what must have been no more than thirty seconds, we were joined at our table by six rather disreputable looking men.

The Teacher explained that these men were refugees from Uganda, attempting to transit through Kenya to reach the coast and eventually Tanzania. Some sort of better life was apparently awaiting them there. Could I possibly assist them with a small donation to their cause?

There were seven of them and one of me. It was my first day in a place far from home and strange to me. Figuring I had just bought a fairly expensive glass of passion fruit juice, I drained my glass, slipped the Kenyan equivalent of about five dollars across the table to the Teacher, wished them luck, and got the hell out of there.

Half a block later, pleased with myself for having extricated myself so easily from a scary-looking situation, I was confronted by two young men dressed in some sort of matching, makeshift uniforms. They informed me that they were with the Nairobi police and had just observed me aiding and abetting some dangerous fugitives. I was to accompany them to the nearest police station where I would be charged for my crime.

Clearly, this was not how I had intended to spend my day. There was, however, another possible solution. They would be willing to forget the whole thing, they said, in exchange for a sufficiently large cash bribe. Just looking to buy some time until I could figure out if these guys were legit, I agreed in principle to their offer. We must go somewhere to discuss the terms.

A few blocks away there was a two-story building housing a bar on the ground floor and more bar upstairs. It was not a touristy sort of place. The locals took little notice of us as we entered and made our way upstairs. I sat at a table with one of the "police" while the other went to the bar, returning with three bottles of Sprite, one for each of us.

An amount of three hundred US dollars was suggested as a fair price for my continued freedom. The Sprite was ice cold and tasted heavenly. I casually asked if they had any sort of ID. They both pulled out wallets and flipped them open to show me. But what I was looking at were ANC membership cards, not police IDs. The ANC is the African National Congress, a political party that originated in South Africa but which has spread its reach to other countries in the region. I guess they were expecting me to be ignorant. I wasn't.

I agreed to pay them two hundred dollars but, of course, I would have to return to my hotel first and cash some travelers' checks. That was fine with them. We would walk back to my hotel and they would wait for me outside. Oh, no, that wouldn't do, I insisted. It would be very embarrassing to be seen under police custody. What would my fellow travelers think if they saw us? No, I would return to the hotel on my own, cash my checks, and hurry right back to the bar while they waited. They could treat themselves to a celebratory second round of Sprites until I got back.

I was quite pleasantly flabbergasted when they agreed to my plan. I went down the stairs and exited the bar, then zigzagged my way through half-remembered streets until I was back at the Intercontinental. These clowns didn't even know what hotel I was staying at. I made my way to my room, threw my bag of batiks on the bed, and sat out on the room's balcony for a while, watching as a rainstorm approached. When the downpour arrived I went back inside and watched a little TV, chuckling to myself as I imagined my two police friends walking home in the rain empty-handed.

In every country I visit I like to check out the local TV offerings. It tells one a lot about the country. In Kenya it was mostly agricultural documentaries. Lots of tractors. Needless to say, when I say I watched a little TV, it was very little indeed. But it was enough to get the flavor. Besides, there was a news channel that actually gave US baseball scores. It was September and pennant races were coming down to the wire. I could at least find out if my Red Sox had won or lost.

After breakfast the next morning my seven-person tour group (nine, counting the driver, Edwin, and our guide, Malik) rolled out of Nairobi, which meant driving alongside seemingly miles of shantytown slums, by far the worst I've ever seen. Little cardboard and tin houses were packed together, with fires burning here and there, clothes strung on lines between sagging walls. As we drove along I told Malik about my misadventures of the previous day. He said that it was too bad that we'd arrived in Nairobi on the weekend. If we'd arrived during the normal Monday to Friday work week the streets would have been filled with regular working people and the hustlers and con men would have retreated to the shadows. They only came out in force on the weekends. Many of them probably lived in the shantytown we were passing. I was pleased to be leaving Nairobi behind as we wound our way down into the Rift Valley and began driving across it toward the town of Narok, a few hours away.

    Let me describe for you the roads in Kenya. Driving, technically, is on the left, as in England. But there are so many holes and ruts in the road that you must drive on whichever is the better side at the moment. Fortunately, most of the roads are dirt, not paved. The holes in the paved roads just keep getting bigger and deeper, whereas the dirt roads get smoothed out a bit from traffic and rain. But there had been no rain here lately on this valley-spanning road and by the time we reached Narok we were all covered in road grit that had somehow managed to make its way into our minibus through its closed windows.

    Narok sits on the edge of the Masai Mara game reserve, the northern extent of what in Tanzania is called the Serengetti. I stood outside a souvenir store, taking in my surroundings, drinking a Coke. Coca Cola must be, after water, the most ubiquitous liquid on Earth. You can get a Coke just about anywhere, from a rest stop high in the Atlas Mountains to a Vietnamese rice paddy. I don't know why they even bother to advertise anymore. In some remote places, I imagine the only English words they know are "regular" and "diet". Actually though, come to think of it, I don't recall seeing diet Coke in Kenya. Needing to lose weight is not a common Kenyan problem.

Word was circulating that someone had been attacked and partially eaten by a lion in Narok the previous evening. Now we were getting somewhere! Africa's dark heart called and we answered, climbing back aboard the minibus and driving into the Masai Mara National Reserve.

As we rolled up the rutted track to the Mara Sopa Lodge we saw, off to our left, a couple of giraffes gazing disinterestedly at us. It was our first real glimpse of African wildlife. From the giraffes' bored looks it was clear that we weren't the first tourists they had seen. Still, it isn't every day that you're driving along and look out the window to see a giraffe looking back.

The Mara Sopa sat along a ridge overlooking the vast open grassland below. From my room's front porch I could see Maasai boys driving cattle through the scrubby brush, and the mountains in the distance were in Tanzania. We settled in and, after dinner, got a good night's sleep in preparation for the next morning's pre-breakfast game drive.

I got aboard the minibus sometime around dawn the next morning, carrying my camera in one hand and my room key in the other, or at least the giant hunk of wood my room's key was attached to. Room keys at the Mara Sopa would surely never get lost – mine was attached to a large wooden carving of a Maasai tribesman that was bigger than my hand.

Lions are most active, and therefore most viewable, in the early morning. Within minutes of setting out we had found a lioness and her cubs shading themselves beneath some bushes. Farther down the track we found an ever-growing array of wildlife. There were antelopes of many kinds, zebras, warthogs, Cape buffalo, hyenas, and birds, some flitting about, some stalking through the tall grass in search of snakes. Our minibus had a raiseable roof, allowing us to stand and observe the shifting scenery. A herd of elephants were on the march. We stopped to let them pass. A proud ostrich mom and dad walked along with their six wobbly chicks, no bigger than ducklings. A lion rested beneath a tree with the newly-killed buffalo it had dragged into the shade there.

      The African plains are exactly like what you see at home in nature documentaries on TV, and completely different. On TV the animals always seem to be right on top of each other, while the reality is that things are a bit more spread out, without the concentrated action of edited footage. And it's quiet out in the grassland, and there isn't much happening in any given place, and a lone acacia tree stands in the distance, silhouetted against the blue sky, so one is lulled into a sense of calm and serenity. And that can be dangerous. Just when you're immersed in that tranquility something will happen. Perhaps a lion will rise from the grass it was hidden in, maybe a snake will strike. Outside the safari vehicle I was prey. Inside it I felt like a canned ham.

      We stopped at the Keekorok Lodge to fuel up the bus and have some refreshments. We watched baboons cavorting as we sipped/ate our drinks – mugs half full of chunks of fruit, topped off with juice, served with a straw and a fork. And we still had breakfast waiting for us back at the Mara Sopa, including passion fruit juice, which I had become passionate about.

      After breakfast we set out again to find more wildlife and the people who live shoulder-to-shoulder with it, the Maasai.

      A Maasai village is a circle of small, square houses made of sticks, mud, and cattle dung. Around the village is another circle, this one made of thorny bushes designed to keep the lions out. Within the circle of houses is a common area where the tribe's cattle, their most prized possession, are kept in the evenings. I paid a visit inside one of the houses, ducking low to enter the front (and only) door and remaining stooped beneath a very low ceiling. Just inside, to the right, was a pen for whatever small animals were being kept, in this case a recently-born calf. Beyond that was a much smaller room where the people lived. The man and woman of the house were there and she was cooking lunch in a small oven in the middle of the room. With little-to-no ventilation, the room was thick with smoke that drove me out again after a brief visit. Just before reaching the front door again I happened to glance up at the lattice of sticks forming the ceiling, where dozens of spiders had spun a gauze of webs that covered it entirely. I was glad that I had stayed low on my way in. Ducking even lower now, I quickly backed out of the house and felt my left foot sink into a gooey mess just outside the door, a fresh wad of cow dung the size of a football. I spent the rest of my time with the Maasai cleaning my shoe.

    Our days at the Mara Sopa were an alternating round of game drives and meals. Breakfast was followed by a mid-morning game drive, then lunch, a little down time, then a late afternoon game drive, then dinner. The equatorial sun would set by 5:30 each afternoon and we would have to hurry back to the lodge. No one was allowed out and about at night.

    That little bit of down time was spent either by the small swimming pool, where red and blue lizards scurried around the edges, or sitting on the porch of my little bungalow, gazing out at the vastness of the Masai Mara. But when a large bat came swooping out of the rafters of Derek and Jeanene's bungalow next door, I decided the pool might be the better option from then on.

    Derek and Jeanene were one of three couples I was traveling with and we had hit it off early on. One of the other men in our group had responded to a hotel staffer's friendly greeting of "Jambo!" by turning to us and asking "what the hell's he saying? Jimbo? Jumbo? Doesn't anyone here speak *English*?" We had quickly turned away, eager to find a place where we could laugh at our very own Ugly American. A bond had formed.

      On our first night at the Mara Sopa I had watched the sun set, quickly and early, as it does near the equator. Then I had set off up the lighted path from my bungalow to the dining room to have dinner. The path was posted with signs advising us not to stray from it. Those signs would prove to be wholly inadequate.

      My attention focused on the still fading dusk where the sun had been just minutes before, I noticed only at the last moment the dark shape moving across the path in front of me. Looking down, I saw that my foot was poised a half step away from a dark snake that stretched across the path, its six foot length spanning the entire width of the path and a couple of feet to each side. Catching myself in mid-stride, I cautiously stepped back and watched the snake as it continued downhill toward the valley below. I had been just about to step on it. Africa's mask of tranquility had almost done me in. I let out a deep breath and continued to dinner, a newly watchful eye on the path ahead.

      As we ate our sweetcorn soup and our grilled talapia, I mentioned the encounter to our guide, Malik. He asked me to describe the snake and then let out a hiss of breath, a look of "yikes" on his face. "That was probably a black mamba", he said. We both knew what that meant. The black mamba is one of Africa's deadliest snakes and a bite could have proved fatal. "But", he continued, "it would probably only bite if you stepped on it". I vowed to keep my eyes on the ground from that moment forward. The rest of Kenya would just be people's shoes for me. And potholes, of course. So many potholes.

      We did the pothole slalom for two hours to reach the Lion Hill Lodge overlooking Lake Nakuru. On arrival I hurried to my room to make use of the bathroom. I wasn't needing just a brief pit stop. I took a quick shower and brushed my teeth as well. These were things that I had flatly refused to do that morning before leaving the Mara Sopa Lodge. There was simply no way I was going back into that bathroom, having seen an enormous spider clinging to one of the walls in there the night before. I had closed the door, stuffed a towel under it, and gone to bed. Spiders are none of my business.

From the lodge we could see Lake Nakuru in the distance, its surface painted with large pink smudges, like there was paint leaking into the water. After driving down to the lake's shore we got our first close-up view of one of the greatest spectacles in the natural world, and the reason the lake looks pink when seen from above – hundreds of thousands, perhaps millions, of pink flamingos. From the shore of the lake the pink smudges became three dimensional as birds scattered into the air and re-settled on the water. Unlike in the Masai Mara, we were allowed out of our safari vehicle here to take in the sight. I have recently read that changing conditions in Lake Nakuru have resulted in most of the flamingos departing for nearby Lake Bogoria, but on this sunny day they were present in full force, a pink blanket extending for miles down the shore. It was almost enough to make us forget about the leopard we had passed along the way, resting in a tree. But I had already peeked behind Africa's mask of tranquility and now kept a wary eye out for danger, though nothing came to disturb us and the flamingos.

Lake Baringo was next on our itinerary and the drive there was remarkably smooth on well-paved roads. According to our guide, the president of Kenya was from the Lake Baringo area, so the road linking it to Nairobi had been freshly paved for his comfort. We stopped along the way when the road crossed the equator so that we could all jump out and stand beside the sign noting its location. Of course a series of souvenir huts had sprung up there as well. An opportunity to sell trinkets to tourists never went to waste. Before long a busload of Chinese tourists arrived, loud and boisterous, and we drove on.

The Lake Baringo Club was our home for the next couple of nights and provided us with a few things we found nowhere else, including mosquito nets draped over our beds, giving them the look of hospital beds. Besides the threat of mosquito bites, Lake Baringo's unique attractions included hippos, camels, a ping pong table, a strange tree it would take me many years to identify, a geothermally active island, and the Mombasa Express, a variety of giant millipede that stalked the club's gardens.

The club's grounds sprouted palm trees and cacti, fruit trees and flowers. Camels ate thorns from tree branches, happily chewing thorns six inches long that could go right through your shoes. Bird nests sat high in trees or dangled above the lake's edge from low bushes. We were taken on a short owl-spotting hike, binoculars draped around our necks.

"What do the owls eat?", someone asked.

"Mostly scorpions", was the reply.

There seemed to be a lot of owls. I was standing in their pantry. Sometimes it's better to not know things.

Pushing off from the club's dock, our boat seemed terrifyingly small as we set out for the lake's volcanic island to see its hot springs and twisted trees. There were crocodiles and hippos nearby and I preferred not being in the water with either of them. We had been advised not to wander around the club's grounds after dark because the hippos often came out to forage then, and an encounter with a hungry hippo would have been most unpleasant. If I didn't want to meet one on land, I certainly didn't want to meet one in the water. The crocodiles seemed almost harmless by comparison.

Ol Kokwe Island is Lake Baringo's largest island, the still smoldering peak of a dormant volcano. Steam bubbled up through small pools of water. The bulbous white trunks of cabbage trees sprouted from boulder-strewn hillsides. The island felt ancient, its stunted life clinging to a crumbling pile of rocks in a sulfurous mist.

Later that day, after some well-deserved time in the pool, Derek and I were playing ping pong when we noticed a strange tree nearby. It was covered with extremely sharp and pointy round thorns, from the trunk to the large branches to the smallest branches, the thorns getting smaller with each branching but remaining needle-sharp. Fascinated by this heavily armored tree, we asked a couple of the club's staff what kind of tree it was. They weren't sure, but thought it probably wasn't native to Kenya, possibly an import from South America. Google was still two decades away, so our question went unanswered until fourteen years later when, on a trip to Costa Rica, I encountered another specimen of this dangerous-looking tree. It turned out to be a kapok tree, which is indeed indigenous to Central America and not Kenya. The one we saw in Kenya must have been a young one, as the thorns gradually fall off as the tree reaches a massive size in maturity, often growing to 200 feet in height, or more.

We spent the evenings at Lake Baringo drinking the local beer, Tusker, and trying to be heard over the deafening sound of millions of insects. Then we would retire to our rooms, hoping not to be run down by a hippo along the way, to slip beneath our mosquito nets until morning.

Sadly, there is not much left of the Lake Baringo Club these days. Sometime around 2013 the water level of the lake began to rise, and kept rising, slowly drowning the club's grounds and buildings until it was forced to close, a fate shared by several other lakeside camps and lodges. And the water continues to rise, reaching as far as the road we had arrived on, now just a highway for hippos.

Getting stuck in mud is an old African tradition, enjoyed at least once by anyone driving around Kenya. That's where we found ourselves, an hour into the drive to Samburu, along with a couple of larger trucks. Our little minivan would be the easiest to get unstuck, so we were first up. We all got out and pushed, our shoes squishing in the mud, trying not to stand directly behind the minivan where mud would be churning and flying. We successfully extricated ourselves but the lost half hour had put us behind schedule to reach Samburu in time for lunch.

The road was horrible for the next four hours, a washboard of dried ruts made all the worse by the speed we needed to maintain in order to not miss lunch at the Samburu Lodge. The hours of constant bumping and bouncing left us shaken, and sore enough that I ate my lunch standing up.

Lizards of all shapes and colors had free run everywhere at the Samburu Lodge. The surrounding semi-desert was a great place to see elephants, giraffes, zebras, impalas, and the very strange-looking gerenuk, an antelope with a long, thin, giraffe-like neck that ends with an oddly tiny head. The Samburu River, famous for its crocodiles, rushed past the lodge. Our game drives here would be the last of the trip.

We arrived at the Ark in mid-afternoon. It was indeed a long wooden construction that looked like I imagined Noah's more famous one had looked. But this was an ark for people, with the animals gathered around it, not allowed inside. Hidden in a mountain forest, the Ark was the perfect place for anyone who was tired of chasing wild animals around, a place where one can just relax and let the animals come to you. Built next to a salt lick and containing three stories of viewing ports, windows, and balconies, the Ark was like the ultimate front porch. Buffalo, elephants, and rhinos came to eat their fill of salt and wallow in the lovely mud while we tried to be as quiet as possible, watching from our multitude of vantage points. On the ground floor there was a room with one wall made almost entirely of glass. One of the panes of glass was heavily taped, though the hole in it was still clearly visible. An elephant had recently tried to break the "no animals allowed inside" rule and had stuck a tusk through the window. It must have made for some lively game viewing that day.

The rooms at the Ark were tiny but we didn't spend much time in them, staying up until very late, conversing in soft voices, to see what might come out at night.

After a night at the Ark we continued on to another unique hotel, the world-famous Mount Kenya Safari Club. The original building was constructed in 1938, but in 1959 actor William Holden headed a group who purchased the parcel and expanded it, opening it as the Mount Kenya Safari Club. It has since been a retreat for movie stars, millionaires, kings, and other members of the world's elite, while continually being upgraded with new layers of luxury. The grounds include tennis courts, a golf course, swimming pool, an animal sanctuary, and more. The equator runs across the property, from which views of snow-capped Mt. Kenya can be had on clear days.

I was standing in front of the sign marking the equator (longitude 37° 7' E, latitude 0° 0', altitude 7000 feet) when I heard a strange, regular "ping" sound coming from somewhere in the direction of the club's parking lot. Investigating, I soon found the source. A peacock was standing behind a parked Land Rover, looking intently at its reflection in the bumper and pecking at its "rival" every few seconds. I could tell that this competition would end in a draw so I eventually returned to my room, just to revel in it.

My "room" at the club was bigger (and nicer) than my apartment back home. The front door opened onto a living room stuffed with cozy furniture, a welcoming fruit basket sitting on the coffee table, a fireplace the only source of heat. While I was at dinner an attendant came around to build a fire in it which was gently blazing when I returned. From the living room a hallway branched left and right, a huge bathroom to the left and the bedroom way down the hall to the right. There was enough closet space to accommodate a fashion show.

After a lavish, dress-up dinner in the club's swanky dining room, Derek and Jeanene and I (and a few bottles of wine) retreated to their "room" in a building far enough from mine that a chauffeured golf-cart ride was available to travel between them. A few empty bottles later I decided to make my way back to my own room. Not wanting to wait for the cart, I decided it wasn't that far to walk. As Derek and I stood at the front door saying our goodnights, for a fleeting moment we both thought we saw something large and vaguely feline disappearing around the corner of another building. Still not wanting to wait for the golf cart, and emboldened by wine, but not *too* emboldened, I hesitated, still not sure if we'd seen a lion, a leopard, or just a shadow. It was then that Derek suggested a ludicrous solution which my inebriated self thought perfectly practical. A couple of days before, Derek had purchased what was billed as a Somali dagger. He now fetched it and put in in my hand. Armed with such foolproof protection, I crept stealthily back to my room, so very prepared for an attack that never came.

The next morning I was up early enough to catch a glimpse of the summit of Mt. Kenya during a fifteen minute window of clear sky before the clouds moved back in. When I saw Derek a little while later I informed him that he had just missed seeing Mt. Kenya, and sheepishly handed him back his dagger.

We arrived back in Nairobi that afternoon and had a few hours to kill before our overnight flight back home via Amsterdam. I was to be given a day room at the

Intercontinental, just someplace to hole up for a while while avoiding Nairobi's scammers. But there were no regular rooms available, so I was given the hotel's Uhuru Suite, which was essentially two huge hotel rooms with the dividing wall removed. It had two enormous beds, at least a dozen chairs and couches, and a kitchenette, all mine for all of three hours. It was like being upgraded to first class on a half-hour flight.

      The next morning Africa was an already fading dream as we touched down at Amsterdam's Schiphol Airport. With an eight hour connection time before our flight to New York, Derek and Jeanene and I decided to go through customs and take the train into central Amsterdam.

      With a steady light rain falling we wandered away from the train station, crossed a bridge spanning one of Amsterdam's canals, and soon found ourselves strolling through the city's notorious red-light district. In the early post-dawn hours the area was closed for business and largely deserted, its quaintness reemerging from its veneer of sleaze. Just around the corner we passed what was billing itself as the world's narrowest building and then walked by the Royal Palace. Mapless, we were just winging it. If we'd known that the Anne Frank house was just a couple more canal bridges away we probably would have gone to take a look. Instead we found a spot, with a view of the narrow house across the street, to sit down and have a nice mid-morning beer. We chose the cheap, local beer, Heineken, over the expensive import, Budweiser.

      And then it was time to return to the airport for the flight home, which would deposit us on what would be our third different continent in less than twenty four hours. It was time for us jet-setters to turn back into pumpkins and return to our homes and our jobs. No one would be coming to build a fire in my fireplace that night. I didn't even *have* a fireplace.

Chapter Four: Iceland – July 1989

From the airplane's window I could see the lights of Albany glowing below. It didn't seem fair – I had spent three and a half hours getting from Albany to JFK Airport in New York City on the airport bus and now, less than an hour after taking off from JFK, I was back in Albany, or over it at least. I looked down and waved at where I thought my apartment might be, then settled in for the overnight flight to Keflavik.

Over the ocean to the east of Greenland, from very high up, the little white spots dotting the water were icebergs, perhaps newly born from Mama Greenland herself. On our final approach to Keflavik the white spots on the water were now boats, mostly fishing boats, I assumed, but there was still no land to be seen. As the long streaks in the water became discernible as wakes and waves, and as we passed low enough over the fishing boats to wave to their captains, a patch of brown wasteland suddenly appeared and the plane set down just beyond the rocky shoreline at Keflavik Airport/Air Force Base.

Until 2006 the United States maintained an air base at Keflavik, which sat on one side of the compound, the airport on the other side, with a no-man's-land of runways separating them. It was six in the morning and a cold breeze was attempting to wake me up as I sat waiting for the bus into Reykjavik, about a forty-five minute ride away.

The bus dropped me off at the Hotel Loftleidir, located directly next to Reykjavik's domestic airport. Like so many places on my travels, the Hotel Loftleidir has undergone a name change. It is now called the Icelandair Hotel Reykjavik Natura. But whatever they call it, the planes keep taking off and landing, making it a rather noisy place to spend the night.

I only had an hour or two to check in and try not to fall asleep in my room before hopping aboard a sightseeing bus for a three hour tour of Reykjavik. While the rest of the country overwhelms the senses with its stark scenery, Reykjavik is a city of low-key highlights – the Summit House, where Reagan and Gorbachev famously met in 1986, the Einar Jonsson sculpture garden, government buildings, the port, packed with boats and reeking of fish, and Laugardalslaug, the largest of Reykjavik's seven public, thermally heated swimming pools. It's an impressive pool and deserves its place on the city tour. Icelanders love to swim, or at least soak. Water in all its forms is Iceland's most striking feature. More about that in a while.

Hallgrimskirkja, Reykjavik's towering cathedral, looms over the city and looks like a concrete rocket frozen in mid-launch. I never went inside it, nor do most Icelanders. Only one in ten of them are regular church-goers. But odd-looking, modernist, one might even say avant-garde churches dot the country. In Iceland, religion seems to be less about god and more about architecture.

Reykjavik spreads out along the coast in splashes of color, brightly colored houses making a picturesque residential rainbow. It looks bright and lovely from a distance but loses a little of its charm close up, when the houses are revealed to have walls of corrugated iron, giving much of the city a look of impermanence.

It was about fifty degrees Fahrenheit on a sunny July afternoon as I strolled the downtown area. Ten minutes later I was back where I started, wondering what to do next. I decided to see what an Icelandic grocery store might have to offer. One thing it surely *didn't* have was beer.

Beer had just become legal in Iceland a few months before my visit and was only available in government-run shops. It was merely one item on a long and quirky list of things that were banned, either in the recent past or still forbidden. Besides beer, the list included dogs, pornography, boxing, turtles, and Basques.

Apparently, if something happens *once* in Iceland, it's considered a trend, or a habit. Some unruly Basques had washed ashore once and made some trouble of themselves, hence the ban on Basques (finally rescinded 400 years later). Someone's pet turtle had sneezed on them or something and given them turtle cooties. So no more turtles. Dogs carried tapeworms. So, much to the delight of Iceland's cats, no more dogs. Boxing – well, someone could get hurt. And the beer and pornography could only result in chronic abuse, so they got the big Viking ax. But now beer was making a comeback of sorts. And dogs were allowed again, under stringent restrictions. Could doggy*style* be far behind?

At breakfast the next morning I had my first taste of a traditional Icelandic staple – skyr. Essentially an extra-thick yogurt, skyr has a slightly sour tang that takes some getting used to. Other flavors are often added to it to make it more palatable but at the places I was staying a bowl of plain white skyr was the centerpiece of every morning's breakfast buffet. Yum. And every other meal, every lunch and every dinner, was fish and shrimp. In a country with almost no farms, Iceland's fishing fleet is its breadbasket. And while the seafood was very fresh, it also became very tedious. But at least it was fresh. We were never confronted with the "opportunity" to try *hakarl*, Iceland's famous rotten-shark delicacy. Buried in the ground for weeks to rot and ferment, then dug out and hung for months to dry out, the resulting chunks of shark meat are said to taste like old cheese soaked in ammonia. There is a reason there are no Icelandic restaurants anywhere in the world. I would describe Icelandic cuisine as "food for the not very hungry".

Heading north from Reykjavik, our first stop was Thingvellir, the site where Iceland's (and perhaps the world's) first parliament was established in 930 AD. If the word "parliament" conjures up images of some grand old palace of government, guess again. At Thingvellir there was nothing more than rock and grass, just a convenient location to meet and speak. To reach it we walked a narrow strip of grass separating two walls of rock. Our little green valley was where the North American tectonic plate was separating from the Eurasian plate. This pulling-apart of the land was why Iceland was a country of volcanoes, geysers, and hot springs. The Earth's innards were rushing up to fill the gap. But today there was just the profound Icelandic silence, a product of the country's almost total lack of people.

One of the most striking things about Iceland is that it is virtually uninhabited. With well over half the island's population living in the Reykjavik area, there are only about one hundred thousand people scattered around the rest of an island the size of Ohio. You are more likely to find the road blocked by sheep or the tiny Icelandic horses than by traffic. A couple of days after leaving Reykjavik we pulled into the town of Blonduos, population 895. It felt like Manhattan. So many people!

Iceland's other most striking feature is water. Everywhere we went in Iceland we saw it in all its forms – liquid, steam, and, of course, ice. The ice was mostly bound up in glaciers, of which there are many. The steam rose from vents in the ground. The liquid water surrounded the island, filled its many swimming pools, and flowed across the land until inevitably plunging over some precipice as a waterfall.

Iceland's flag is a cross of red and white on a field of blue. I believe the flag should simply be a painting or a photograph of a waterfall instead. They are everywhere. As we drove along between small mountains to either side of the road, ribbon waterfalls cut paths down the slopes every hundred yards or so on both sides, their narrow channels bordered by fluorescent green moss. Every so often we would arrive at a large waterfall and hop out to commune with the cold, misty spray.

In between what might count as towns, Iceland is dotted with small settlements. Anywhere there is steam venting from the ground there is a settlement. Typically, these consist of a greenhouse (built over the hot spring), a one-room school, a small church, and three or four houses. This is how urban blight begins. Gather a few people around a hot spring, wait a thousand years, and presto! Instant megalopolis! It was no wonder that Blonduos felt like a return to civilization. Blonduos had *streets*!

Continuing our clockwise circuit of the country, we soon arrived in Iceland's second city (the Chicago of Iceland?), Akureyri. There are a couple of other "cities" that are larger, but they are just satellites or suburbs of Reykjavik. Although located on Iceland's north coast, Akureyri tends to be warmer than Reykjavik (winds from the south pass over the island, gaining warmth as they move north). It has a large and lovely botanical garden and, with a population of nearly 20,000, it feels like an honest-to-goodness *town*. As I took a stroll one evening in search of dinner, I was struck by how much it reminded me of small town USA.

It was like *Happy Days*, Icelandic-style. Motorcycles buzzed around a hamburger stand. Teenagers slouched in small groups, rebels without a continent. There wasn't much else to do in Akureyri on a Friday night, or any other night. And here I use the word "night" to denote a time, and nothing else. There is no real night in Iceland in the summer.

I emerged from the hamburger stand with cheeseburger and milkshake in hand and made my way through the motorcycle fumes. It was nearly ten p.m. and the sun was still hovering in the sky. By midnight it still hadn't set so I snapped a picture from my hotel window. No one has ever guessed correctly which of my Iceland photos was the one taken at midnight. It looks like noon. The sun would eventually set sometime around one a.m. and rise again an hour later, never having fallen far enough below the horizon to bring on full darkness. After the bed, the most important feature of any Icelandic hotel room was its shades.

From our base in Akureyri we explored the volcanic sights of northern Iceland. There were hot springs and boiling mud pots, piles of rocks venting steam, dark volcanic rock twisted into bizarre formations. There was an active volcano we could climb, Krafla, with a perfect, hikeable volcanic cone, from the rim of which we could see the deep blue lake nestled within it, a wedge of ice covering the lake's more shaded end. Here was all of Iceland in one easy view – water and ice, with magma just below, waiting to turn it all into steam.

At one point we pulled over to the side of the road and the busload of us all piled out. We were going swimming! Picking our way down a slope, we came to a ladder. We descended the ladder to a lower level of grassy ground and walked along until we came to the changing room, which was a collection of large, scattered boulders. We each picked a rock to duck behind and changed into bathing suits. We still had one more level to descend. An opening in the rocky ground was the entrance. Half sliding, half falling down the wet, slippery rock, we plopped into an underground hot spring. Several other such places in the area had been closed to visitors because the water had become too hot. Ours was a pleasant 115 degrees. There was enough room in our hot tub for a whole busload. While bobbing in this basalt bathtub I looked up and could see, through a crack in the roof, green grass growing, and blue sky beyond.

Exiting the hole proved just as ungraceful as entering it, and much more difficult, requiring the assistance of a rope and a helping hand or two. Back in my changing room I dressed quickly, then kept my eyes politely diverted as I made my way back to the ladder and back to the bus.

Located about a hundred miles east of Akureyri, our next major sight was Dettifoss, Europe's most powerful waterfall. In Icelandic, "detti" means "fall" and "foss" means "waterfall". So Dettifoss is literally "Fall Falls". Located in the middle of nowhere (even by Icelandic standards), we would find there a dirt parking area for about a dozen cars. There was a trash can (keep Iceland beautiful!). We were the only people there. It was about as un-Niagara Falls as it could be. From the parking area we walked along a bluff above its river, the Jokulsa a Fjollum, just downstream from the falls, approaching from below. Land on either side of the river had broken off and fallen in, and there were deep ruts in the ground to show where the next chunk of ground was likely to disappear. Spray from the falls had been visible from a mile away and was now a curtain of mist being blown over us. The roar of the falls grew louder as we got nearer.

Unlike tourist attractions in the USA, Iceland doesn't seem to feel the need for luxuries like railings or large signs saying "Danger! Do not go past this point!" Iceland assumes that you're an adult, and one who hasn't been drinking too much. It is also assumed that, should you fall in, someone will eventually fish your body out of the river. Probably. It happens every year.

This was why I was able to walk right up to the top of the falls, look straight down into the roaring mist, and even stick my hand into the water just as it went over the edge. Five hundred cubic meters of water every second were plunging 150 feet to the river below, and I had my hand in there like an overwhelmed Dutch boy trying to plug a hole in a dyke. I conceded defeat and scrambled away from the falls, not wanting to become this year's fishing project.

We continued our circuit of the island (since "Island" is Icelandic for "Iceland", I frequently found myself wondering why the country had such a generic name!), stopping at all the major waterfalls (Selfoss, Godafoss, Skogafoss, Seljalandsfoss, Svartifoss). The land was treeless and green (and a very bright green where the moss was growing), shards of basalt sticking out of the ground everywhere.

Walking in Iceland will grind your shoes down to nothing. The volcanic rock that makes up the island is uneven and razor-sharp. To stumble and fall is to require stitches. Even to just sit down requires padding. But one day we stopped by the side of the road to go frolicking in a lava field, and I fell repeatedly, and joyfully, without any harm coming to me. It was the moss.

The lava field extended as far as I could see in all directions. It was jumbled and uneven, split by crevices, but was completely covered by a layer of moss at least a foot thick, even down into the deepest cracks. Walking on it was like walking on a trampoline made of sponges, while drunk. I wobbled, I fell, I sank into the crevices up to my hips, I extricated myself and lay on my back, looking up at the sky, laughing. All around me other people were doing the same. We looked like escapees from a lunatic asylum. It was tremendous fun.

Of course, we shouldn't have been trampling the moss at all. Iceland frowns on the damage visitors can do to its natural wonders. But it was an Icelandic tour company that had brought us there and so we just assumed it was all right to do.

We hadn't seen any "keep off the moss" signs. Fortunately, we left before the moss cops showed up and made our way to our stop for the night, Kirkjubaejarklaustur. Okay, everyone, say it with me: "Kirkjubaejarklaustur". You say it just the way it's spelled. Easy, right? Come on, you can do it: "Kirk you buyer clauster". See? Nothing to it!

We were on the home stretch back to Reykjavik, having completed almost the full clockwise circuit around the country. Two major sights still lay ahead, Geysir and Gullfoss.

Geysir is the original *geyser*, an erupting fountain of boiling water. That's where the name comes from. Surrounded by smaller geysers and hot springs, the big one, the Great Geysir, no longer erupts much anymore. But neighboring Strokkur, now the main attraction, still erupts every five to ten minutes, sending a jet of steamy water fifty feet skyward. It went off eight or ten times while we were there.

Just down the road from Geysir is Iceland's loveliest waterfall, the incomparable Gullfoss ("Golden Falls"). Changing directions down a series of drops and cutting through a lush green landscape, Gullfoss almost glows as the sunlight reflects off the misty spray. All that was missing was a rainbow, and maybe a flying unicorn or two. And, like at Dettifoss, we were able to walk down to a rocky area between cascades and stick our hands right into the falling water. I would leave Iceland with very clean hands.

The greenhouses of Hveragerdi were our last stop before returning to Reykjavik. Built directly above hot springs, the town of Hveragerdi harnesses all that hot water in the usual Icelandic way, by building greenhouses over it, giving them a year-round growing season. What sets Hveragerdi apart is the scale of the operation. Most places around Iceland have a small bit of venting steam, a single greenhouse, a population of less than a hundred. Hveragerdi is home to over two thousand people, and dozens of greenhouses sit in rows. Steam rises from the landscape everywhere, and boiling water bubbles to the surface.

We saw stubby Icelandic bananas growing, just like the ones I had seen for sale in Reykjavik markets. But it was getting late and, although there was no darkness descending, we needed to reach Reykjavik in time for dinner.

Later, on my last night in Iceland, I relaxed in my room and watched a little Icelandic TV. The game show I watched tells you everything you need to know about Iceland. Although I couldn't understand a word, the one thing I understood was that the game's grand prize was a book. That's all. Just a book. It was a very nice-looking book, hardcover, probably set you back twenty bucks at a bookstore. It proved two things about Iceland: that Icelanders love to read and that they are content with small things – small towns, small island, small horses, small bananas. Only the swimming pools are huge.

I was sitting on a bench at JFK, waiting for the shuttle back to Albany (which, of course, I had flown over a mere two hours before), when I began to realize there was something, uh, not quite *right*. There was definitely something funny going on but I couldn't quite figure it out. It took a few minutes but it finally hit me – it was beginning to get *dark*. Honest-to-goodness *night* was falling, complete with black skies and, once I got away from New York City, stars in the sky. I had returned from the land of the perpetual chilly summer day and now a sultry summer night was about to begin. When the shuttle arrived I hopped aboard and was soon napping as we rolled north up the Thruway. I didn't even need to pull down the shade.

Chapter Five: Morocco – October 1990

We were already in Rabat and I was feeling dehydrated, and more than a little pissed off.

I had arrived in Casablanca that morning for what would turn out to be my last big-bus tour; this would be the one that broke *that* camel's back (how appropriate, as Morocco is teeming with camels). I had been stuffed into a bus with forty others and driven to the beach, to see the Atlantic Ocean pounding the shore, with Casablanca's almost uniform whiteness spread out and away from it. The single-color city was a repeating theme in Morocco – Casablanca was all white, as was Rabat. Meknes was all yellow, Fes was tan, and Marrakesh was brown. There were at least six different nationalities represented in our motley group, including a large Italian family whose various members insisted on questioning me in fractured English about my feelings toward my president, George *Boosh*. Our tour guide, Abdu (who we all eventually started calling "Tojo"), conducted the tour in three languages – French, English, and Italian. The Italians seemed to understand him fairly well, as did the French, but his

English sounded to me like just more French, but with a different accent. The bus's lousy sound system didn't help matters. Most of the time I relied on the French to translate for me, as many of them spoke passable English.

After half an hour in Casablanca we began driving north toward Rabat, Morocco's capital. We had not been offered an opportunity to change any money into the local *dirhams* and consequently had not had a chance to buy water. As we made a brief pit stop in some small town along the way, it began to rain. I tilted my head back and caught a few drops. It was better than nothing.

By the time we arrived in Rabat we were all thirsty and aggravated. All we needed was a little local currency. None of us felt like begging on the street but the hotel said they would have no money until the morning. Tojo was no help at all. I decided to take a walk, along with a handful of others from the group, and look for some place to change money. There was a train station nearby with a currency exchange. It was closed. We slumped back to the hotel dirham-less. At least the fridge in my room had a couple of bottles of water in it. I brought them both with me for our tour of Rabat's attractions, the most memorable of which was the Tour Hassan.

The Tour Hassan, or Hassan Tower, is a 140 foot high rectangular minaret made of red sandstone. It looks like a huge brick standing on end. It was originally supposed to be twice as high and was to be the centerpiece of what would have been the world's largest mosque. Construction began in 1195 AD but ended just four years later with the tower half built, a couple of wall sections completed, and over three hundred stone columns standing in neat rows, ready to bear the load of a roof that was never to be raised. It didn't matter anymore. After nearly a thousand years there's not much difference between a half built mosque and a half demolished one.

The next morning the hotel said they were

sorry but they still had no money to change and soon we were on our way to Meknes. I didn't bother to mention the overpriced bottles of water I'd taken from the fridge and no one dared to ask. At our lunch stop later that day we were at last able to change money. There should have been a banner there reading "Welcome to Morocco, *finally*".

The rain had stopped by the time we reached Volubilis. Founded long before the Romans arrived there in the first century AD, the ruins were nonetheless dominated by the remains of Roman construction and featured some impressive arches, columns, and mosaics. It would have been nice to stay longer but a violent thunderstorm was rushing in and the rain began again as we were sprinting back to the bus, wetting the fastest of us and soaking the slowest. The rain persisted all the way to Meknes.

By the next morning I was coming down with a cold that would plague me for the rest of the trip. I took to carrying a roll of toilet paper with me everywhere as surrogate Kleenex. The sneezing and blowing were nearly continuous. I sure was enjoying this trip!

We would be spending the day in the medina of Fes, a day that would be the highlight of the entire trip. Fes, with a population of over a million, is Morocco's second-largest city. Its walled-in medina, or old original part, is one of the world's largest and is home to over 150,000 people. Spending time in the medina is a bit overwhelming. It's a mental juggling act.

The medina is a huge maze of narrow streets and alleyways filled with more hazards and distractions than a video game. Without a guide, getting lost is almost a certainty. And having a guide as short as Abdu didn't help. So I did my best to keep one eye on Abdu, or at least on a few stragglers from the group, as I tried to navigate the obstacles and novelties in front of me, and behind. Fully-laden donkeys were led through the narrow lanes by men dressed in djellabas, children scurried on errands, craftsmen pounded copper and brass, flies swarmed, sellers of everything from slippers to swords hounded me in groups, dates and other produce were arrayed in heaps, sheep intestines dangled from wooden beams, the air smelled of fruit, spices, donkey droppings, and sweaty djellabas. It all came at me fast, from all directions.

Oh, look, a goat's head hanging on a string, look out, here comes a donkey, squeeze against the wall and let it by, damn these flies, shoo, get away, no I don't want any slippers, how much?, you're joking, I'll give you thirty dirhams at most, look out, here comes another donkey from behind, oh crap, there are donkeys coming in both directions, squeeze extra hard against the wall, oof, a donkey's load rubs across me as it passes, I'll give you forty dirhams, that's my last offer, look out, donkey crap ahead, step over, damn these flies, oh, look at this guy pounding brass plates, uh-oh, where the hell is Abdu?, oh, there he is, didn't see him down there, look, I don't even want any damn slippers, how much for that dagger?, you're joking, I'll give you fifty dirhams, look out, donkey coming. It went on like that all morning.

By the time we arrived at a small restaurant for lunch, the dagger, original asking price 500 dirhams, was down to a mere one hundred but I was holding out at sixty. I really didn't want it anyway and was relieved to be away from the incessant haggling as we entered and sat down at our reserved table. As a covered platter was set on our table we were told that we'd be having something special for lunch – drumroll, remove cover – mutton and couscous! Everyone groaned.

It looked like the leftovers from last night's special dinner of mutton and couscous, which looked like they'd reheated yesterday's special lunch of mutton and couscous. At least they never dared try to serve it to us for breakfast. The groans would only get louder, though. We would be treated to mutton and couscous a dozen more times over the next couple of weeks. I haven't touched either one in the almost thirty years since.

Emerging from the restaurant, I was chagrined to see my would-be dagger salesman lounging outside waiting for me. I needed to get this over with.

"Seventy dirhams, old buddy, old pal, and not a single centime more".

"I make you special deal – dagger, slippers, one twenty for both."

I walked away and followed the group. My friend waited a few seconds, then came running after me.

"Okay, okay, seventy", he said, waving a dagger at me. I had always imagined myself in straits much more dire than this when accosted by a strange man with a dagger in an exotic foreign alleyway. But I quickly disarmed him by giving him seventy crumpled dirhams and suddenly it was I who was in command of the situation, dagger in hand. Looking around me, I noticed the fat Italian man from our tour bringing up the rear of a shuffling group. I fell in behind.

Our next stop in the medina was a carpet shop, as common in Morocco as Starbucks in the USA. We were led inside and seated in a semicircle around the carpet display area. Shot glasses of mint tea were handed out. It was very tasty. And then came the men with carpets.

One by one by one, carpets were unfurled in front of us and laid out on an ever-growing pile. Surely each and every one of us would want to buy one of these beauties, free shipping to Europe or the USA. Prices started at around three hundred dollars. There were dozens and dozens of them. The heap continued to grow. Having no interest in buying a carpet and growing bored with looking at the assortment, I quietly got up and began nosing around. I saw a set of steps leading to a second floor and decided to poke around up there. No one noticed me leave.

The second floor ran around an atrium – I could look down upon the carpet sellers, see the summit of Mt. Carpet Heap. I passed an open door to my left and peeked inside. About thirty young girls, ages roughly nine to thirteen, sat at looms, weaving carpets. One of them beckoned to me to come in and sit beside her. She showed me how the loom worked and instructed me as I wove my own little section of the expensive carpet. This was surely more fun than shooing away salesmen.

After a few minutes I saw a woman walk past the room's open door, do a double-take, then turn around and enter the room, gesturing at me. It was clear that she wanted me to leave. I had discovered their dirty little secret.

Back downstairs, I told a few others in the group, the English-speakers, what I had seen upstairs. No one was surprised. I hadn't been either.

There was one more thing we couldn't miss seeing before leaving Fes. We were ushered to the top floor of a building and then out onto a balcony overlooking a tannery. The tanneries of Fes are the world's oldest. Laid out below us were vats of dyes of all colors. It reminded me of a watercolor paint box I had when I was a kid. There were other vats containing a blend of saltwater, cow urine, and pigeon droppings, an essential first bath to soften the hides before dyeing. Already dyed hides were drying in the sun around the periphery of the site. The stench of urine, droppings, and dyes was overpowering. Men stood knee-deep in some of the vats, turning pieces of hide over and over. Working in an office suddenly seemed like a pretty sweet deal.

The Atlas Mountains cut a diagonal slash across Morocco, separating the more temperate coastal half of the country from the hotter, drier desert half. We went up and over the mountains, stopping midway for lunch in Midelt. The road ran up, down, around, and through the mountains, which kept getting a darker and darker brown. It was scenic, but not quite spectacular. The road eventually flattened out into desert, the beginnings of the Sahara, a landscape displaying the full spectrum of shades of brown, like a chocolate rainbow. And every so often along the road there would be a brown town, a string of market towns and sandcastle fortress outposts leading out into the sea of sand – Er Rachidia, Erfoud, Tinerhir, Ourzazate, Rissani, Tinsouline, Zagora, Tagounit. A few times we passed fields of small rocks sticking up out of the ground just a few inches, black stones casting tiny shadows on the ground. These were cemeteries. There were camels and sand dunes, and vivid sunsets, traditional desert postcard stuff.

In Tinerhir, Abdu led us to what he said was a traditional Berber house to have a look-see. To no one's surprise, it turned out to be another carpet shop. About three quarters of the group immediately walked out, demanding to be taken back to our hotel, determined to walk back if necessary. Our driver took pity on us and went to fetch the bus. While we waited I had a nice conversation with Abdul, a young man who wanted to practice his English, which turned out to be much better than our guide's. He told me he would be attending the University of Maryland the following year and wanted to know if there would be much snow. I told him there might not be much, but there *would* be snow. He was very pleased at the prospect of such an exotic adventure.

By the time we got to Zagora my cold had eased up a bit but I, like many others in the group, had been struck down by a case of "Mohammed's revenge". The rolls of toilet paper I had been using as tissues took on a new and more insistent role.

I had become tour bus seatmates with a middle-aged woman from Atlanta named Betty. We had a few things in common – we spoke English, we hated Tojo, we liked puzzles, and we thought the Italians were hilarious. That night in Zagora I took advantage of a lull in the "revenge" and joined Betty and a few others for a stroll around the town.

Zagora was dark and quiet, the night sky filled with more stars than I had ever seen at once, so many and so bright that it was hard to look away from all the dazzling diamonds on display. There was almost no one else out on the streets, but a couple of young boys approached us and tried to sell us an exotic coin. It turned out to be a one deutsche mark coin, a clear sign that German explorers must have been here in the recent past. The archeology of tourism.

Zagora felt like the end of the line but there were a few more end-of-the-line places a little further on.

I dropped to my knees in the side of a soft, sandy dune, plastic bag in hand, and scooped up a bagful of Sahara Desert sand, a powder so fine that it poured like a liquid, flowed without friction. This would be my best souvenir of Morocco, better than that crappy necklace I bought in Erfoud. We had stopped along the road leading south from Zagora where a few small dunes marked the western fringe of the daunting Sahara. I would bring my sand home and put it in small vials to give away to family and friends, little samples of a faraway world they might never otherwise see.

A few more miles south the road simply ended, expiring in the square of a little village called M'hamid, the last outpost before the Algerian border, the last tiny place before miles and miles of nothing at all. The village was centered around a single well, without which there would have been no village at all. Women and children gathered around it, hauling up the blood of the desert in buckets of leather; life would continue for another day. Sand drifted up the sides of the homes in M'hamid, buried them up to their second-floor windows, making the whole place look like a sand castle dissolving.

There was not much else to see or do in M'hamid. It seemed to be there mainly as a place to turn around. This was where the road ended but, turned around, it was where the road *began*, the road back to the relative splendor of Zagora.

Back in Erfoud I'd gone shopping for trinkets with Betty. For reasons I can't recall and have no explanation for, we had both been drawn to the same heavy, chunky, clunky (some might say *ugly*) necklaces hanging high on a wall in a shabby, dusty little shop by the side of the road – wooden beads and chunks of metal, shish kabobbed on thick maroon strings.

"If we each buy one we can haggle for a discount", Betty suggested.

"Yeah", I agreed. "But what in the world would I *do* with it?"

"I'll tell you what you should do with it", Betty drawled in her Georgia accent. "One of these days you're going to meet a nice girl, somebody special. Give her the necklace and tell her you've been waiting for just the right person to give it to. Tell her some romantic story about finding it in the desert under a night sky filled with a million stars".

"It's cloudy tonight", I protested.

Betty chuckled. "Just give it to her".

On the way to Marrakech we stopped in Tinsouline to visit another weekly market. In addition to piles of every type of local produce, there was also a fascinating slaughter area. I walked along a row of stalls – empty, empty, empty, goat. Well, what used to be a goat. Its disassembled parts were neatly piled in the middle of the stall, with its head perched proudly on top.

The drive back over the mountains to Marrakech was prettier than our first mountain crossing. We pleaded with Abdu to stop at a particularly scenic location overlooking a gorge. Instead we drove on another mile and pulled up next to what we were all by then referring to as another "junk stand", a shop selling the usual assortment of brass plates, camel key chains and other tourist crap. We all suspected that Abdu was getting a kickback from all the places he steered us to. Perhaps he hadn't wanted to stop by the gorge for fear we might throw him in. His fear was not unfounded.

After so many days in dusty little desert towns, Marrakech was an actual city, a sudden swarm of traffic and hucksters. But Mohammed was having his revenge again the next morning and I didn't have the energy to explore. By lunch it had passed and I was feeling better. I wandered the Jemaa el-Fnaa with Betty that afternoon, taking in the exotic sights.

The Jemaa el-Fnaa is Marrakech's old central square. Surrounded by merchants selling just about everything, the square itself is a human circus. Snake charmers, jugglers, acrobats, monkeys, and magicians performed their various tricks. Pickpockets profited from the multitude of distractions. There was even a dentist with his chair and some medieval-looking tools. I was glad that my ailments didn't include a toothache.

It felt good to finally reach the Atlantic coast again. The air was cooler and wetter, the cities were ocean-front white instead of desert brown. We made our way up the coast from Essaouira to Safi to El Jedidah and finally back to Casablanca. It was all a blur of fish markets and old Portuguese fortresses, their cannons pointed out to sea at invaders long since gone. The mutton and couscous had mercifully been replaced by a steady diet of bony fish. This dangerously cheek-piercing food was a welcome change at first but the novelty wore off quickly. Guess what we're having for dinner tonight. Fish again! Yay! With just a couple of days remaining until my escape from Morocco, I was hoping I could just make it to the end. I hunched over my dinner plate and began searching for bones.

On our last night in Morocco some members of our group discussed Abdu's tip over drinks. Most of us felt he deserved much less than the standard amount, perhaps nothing at all. We figured he had already made his money from every one of his friends who had a junk stand or a carpet shop. We drank a toast to being rid of him.

So here's my quick and handy summary of Morocco for those who might be inclined to follow in my intrepid footsteps:

> Bring some water with you.
> Morocco is mostly brown or white.
> I got sick and then I got sicker.
> Mohammed is vengeful -- always carry a roll of toilet paper.
> Never follow a little man in a djellaba named Abdu.
> I will never eat mutton and/or couscous again.

At JFK I walked Betty over to her gate for her flight home to Atlanta, then sat outside waiting for the shuttle and the three-hour drive back to Albany. It was October and the autumn leaves were showing their full range of colors -- oranges, yellows, and reds. It was the perfect antidote to Morocco's inland sea of brown and coastal whitewash, its brown mutton and white couscous, its monochrome cities. I felt like Dorothy arriving in Oz and opening a door to a world of colors. I just sat and looked out the window until the light began to fade somewhere around

Poughkeepsie.

Chapter Six: Vietnam – February and March 1999

"Ha Long City? Mr. Koo? What? No, no, no! Go back! Turn around! Back to the airport! Back, back, back!"

I was making turn-around-and-go-back hand gestures, making loops with my finger and jerking my thumb over my shoulder.

"No, I'm not Mr. Koo and I don't want to go to Ha Long City", I was shouting. Ha Long City was a few hours away, a very long taxi ride. Mr. Koo must have had a fistful of dong. Of course, just changing a few dollars would give anyone a fistful of dong. I would soon be a Vietnamese millionaire myself. I don't recall the exact exchange rate, but it was at least 10,000 dong to the dollar. But I didn't want to blow my soon-to-be fortune on a four hour taxi ride. Something had gone spectacularly wrong.

Booked on a small group tour, my flight had touched down mid-morning in Hanoi. My flight seemed to be the only arrival at the baggage and customs area and within a few minutes most of the passengers had made their way through and were gone. I looked around for the tour representative who should have been there to meet me. I looked for possible fellow tourists who might be as perplexed as I was. There was no one. Outside the arrivals terminal, half a dozen taxi drivers leaned against their cabs, smoking, chatting, waiting for a customer. They waved at me competitively, beckoning me to their cabs. I kept looking around. Surely there must be someone coming for me, perhaps a clipboard-encumbered tour rep in a company t-shirt, maybe just a van sent by the hotel? Shouldn't there at least be some other bewildered tourists milling around like me, wondering what the hell to do? There wasn't even anyone I could ask. No one here spoke English.

A man suddenly approached me with great enthusiasm and a handshake. As he ushered me to his vehicle I imagined his unintelligible Vietnamese babble was saying something like "welcome to Vietnam, so sorry to have kept you waiting, we go to hotel now". Thank goodness, someone was finally taking charge of things! I climbed into the back seat of the car with my luggage and leaned my head back. Everything was sorting itself out. I would be at the hotel soon.

"Do I look like Mr. Koo to you? Back to airport". My finger was still doing that twirly "turn around" motion. The driver slowed and pulled to the side of the road. I breathed a sigh of relief that he seemed finally to understand.

Comically, we had to go back through the same set of toll booths we had only minutes before paid to go through the other way. Twenty minutes later we were back at the airport, where I paid the driver in dollars for the ride, plus tolls. But now I was back where I started. I decided to phone the hotel.

Now understand, this was in the days before everyone carried a phone. And a quick search found no public phones in the terminal. Back outside, one of the taxi drivers did happen to have a phone and offered me its use. Ten dollars. Take it or leave it. I had been in Vietnam for about an hour and was not having a good time. It was a strange start to what would turn out to be my favorite trip and my favorite foreign country. I paid the ten dollars and called the hotel. They sent a car for me and an hour later I was at the front desk of the Royal Hotel Hanoi.

The Royal Hotel Hanoi was a nice old creaky-floored hotel in the heart of the city. I checked in to my room but no one at the desk had a clue about the tour or where the hell the guide was. They changed a hundred dollars for me and I became an instant Vietnamese millionaire. There was nothing left to do but go out and explore, and maybe spend a little of my windfall of dong. Maybe by the time I got back there would be some answers.

I walked over to the nearby Ho Hoan Kiem park, a small park in central Hanoi with a lake in the middle. Getting there was my first grand Vietnamese adventure. Traffic in Hanoi consisted of the usual assortment of cars and trucks, plus bicycles and cyclos, the ubiquitous bicycle rickshaw, all surrounded by a swarm of motorbikes, some with solo riders, some carrying up to a family of five. Hanoi's dominant sound is the constant beep beep beep of motorbikes, night and day. The traffic *tends* to stay to the right but opposing streams of traffic often flow through each other, some left, some right. The lack of any sort of traffic signals adds to the chaotic fun. To cross the busy avenue to reach the park I had to do what the locals do and simply *take the plunge*. The technique is as simple as it is nerve-wracking – you simply wade out into traffic, maintaining a slow and steady pace, and allow the traffic to flow around you. As long as you don't panic and run you should be okay. If you run, your position is harder for drivers to gauge and, well, accidents happen. I waited for a narrow gap in the traffic and stepped off the curb. Thirty seconds later I miraculously arrived at the other side, realizing I would have to do it all over again to get back to the hotel.

As I walked around the lake I was assaulted by a steady stream of Vietnamese kids selling postcards, t-shirts, shoe shines, books, and other souvenirs. But instead of swarming me they seemed to wait and take discrete turns. Unlike the tenacious Moroccan hucksters, who fell upon me in relentless, desperate hordes and wouldn't take "no" for an answer, these kids were fairly laid back. If they could make a sale, that was great. If not, oh well. They were trying, just not trying too hard, and they were all smiles and giggling laughter, like this was just the most fun game they'd ever played.

"Postcard mister?" a girl of about thirteen asked as she fell in beside me. I told her I didn't need any more postcards, having just bought a stack of them from another girl. She frowned.

"You not buy my postcards, you a very bad man", she said as a smile brightened her face, giving her away. We walked together for a while, exchanging names and smiles until another potential target caught her eye.

"How long you be in Hanoi?" she asked me. Two more days, I told her.

"Maybe I see you tomorrow, you buy postcards then, okay?"

"We'll see", I said with a chuckle.

By the time I left the park I had a Ho Chi Minh t-shirt, a collection of old Indochinese coins, and a collection of old Indochinese paper money, in addition to my wad of postcards. Let that be a lesson to you my Moroccan "friends".

After leaving the park, and surviving another street crossing, I spent some time wandering around Hanoi's old colonial French Quarter. A group of young boys suddenly came running toward me. I was wondering what they were going to try to sell me but they simply ran up to me, shook my hand and said hello, one by one, then ran off again. A short while later as I was walking along I approached two boys kicking a soccer ball back and forth. Just as I was about to pass them, one boy's shoe flew up in the air after a mighty kick. Without breaking stride I caught the shoe, handed it back to him, and kept walking. The boys fell to the ground in hysterics, like it was the funniest trick they'd ever seen.

By the time I got back to the hotel I had fallen in love with Hanoi. The traffic was a nightmare, the beep beeping was incessant, old women carried loads that weighed more than they did, the buildings were grimy and crumbling, and loudspeakers perched up high on power lines were broadcasting Communist Party dogma constantly. But everything was clean, even the grime, and the children were happy and smiling, the city lively and vibrant. I was happy to have had this time on my own. It was about to end.

I walked into the Royal Hotel Hanoi to find three people waiting in the lobby to meet me. One was our guide (who I will call "Tuan", though I unfortunately don't remember his actual name). The other two were the Salinas sisters, Elvira and Josefina, who would be my companions on this tour.

The Salinas sisters were a couple of Mexican ladies living in New Jersey. They had been almost everywhere and in the years to come I would regularly receive postcards from them from the most random assortment of places – Yemen, Ethiopia, Jordan, South Korea, and others. Elvira's English was good but Josefina communicated mostly in Spanish. As I was best able to decipher Tuan's Vietnamese-accented English, the chain of communication went like this: Tuan would tell us something, I would transfer it to regular English for Elvira, and she would translate that into Spanish for Josefina. It worked very well because, aside from our driver, there were only the four of us in our little group.

Tuan explained that I had originally been scheduled on a flight that arrived in Hanoi in late afternoon but my flight had been changed to the mid-morning arrival. Of course I knew that, having been on the flight after all. But apparently no one at the tour company had bothered to tell Tuan, which explained the lack of a welcome at the airport. After being reimbursed for my wild taxi ride to nowhere, I was feeling much better. Our tour would properly begin the next morning with the official city tour of Hanoi. Until then I slipped away to a quiet dinner in the hotel dining room and then to my room to begin a trip-long battle with jet lag.

      Our first stop the next morning was to visit dear old Uncle Ho. I won't attempt to encapsulate Vietnam's long and complicated history but communist revolutionary leader Ho Chi Minh remains the most revered person in the country. The country's largest city, Saigon, is now named Ho Chi Minh City. And Uncle Ho himself remains quite visible, his embalmed body lying on display inside the Ho Chi Minh Mausoleum. The huge mausoleum sits by itself, surrounded by a large public square. Visitors line up to enter and pass Uncle Ho's remains single-file. Solemnity is demanded. Hats are to be removed. There is to be no smiling, but grief-stricken sobbing is allowed. By the time I arrived to pay my respects, Uncle Ho had been dead for thirty years. Every now and then, when he begins to look a little tattered and frayed, Uncle Ho is shipped off to Moscow for a makeover, like the scarecrow in The Wizard Of Oz getting some new straw. He had recently returned from his latest trip and was looking tanned and rested.

      We also paid a visit to Uncle Ho's house in Hanoi and an old Vietnamese university before continuing on to the Hanoi Hilton. Along the way we passed a number of things that had me scribbling in my little notebook. We saw a man relieving himself inside a busy traffic circle, saw a cow sitting on top of a wall, and drove past "dog restaurant row". We passed a restaurant advertising "fried bird, eel, and frog in plaster". We passed a shop selling "Swiss or Russian watches" and also drove by the "Western Canned Food and Wine Shop". I wanted to visit them all but there was no time. We pulled up in front of the Hanoi Hilton.

Above the entrance were the words "Maison Centrale", French for "central house", a common name for French prisons. After the North Vietnamese had rid themselves of the French it became Hoa Lo Prison. In the 1960s Hoa Lo became a place to hold (and frequently torture) American POWs, who dubbed the place the "Hanoi Hilton". Only a remnant remains, the bulk of the prison having been torn down just a few short years before my visit. But within that small remnant we saw dank cells equipped with chains and leg shackles, displays presenting the plight of the POWs in the rosiest light the Vietnamese government could shine upon it, and an old French guillotine. Dummies had taken the place of real prisoners here and there, their shackled dummy legs preventing them from rising to greet us when we visited their cells. I felt a renewed sense of good fortune that the Vietnam War had ended when I was fifteen.

That evening we walked to dinner in the old French Quarter and then strolled over to the local water puppet theater to see one of that night's performances of the traditional northern Vietnamese art form.

The puppeteers were hidden behind a screen as they manipulated the puppets using long rods. The action played out on a small pool of water in front of the screen as a small orchestra sat to the side playing Vietnamese music. There were a multitude of characters, boats, dragons, and boats shaped like dragons telling stories of rice harvesting, village life, and, of course, dragons. Firecracker explosions punctuated the action, smoke dissipating slowly across the water. A note I jotted down later called it "cute", although I'm not sure the Vietnamese would appreciate being culturally summed up that way.

   The next morning we began driving south, our destination the Ninh Binh area a couple of hours from Hanoi. The city faded away ever so gradually, thinning to a line of businesses on either side of the road for a few miles before finally giving way to rice paddies, farmers in conical hats pulling water buffaloes through the muck. It was iconic Vietnamese countryside. The people could have been water puppets, playing out the traditional scenes.
   At one point along the way we saw a small crowd of people gathered around something floating in a rice pond. It appeared to be a farmer, the story of his traditional life having ended here, perhaps from a heart attack or stroke, some short time before we passed.

   As we drew nearer to Ninh Binh the land began to display bumps, large limestone humps rising from the paddies and towering over them, green with vegetation. We turned off the main highway and followed a dusty track through the paddies until we arrived in a small village. We were there to take the Tam Coc boat ride, a serene two-hour paddle through rice fields, between the limestone outcroppings, and through three tunnels dug beneath them by the gently flowing water, the rough rock of the ceiling just a few feet above our heads in the sudden darkness. I sat in the front of my small boat, Tuan behind me. Behind Tuan a woman in a conical hat sat and rowed while a man stood behind her with a pole, steering. Elvira and Josefina floated nearby, with their own hat lady and pole guy. After an hour we reached the turnaround point, where a woman in another small boat waited to sell us cold cans of Coke from a cooler, along with a variety of other snacks and trinkets. Then we turned around and went back the way we came, back through the tunnels, back through the quiet tranquility of the rice fields, and, ultimately, back to Hanoi. Before we left we visited three temples nearby, perched up on a limestone mountain, their altars adorned with gold and flowers and candy and incense, so much opulence in the middle of so much beautiful nowhere. As we drove north to Hanoi, a few hours after we had first passed the spot, the deceased farmer still lay face down in the pond, but the crowd had returned to their planting.

      The next morning I was on my way to Ha Long City and this time it was no mistake. Maybe I'll look up Mr. Koo when I get there, I mused, as I looked out the window at the misty, pastoral northern Vietnamese scenery – more rice paddies, more water buffalo, more conical hats. It looked like a painting. We stopped to take pictures.

      We arrived late morning and went directly to the boat that would be taking us on a five-hour tour of Ha Long Bay. Just as limestone peaks rose from the paddies of Ninh Binh, similar limestone rocks rose from the water of Ha Long Bay, thousands of them. We ate lunch aboard the boat as it chugged toward one of them, the first stop on our tour.

      We had not been told what to expect, and it was amazing. Disembarking on this huge lump of rock, we climbed some rough steps until we came to an opening in the side. We stepped inside and found ourselves in a cavernous wonderland. If you've ever visited caves or caverns, the sights would have been familiar – rock formations of all sizes, shapes, and colors, drooping from the ceilings and rising from the floors. But these were above ground, or at least above sea level, nestled in large expanses within this chunk of rock rising from the bay. And now it was a tourist attraction, well lit and full of people roaming around widened paths checking out the weird formations.

      We motored for miles around the bay,

zigzagging between the limestone gumdrops rising from the water. The closer ones were reflected in the water, clear, crisp double images kissing at the surface. Farther out the gumdrops were wrapped in low clouds and mist, almost invisible.

    As we stood gazing out from our boat's rail we saw a small raft approaching, paddled by a woman in a conical hat, her young daughter sitting beside her. Our taxi had arrived.

    Josefina preferred not climbing up or down things if she didn't need to, so Elvira and I climbed aboard the raft. No one told us where we were going, but we headed toward the nearest limestone gumdrop.

    As we got close we could see a low opening in the rock, a short tunnel to the interior. We passed through, heads ducked to avoid the rough ceiling, and came out into the middle of the flooded ring of rock.

    Ha Long Bay's limestone gumdrops existed in various states of dissolution, centuries or millennia of ocean tides and rainwater having hollowed out their interiors. Some, like the one with the caverns, were hollow inside but still largely intact. But the inside of the one we were now entering had completely collapsed and been flooded by the ocean through the small opening we had just navigated. What was left was a towering ring of rock encircling us, hundreds of feet high, crusted with green growth, blue sky above. And we were floating inside it.

    We all just sat there, the little girl playing with Elvira's hair, almost overwhelmed by the quiet, the serenity, the feeling of seclusion in such a crowded country. But after a few minutes it was time to play with the acoustics.

    Wanting to hear what sort of echo I might get, I clapped my hands together just once. A gunshot exploded. The ring of rock was not so much an echo chamber as an amplifier. That single clap came back to me as a rifle shot. I tried a short whistle. The whole bowl filled with a piercing siren blast. This was fun. I wished I'd brought a gong with me, but it would have been impossible to get one on the raft. I wondered what a harmonica would sound like, or a violin. Having left all of my fantasy instruments in my imaginary suitcase, I contented myself with clapping and whistling, apologizing each time to the serenity for my intrusion.

And then it was time to go, back through the tunnel and back to the boat to tell Josefina about the wonderful place we had been.

As evening fell I stood on the third-floor balcony that wrapped around the hotel and looked out over the bay. I was staying in room 308 of this hotel (whose name escapes me). The room just below mine, room 208, had a plaque beside its door informing one and all that Uncle Ho himself, Ho Chi Minh, had once stayed there, as had the actress Catherine Deneuve (not, I assumed, at the same time).

The next morning we drove back to Hanoi for our flight south to Danang.

We traded in the gray, sixty-five-degree days of the north for the warm and sunny eighties of central Vietnam. We were met at the airport in Danang by our guide for this part of the country, Hoa, also known as Flower. She was easily the friendliest tour guide I've ever had and, needless to say, we all took an instant liking to her. She told us that she was originally from Hanoi and had studied to be a doctor, but the only jobs available were in small villages. So she had become a tour guide, which, she told us, was often a better-paying job than doctor anyway.

We drove from the airport into Danang itself, which had a ramshackle, impermanent feel to it, like it could all be folded up, loaded onto trucks, and moved somewhere else if needed. Stone-working and sculpting were major activities. That made sense, as the Marble Mountains stood nearby, a handful of limestone mountains rising individually above the otherwise flat oceanfront, more rocky pimples bursting from Vietnam's skin. We drove to the bottom of one of them, Thuy Son, and began climbing the seemingly endless steps to see what was up there. Even Josefina came along.

What was up there was an array of grottoes, pagodas, temples, gardens, statuary, and tunnels. It had long been a sacred sanctuary and during the Vietnam War one of the grottoes had even served as a Vietcong hospital, within earshot of the US air base. From the top we could see Danang spread out below us and, in the distance, the beach known during the war as China Beach.

We were joined by a gaggle of young girls who, having failed to sell us anything, were determined to earn a dollar or two by being our unofficial guides. One girl in particular attached herself to me as we ascended the 180 stone steps. She seemed to have an Americanism for any occasion.

"Where you from?" she asked.
"New York", I replied.
"Totally awesome!"

Later, as I struggled up the endless uneven steps, she chided me. "No pain, no gain". I tipped her two dollars at the end, mostly for making me laugh.

Right from the start of the trip I had been pleasantly surprised at the warm reception I received when I told someone I was an American. As a general rule, the Vietnamese seemed to love Americans, like Brits, and loathe the French. But they had a special contempt for the Chinese and the Russians, their two overbearing and meddling rich uncles. I was called "G.I. Joe" more than once, and with a thumbs up and a smile.

It was dark by the time we reached nearby Hoi An and checked into our hotel. Wanting to be a good guest, I read the notice on the nightstand, which listed the hotel's regulations. The seventh and final rule was this – "Bicycles, motorbikes, pets, fire, arms, explosives, inflammables, stinking things, and even prostitutes are not allowed in the hotel." Okay, okay, my cat won't blow up anything while I'm cycling around my room. But even prostitutes? I don't know...might be a deal breaker.

    The mention of "stinking things" was clearly a reference to durian, a fruit common in Vietnam and whose odor has been compared to a rotting corpse. I had seen notices in other hotels that were more direct – "Absolutely no durian!!!!" It would be quite a few years later that I would have a chance to experience this fruit treat myself. It would turn out to be worth the wait, sort of.

    Hoi An was a brief respite from the crowds and the insane traffic. We walked around the old town and viewed the centuries-old Chinese and Japanese neighborhoods. We floated by boat to a small neighboring village, completely submerged by floods just three months earlier, where pottery was the main business and where you could buy just about anything made out of coconut husks. I found time to enjoy the hotel's swimming pool, lounging in the water, looking up at the palm trees, thinking "this is the life". Lizards scuttled across the ceiling above us as we ate dinner that night. In the morning we drove back north to Hue.

    The road to Hue wound and ascended through mountains that rose almost directly from the South China Sea, reflecting the morning light in the near distance below us. For part of the way we followed a Pepsi truck, playing hide-and-seek with it as it disappeared around the many bends in the road, which gradually descended again to the coastal plain.

    Hue was once and for many years the capital of Vietnam and featured a large ex-Imperial City as its centerpiece.

We visited what was left of it. The War had not been kind to Hue. It had been the center of a long and bloody battle. Bombardment, street-to-street and house-to-house fighting, and mass executions by both sides left Hue a broken, depopulated shambles. But that had been thirty years before and now Hue was alive again, some rubble and a few bullet holes being the chief reminders of times past.

The city is bisected by the Perfume River and we floated down it, past the many shrines, citadels, and pagodas that loomed above its banks, durian hanging from trees like green footballs, ghosts of the war hanging over the city like mist. But it was a fine and sunny day and children played soccer outside the pockmarked walls of the Imperial City.

On our way to dinner that night Elvira had a special request. Though having no desire to do so herself, Elvira had a fascination with the concept of eating dog. She asked if Flower knew of any dog restaurants in Hue and, if so, could we stop and visit one. Flower conferred with the driver for a minute. He thought he might know a place and it was on our way. As we drove along we asked Flower about her own relationship with dogs. She told us she had one as a pet.

"Would you ever eat your dog?" I asked teasingly. She looked horrified and shook her head "no" emphatically.

"Of course not!"

"So", I asked, "what kind of dog is best to eat?"

"Young dog!"

It turns out that dog is something of a luxury item. Unlike other meat animals, dogs are meat eaters themselves. That makes them expensive to raise. I suddenly felt underdressed to be visiting such a ritzy place.

Our minibus turned down an alley and

stopped in front of a nondescript building. The driver went inside and came back out a moment later, motioning for us to come in. Inside there was a party of five or six men sitting around a low table, various dishes arrayed in front of them, apparently in mid-meal. They waved to us to join them.

Elvira and Josefina hung back, not wishing to partake, wanting only to observe and shoot video. The sisters offered to buy the table a bottle of rice wine, which was readily accepted. It would not be the first bottle to be drained at the table that night.

I accepted their invitation to join them at the table and they made room for me on a low bench. One of the men handed me a cup of rice wine, which tasted like varnish and burned like a Molotov cocktail. They showed me some of the dishes they were eating while refilling my cup. The dog intestine was black and uninviting, but the leg of dog looked okay. They put some on a plate for me and handed it to me along with my refill. It was tasty and fatty and reminded me of lamb. The second rice wine tasted no better than the first but burned considerably less. Elvira got it all on video.

Before I could finish my third rice wine (or the other way around), Flower said we needed to be going, dinner awaited. I knocked back the rest of the wine, thanked our hosts, and staggered back to the minibus to return to our regularly scheduled dinner.

Dinner was a ridiculous affair at an old palace from imperial days, the emperor's mother's residence. I was given an emperor costume, complete with multi-colored robe, silk pants, and tasseled hat. Elvira and Josefina were dressed up as queens. I had become rather proficient with chopsticks and could pick up half a peanut with them. I practiced picking peanuts off my dinner plate while court musicians played and singers sang traditional songs, ending with that old Vietnamese standard, "Auld Lang Syne". It was a good night to have a rice wine buzz.

That night I sat out on the terrace of the Huong Giang Hotel, watching the lights of the boats gliding by on the Perfume River, shadows in the inky darkness. Mosquitoes swarmed but my repellant was keeping them at bay. Sometimes just sitting and watching lights sparkle on water is all I need. Passengers and cargo motored up and down the river. Lizards scurried up and down the walls and across the ceilings. After a while I said goodnight to Hue and went to bed.

We reluctantly said goodbye to Flower and boarded our flight from Hue to Ho Chi Minh City, formerly (and still) known as Saigon. The North had won the war and renamed Vietnam's largest city, the capital of the former South Vietnam, after dead Uncle Ho, but the southerners who called it home still called it Saigon. And who wouldn't? It's so much less cumbersome, and so I will use it here.

Upon arrival in Saigon we were taken directly to lunch — the usual array of rice, fish, pork, chicken, hot sauce, various vegetables, and the ubiquitous french fries, with the standard dessert of watermelon. The Vietnamese may not have liked the French, but they sure did love french fries, which were served at virtually every meal, even breakfast, and came accompanied by a small dish containing coarse salt and a lime wedge. As someone who has long considered french fries mainly to be a great way to eat large quantities of ketchup, I have to admit that I found the potato, salt, and lime juice combination a tasty one.

We emerged from lunch to find three cyclos and their drivers waiting for us, one each. Our southern guide, Huie, told us to hop aboard, we would be taking a three-hour tour of Saigon by cyclo, and he would see us later at our hotel.

The cyclo is a bicycle rickshaw — the

passenger sits in a little open cab up front, with the driver pedaling the bicycle part behind. With two wheels on the cab in front, the whole contraption forms a fairly stable tricycle. We merged into Saigon's traffic, twice as crazy as Hanoi's, and were soon engulfed in the maelstrom of cars, trucks, motorbikes, and other cyclos.

It is my understanding that Vietnam's traffic has become much worse in the twenty years since I was there and that cyclos have mostly been forced off the roads by the explosion in car and motorbike ownership. The pace of life has quickened and the old cyclos were just getting in everyone's way. And that's a shame. But for three hours I had a front row seat for Saigon's traffic madness, most on display at busy intersections, where all the traffic would merge head-on and pass through itself, like the stars in two colliding galaxies. We hardly stopped at all. I felt like the prow of a ship as we parted the beep beep beeping waves.

It is a testimony to the power of jet lag that I actually dozed off for a while in the midst of all that chaos. Even then, more than a week after I arrived, I still had the three-in-the-afternoon sleepies, as I had every day. Elvira, in her own cyclo nearby, got my nap on video for posterity.

The cyclos dropped us off at our hotel, the Omni Saigon Hotel, where Huie awaited to tell us that we should make our own way to dinner that evening, where he would meet us. He gave us the address and instructed us to have the hotel desk call taxis for us, which he would reimburse us for later.

The Omni Saigon Hotel was an overly-ornate, overly-spacious exercise in pointless opulence. It looked and felt expensive but uninviting. It had a rooftop swimming pool. I decided to go for a walk instead.

Every afternoon in Saigon, somewhere around four-thirty or five, there would be a torrential downpour lasting about ten minutes. I set out to explore the small neighborhood behind the hotel, figuring I would easily make it back before the rain came. My route was essentially a rectangle – two blocks behind the hotel, right turn, two blocks, right turn, two blocks, right turn, and two more blocks would have me back on the hotel's doorstep. Fifteen minutes later I had completed the rectangle and had no idea where I was, or where the Omni Saigon was. It had disappeared, along with the busy road that ran in front of it. I decided to retrace my steps. Back two blocks, left turn, over two blocks, etc. Nope, nothing. I felt like a rat in a maze. As I turned on to a dead end street the rain suddenly came down like a curtain, bringing Act One of *Lost in Saigon* to a close.

    There was nothing to do but stand there and take a cold shower. Ten minutes later it stopped as suddenly as it had started. I was glad that I hadn't brought my camera with me. I was as wet as if I'd just climbed out of a swimming pool. As I stood there, still on this dead-end street, a man emerged from one of the small houses and approached me, saying something in Vietnamese. I shrugged at him that I didn't understand. He reached into a shirt pocket and pulled out a small scrap of paper and a pen, offering them to me. I got the point and wrote "Omni Hotel" on the paper and handed everything back to him. He motioned for me to wait and then ducked back into the house. Five minutes later he returned and handed me another piece of paper, folded in half. Unfolding it, I found a crude map with directions back to the Omni. I thanked the man profusely and five minutes later I was back at the hotel, looking like something the rain had washed into the lobby.

    Back in my room I got out of my wet clothes and dried off. It felt so good to be dry and curled up on the bed that I decided not to bother going to dinner. I went downstairs and bought a big chocolate chip cookie instead.

    As it turned out, Elvira and Josefina also hadn't made it to dinner. A little tired and not feeling like dealing with a taxi ride, they had called it an early night. And Huie hadn't gotten to the restaurant either, having been involved in a minor motorbike accident on the way in which he'd injured his ankle. If I hadn't gotten soaking wet I'd have been at the restaurant alone, not speaking the language, and wondering where the hell everyone was, just like at the airport in Hanoi. Perhaps Mr. Koo had eaten there that night in our place.

Huie's injury turned out to be minor and in the morning we drove to Cu Chi, on Saigon's northwestern outskirts. Along the way Huie told us what life had been like for Southerners such as himself after the fall of Saigon almost twenty-five years earlier. He had been sent to a "re-education" camp for a time, to unlearn his wrong thinking and to get with the victorious North's program. Like so many other southern Vietnamese at the time, he pretended to believe, well enough anyway, and confessed to whatever he was asked to confess to, and so was released to resume his life. But many had been tortured, many had died in those camps. Huie showed us the physical scars of his time there. His distrust of the government was obvious, his disdain for it permanent. He told us that while we were riding in the van he would answer any of our questions truthfully. But outside the van, where ears might be listening, would not be the time or place for difficult questions. And so as we drove to Cu Chi he told us about the re-education camps and the fates of some of the people he had known, either fortunate or tragic. We learned that in some ways the south had never fully surrendered. They still called their city Saigon, after all, no matter what the government's maps called it now.

We were about to visit the tunnels of Cu Chi, one of the most extraordinary chapters in the annals of warfare. Dug mostly by hand and begun back in the '40s when the French were still pretending to be in charge, the tunnels had been expanded during the Vietnam War era to hundreds of miles and several levels and included underground living areas, meeting rooms, kitchens, hospitals, and even entertainment venues. Thousands of people lived underground there while the war raged above. The tunnels crisscrossed the region to the west of Saigon, surfacing at well-camouflaged exit holes, including exits within the perimeter of the nearby US military base. Sometimes a Viet Cong soldier would pop up, fire a few rounds, and disappear again. The US Army made a concerted effort to eradicate the threat posed by the tunnels – the North's soldiers and weaponry were able to move freely, unseen. The area was heavily bombed. And tunnel rats were sent in.

  The job of "tunnel rat" was one of the most dangerous and uncomfortable for American soldiers. Tunnel rats were accepted on a volunteer basis and had to be small enough to fit in the narrow spaces below ground. When a tunnel opening was discovered, they were sent in to flush out and kill any enemy combatants they might find. The conditions were frightening – in addition to the possibility of encountering enemy gunfire, there were also numerous booby traps waiting to impale them, as well as snakes, spiders, scorpions, and centipedes, all crammed into spaces too small to stand or even turn around in. The air was foul, the heat and humidity intense. Once the tunnel was cleared, explosives were dropped in and that section was demolished. But much of the tunnel complex remained undiscovered during the war. And now it was on display.

  There are two sets of tunnels, located a few miles apart. One is a reconstruction, a fake, for demonstration purposes. The other is the real thing, the tunnels having been enlarged to allow visitors entry. We went to the real one.

  Before going in to the tunnels, we enjoyed a few above-ground diversions. There was a small building with a bunch of empty chairs facing a TV showing some really juicy propaganda, plenty of stuff about the aggressive American "dogs", our evil, imperialist aims, and our cruelty and joy at the slaughter of the peaceful, fun-loving Vietnamese. There was an old, rusty

American tank nearby, sitting where it died. I scrambled up and sat atop it, posing for a picture. There was also wine for sale – bottles of rice wine, each one containing an entire cobra. But the primary entertainment was the large display of booby traps.

There was a whole row of them on display, a cheerful Vietnamese man demonstrating their ingenious effectiveness. There were trap doors dropping into spikes, trap doors swinging from doorways, laden with spikes, spikes on rollers, ankle-snaring pits of spikes, grenades on trip wires. Old war-era bombshells and weapons lay scattered about, hands-on history.

Then it was time to go down in the tunnels. I went down one level and duck-walked through a tunnel that was now several times wider than it had been during the war. It was hot, humid, dirty. I tried to keep my knees from scraping the floor as I looked for the way down to the second level.

I eventually got down to level three, crawling in the increasing heat and humidity, dirt smeared on my shirt, looking for the ladder back up to the surface. My time as a tunnel rat was over; I breathed the fresh air again, happy once again that I had only been fifteen when the war ended.

The next day would be my last in Vietnam, my flight home leaving the following morning. Elvira and Josefina would be traveling on to Cambodia for a few more days. Part of me wished I was going with them. Part of me craved a pepperoni pizza.

We drove south out of Saigon, which sprawls so far in all directions that you lose any sense of it even being a city anymore, on our way to the market town of My Tho, on the banks of the Mekong River. Our first stop was the huge, overflowing market, where we stopped to sample exotic fruits the names of which I had never heard before. After a lunch overlooking the river, we boarded a small boat and set out onto the wide Mekong. We were dwarfed by the cargo ships sailing up and down the river, which was full of craft of all sizes. Crossing to the far bank, we found a canal leading away from the river and into dense vegetation, which overhung the narrow canal like a green ceiling. After a while we came to a clearing where we disembarked to visit a beekeeper.

     Plastic water bottles, repurposed for honey, filled a wooden table. It was good to see that there were no cobras coiled up in the honey bottles. The beekeeper, a smiling young woman, stood beside a large wooden box raised on four spindly wooden legs. This was a beehive and inside it were four trays, wooden frames with wire mesh for the bees to build their honeycomb in. The woman removed one of the trays and stood it atop the box. It was a solid mass of bees. In gestures, she motioned me to hold out my arm and extend one finger toward the tray. As I did so she took ahold of my hand and guided my pointing finger through the quivering bees and into the honeycomb. I pulled my finger back out covered with honey and licked it off. She then handed me the tray. I stood holding it, looking down at the hundreds of bees dangling from my hands, the look on my face saying "okay, you can have this back now". It was symbolic of Vietnam itself, a swarming hive of activity that had given me some of my sweetest memories as a traveler. But the bees had to go back in their box now, and I had to leave Vietnam in the morning.

     It took four flights to get home, with connections in Hong Kong, Vancouver, and New York City, but it would be days before I could call the trip finally concluded. With a very short connection time in Hong Kong, I barely made the flight but my suitcase didn't. I stood at the baggage carousel at JFK, waiting and waiting for something that wasn't coming. The crowd got thinner and thinner until there was just me standing there, and a couple of mystery suitcases going around and around. It felt like Hanoi all over again, but at least this time there were English-speakers around. And there was no sign of the mysterious Mr. Koo.

At the baggage office I was shown pictures of suitcases, a lineup of luggage, like I was there to identify a suspect. "Which one looks most like yours?" I pointed to one of the pictures. The real answer, of course, was "the one with my name tag on it", but they didn't have a picture of that. They told me they'd ship it up to Albany when they located it and to check with the local FedEx office.

Three days later I retrieved my luggage and drove back home, the trip finally complete. A few weeks after that I received a package in the mail from Elvira. It was a videotape copy of all the video she shot in Vietnam and Cambodia, including scenes of my cyclo nap in Saigon. It was, as the girl at Marble Mountain had said, "totally awesome".

Chapter Seven: Ecuador/Galapagos Islands and Peru – October 2001

In October 2001 traveling had become tense. It was just thirty-three days since the 9/11 attacks, airport security was hyperactive, and all the rules had changed. There were bombs in every suitcase, boxcutters up every sleeve. Flying wasn't fun anymore. It was a good time to go to South America, far from all the madness.

My flight had touched down in Quito, Ecuador after dark. I sat on a bus parked outside the terminal with a few other people, waiting for the rest of my group to clear the maze of baggage claim and Customs. I could barely breathe. Quito, at about 9,300 feet above sea level, was the highest place on Earth that I had yet been. Just walking from the terminal to the bus and climbing aboard had left me gasping. And Cusco would be even higher.

When the bus reached the hotel and we walked into the lobby, we were greeted with trays of glasses of a minty tea, not unlike what I had been served in Morocco. But this tea had a special ingredient and the mint was there to mask its bitter taste. That special ingredient was coca leaves.

Coca leaves, from which cocaine is processed, have long been a staple of the Andes. Chewing coca leaves gives relief from the altitude, the dizziness and shortness of breath. The tea was just what I needed and soon I was feeling better, breathing easily. There was no jet lag on this trip, as I hadn't changed time zones from Albany to Quito. I was soon asleep, ready to see some sights in the morning.

The old colonial part of Quito is the best-preserved site of its kind in South America. It was one of UNESCO's first dozen world heritage sites selected in 1978, a list that now exceeds 1,100 places around the world. Colonial Quito is crammed with cathedrals and other old buildings, some dating back to the city's founding in the early 1500s by the Spanish conquistadors, yet still has spacious plazas as well.

Stepping inside the church known as the Compania de Jesus, it was obvious what the conquistadors had been after when they came here, and it was obvious what they had done with it. The walls, altars, columns, ceiling, and just about everything else was covered in gold leaf. It was like visiting Fort Knox, but without all that annoying ultra-high security. Construction of the church had begun in 1605, two years before the English established their first permanent settlement in the New World, Jamestown. The English clearly had a lot of catching up to do. But by the time the Compania de Jesus was completed in 1765 the Brits had managed to close the gap and pull ahead. Squinting in the golden glare, I put my sunglasses on and had a look around the place.

Besides the ubiquitous gold, there were paintings, carvings, and bizarre statuary, faces sprouting out of shoulders, grimacing skulls. It was like the home of an eccentric billionaire hoarder. I took off my sunglasses and stepped back out into the bright morning sunshine.

A few miles to the north of Quito stands the world's largest monument marking the location of the equator. And it's no wonder – Ecuador is so proud of being located on the equator that they named the whole country after it. The monument rises several stories and contains an ethnological museum within it. Outside, there is a line extending from either side marking the actual location of the equator. I stood there straddling the equator, one foot in the northern hemisphere and one foot in the south, and had my picture taken. There is just one problem with this – I wasn't actually standing on the equator.

The real equator is located about 250 yards north of the monument and is indicated by a much smaller marker. Or maybe not. More precise measurements seem to suggest that the equator is yet another 140 or so yards farther north. And then there is this – not to get too technical, but the equator is a line that is perpendicular to the planet's axis of spin, which wobbles a bit. That means that the exact location of the equator meanders by a few feet. Also, because of continental drift, Ecuador itself, and its equator monument with it, will one day, far in the future, no longer be anywhere near the equator. But I know that I at least *crossed* the equator on our way up to Otavalo, and again on the way back. That's good enough for me.

We were left on our own for lunch later that day. Did I seek out some exotic Ecuadorian cuisine? No. I take no pride in admitting that I went for a quick meal at the food court of the mall that sat just down the street from the hotel. I don't speak Spanish but I found a place that advertised its food in a language we both spoke – Menu Italian. I ordered a plate of fettuccine alfredo and took a seat at a Formica table with plastic chairs. Ah, the allure of far-off places!

Five hundred miles west of mainland Ecuador, out in the Pacific Ocean, our plane touched down on the island of Baltra. We had arrived in the fabled Galapagos Islands (or, as my tour-assigned roommate Gene kept calling them, the *Gawapalos* Islands). To guard against the importation of invasive species, we all had to step onto some sort of disinfecting mat before leaving the airport for the short bus ride to the boat.

Baltra was the logical place for a Galapagos airport. A mostly barren chunk of desert rock, just ten square miles, a few cacti filled in the spaces between concrete bunkers, leftovers from World War Two, when Baltra was the location of an American Air Force base. Flat, brown, and mostly lifeless, the departing and arriving planes had little to disturb here.

A few minutes after leaving the airport we arrived at the dock to take the ferry across to Santa Cruz Island.

It took twice as long to put on and take off our life jackets as it did to cross the narrow channel, no more than a quarter of a mile wide, separating Baltra from the island of Santa Cruz. Another bus awaited us.

The road from the north of Santa Cruz to the southern end was almost a straight line, only one or two small bends to negotiate on the entire forty-five minute drive. At the end of the road sat Puerto Ayora, the largest town in the mostly unpopulated islands, with a population of about twelve thousand, spread out around Academy Bay, which was crowded with boats. We boarded a water taxi for the short trip to our hotel's private dock. A five minute walk, overseen by black iguanas watching from atop a low stone wall, brought us to the Hotel Delfin, quiet and secluded, with a swimming pool and a private white sand beach. The pool and the beach were of little use, as we soon learned. There is a quirk to the weather on Santa Cruz, true of the Galapagos Islands in general – the north end is sunny and warm, but the south end tends to be cloudy and cool, not ideal weather for a dip in the pool. Besides, we would leave the hotel every morning and return after dark. We didn't need a pool and a beach; there was water, water everywhere.

As is so often the case in my travels, the Hotel Delfin can no longer be found. It has been upgraded and renamed. It is now the Finch Bay Galapagos Hotel. In pictures, the pool still looks like I remember it – beautiful and empty.

Before we began exploring the islands we sailed across the bay in our private yacht, the *Delfin II*, to visit the Charles Darwin Research Station. The Galapagos Islands are most famously home to the giant Galapagos tortoise, which can live to be two hundred years old or more. They live in remote areas scattered around the islands. They're not easy to find and visitors are prohibited from tramping around unsupervised, so the Darwin Research Station was the place to go to see one (several actually). From there we eventually walked back into Puerto Ayora, a charming town full of eateries, souvenir stands, and a small graveyard full of white tombs and headstones. But Edith Bunker was interested in only one thing – refrigerator magnets.

I don't recall her real name, but everyone in the group pretty quickly took to calling this particular woman "Edith Bunker", because she sounded exactly like the well-known TV character. It was not a term of endearment. She was ponderously slow, frequently confused or distracted, and constantly on the lookout for refrigerator magnets, the Holy Grail of her travels. She was like a stone in our collective shoe. I pitied our guide for having to look after her like she was a toddler at the county fair. We left her behind to haggle for magnets as we returned to the dock to take the water taxi back to the hotel. She straggled in an hour later, beaming with delight at the treasures she had found.

The trick to having a private yacht without being a millionaire is to share it with a group of strangers and to get the hell off it when your time is up. We had four days to visit four islands. Sailing back to the north end of Santa Cruz, we had just finished lunch aboard the *Delfin II* when we arrived at our first stop.

Ghost crabs scuttled across the sand and into their holes as we set foot on the beach. We were going to hike inland to look for yellow iguanas. Bright red-and-yellow crabs stood out against the black volcanic rocks jumbled on the shore, pink flamingos picked their lunches out of a shallow lagoon a few yards inland, and the ocean was like a blue and green rainbow, the shallow green water near shore gradually darkening to the light blue of slightly deeper water, then to darker and darker blues out to sea, where the snow-white *Delfin II* bobbed in the gentle waves. It looked like the Crayola crayon factory had exploded, or simply melted. There was color, color everywhere.

It took another couple of hours to reach our next destination, Rabida Island. But we had good company – a pair of dolphins swam with us almost the entire way, one just off the front of each side of the boat, guiding the way. On arrival we hopped into Zodiacs and soon made a wet landing, wading onto a strikingly red sand beach. Sea lions lounged by the water, pelicans nested in bushes just behind the beach. Careful not to come between the young sea lions and their potentially cranky moms and dads, some of us headed up the beach to where a sea cliff rose from the water, deemed a good spot to go snorkeling. Despite never having been snorkeling before, and my deep distrust of the ocean, I decided to give it a go.

The first thing I learned was how to walk in flippers – backwards. Walking forward, your flippers dig into the sand. The second thing I learned was that I'm not a natural-born snorkeler. I lagged behind the others, spitting water, clearing my mask and mouthpiece again and again. I decided to just stay in one place and float face down, which worked pretty well for a minute or two at a time before I came up spitting out seawater again. I watched fish darting back and forth in the clear water below me until the novelty had worn off, then returned to shore and tried to get dressed with a minimum of sand getting into the wrong places. After rejoining the rest of the group that had opted out of the snorkeling, I learned a third thing -- while I had been floating in the water, they had seen a shark's fin cruising up and down a few dozen yards from shore. I was happy not to have known that while I was out there – panic tends to spoil the fun. But I've told you before and I'll tell you again – the ocean is no place for people.

    The first time I ever got seasick was on the return trip from Rabida to Santa Cruz, in the *Delfin II*'s tiny bathroom. Thanks again, ocean!

    The next day we had North Seymour Island on our schedule, followed by more of Santa Cruz, Depending on logistics, on some of the mornings the *Delfin II* would be waiting for us out in Academy Bay, other times we would make the forty-five minute straight-line drive to the north end of the island to catch up with it there, with Baltra an arm's length away, as we did this morning.

    North Seymour was a tiny island, just one square mile, lying just to the north of Baltra, which itself had formerly been known as South Seymour Island. We were there, of course, for the boobies.

    We had already seen them advertised on t-shirts for sale in Puerto Ayora, t-shirts with phrases like "who wants to see my boobies?", "show me your boobies", "stop staring at my boobies", and the straightforward "I love boobies", all illustrated with the same goofy-but-cute birds with bright blue feet. I was tempted to buy one but figured I'd have too much explaining to do when I wore it back at home.

    The blue-footed booby is one of the most popular animals in the Galapagos, if measured only by t-shirt sales, and we stepped out of our Zodiac and onto a rocky, makeshift landing spot, Just a few yards inland there were boobies on display everywhere.

The boobies were nesting in an area with boulders of all sizes scattered about, almost every surface covered with a white layer of accumulated booby droppings. Standing two to three feet tall, white and brown, with big, bright blue feet, they largely ignored us as we trespassed through their turf. There were many booby chicks, fluffy white fuzzballs whose feet were still a dull off-white, yet to blossom into full blueness. Behind the boobies, in the center of the island, frigate birds were nesting in dense bushes. Walking past these we were suddenly at the other end of the island, nothing but ocean in front of us. That's all there was to North Seymour Island. A few sea lions lazed on the beach as we circled the island and arrived back at our landing spot. A couple of red-footed boobies stood on the rocks there, displaying their alternative booby fashion.

Sailing back down the west coast of Santa Cruz, we stopped for a while at a nice white sand beach with what were becoming the familiar ingredients: red-and-yellow crabs on black rocks, pink flamingos pecking at shrimp in shallow lagoons, and all the ocean shades from green to deep blue, the *Delfin II* waiting just offshore. Some of the group enjoyed snorkeling there. I walked the beach and watched for fins in the water.

The next morning we sailed out of Academy Bay, heading south for the island of Floreana. Our first landing was at a place known as Post Office Bay. The major attraction at Post Office Bay is an old barrel. Since the 1700s sailors have been using that barrel to send letters home. English whaling ships were often away from home for a year or more and the barrel on Floreana was established as a mail drop. Outbound sailors would leave their letters in the barrel and homeward-bound sailors would pick them up, bring them home, and deliver them. Now it is mainly tourists who use it.

While on the mainland of Ecuador I had spent a frustrating amount of time trying to find a post office to send a few postcards home. There just didn't seem to be any in the whole country and our guide had no clue either. At the airport in Quito, just before boarding our flight to Baltra, I found what may have been the only post office in mainland Ecuador, tucked away in a dusty corner of the terminal. I mailed my postcards but held one in reserve to test the barrel method on Floreana.

The cards I mailed from the Quito airport took about two weeks to arrive back home. The card I left in the barrel took one week, and required no postage. The recipient never met the deliverer – the card just showed up in his mailbox one day.

Before leaving our mail there our guide pulled a handful of cards and letters from the barrel and began reading off the addresses. Whenever a member of our group heard an address near them, they would raise a hand and say "I'll take that one". I took one addressed to someone in Manhattan and, back home, I passed it along to a friend who was traveling to the city and could deliver it for me. If I'm ever in that part of the world again, I will send all of my postcards postage-free.

It's a bit of a shame that these days postcards are largely obsolete. People just take pictures of where they are with their phones and send them home in seconds. What we gain in expediency we lose in experience.

An extended Zodiac ride just offshore showed us some of the islands' more hidden wildlife. Sea lions, sea turtles, stingrays, and even a small Galapagos penguin patrolled the water and the shore. Landing at Cormorant Bay we walked a beach that sparkled green with olivine crystals and which was strewn with dead, washed-ashore jellyfish. Sea turtles lurked just beneath the breaking waves and the usual flamingos stood in a lagoon, stepping and pecking. Our time in the Galapagos was almost at an end. We would be flying to Peru in the morning. But my tour-appointed roommate, Gene, had opted not to take the trip's Peru extension. He had been in Peru just a few months earlier and gotten himself engaged to a Peruvian girl. He planned to visit her again in a few weeks. So Gene bid farewell to us (and to the "Gawapalos" Islands) and we continued on without him. I would now have a room all to myself.

Our evening arrival in Lima, Peru should have been simple and uncomplicated. It turned out to be neither, all because of a brief nap.

A Customs and Immigration form had been given out to everyone on the flight, to be filled out and handed in on arrival in Lima. I had been napping at the time and was passed over. Lacking the required paperwork for entry, the Customs official pointed me back toward a supply of blank forms. In the ten minutes it took for me to get the form and fill it out, at least four full planeloads had arrived, hundreds of people now forming a huge line that I had no choice but to take a place at the back of. While the rest of my group waited for me on a bus, I stood and waited in line, the faint sound of passport-stamping growing slowly louder as I inched forward.

Finally through to the baggage claim area, my flight's baggage carousel was now being used for two more flights. Watching as hundreds of pieces of luggage went around and around, I figured mine had to be in there somewhere. But as the baggage dwindled to nothing over the next half-hour, I came to realize that my suitcase was not playing on this merry-go-round. Widening my search, I finally found my suitcase hidden in an out-of-the way corner of the baggage claim area. By this point I imagined that my tour group had assumed I'd been arrested for smuggling booby eggs and left me behind to rot in a Peruvian prison. Fortunately, our guide, a new one for the Peruvian leg of the trip, was still waiting patiently for me, clipboard in hand, needing one more check-mark on his list.

We were only in Lima for the night, with a flight to Cusco the next morning. *Cusco* is one of those place names that no one seems quite sure how to spell. "Cusco" and "Cuzco" seem to be used interchangeably. I will stick to the official Peruvian government spelling.

Cusco sits in the Andes at an elevation of over 11,000 feet. The approach to the airport is breathtaking, with snow-capped Andean peaks giving way to brown folds of mountains, the airport a flat postage stamp in the distance on which to stick a landing. But after four days in the Galapagos we were no longer acclimated to the altitude and the coca tea they gave us on arrival at the hotel was much needed. Unfortunately, they hadn't sweetened the tea as had been done in Quito and it took me a while to gag down the bitter brew. But it was well worth it. My initial lightheadedness and difficulty breathing gradually subsided as I took a slow, short walk around the hotel's neighborhood.

We toured Cusco and some of the nearby Inca ruins that day. Cusco had been the capital of the Inca empire and they had left behind some very impressive stone work, both outside and within the city. At one point as we were driving we crested a hill and were informed that we had just reached an altitude of 12,000 feet. That was the highest point on Earth that I had yet ascended to.

We were on our own to find dinner in Cusco that night. As it turned out, dinner found *me*.

Cusco is a major tourist destination and its city center is packed with restaurants and nightclubs. The competition is fierce and many of the restaurants hire people to walk around the streets and almost literally pull people into their establishments. Young men and women with clipboard menus accosted me as soon as I set foot in the area. "Best food, special deal, free drink". They all had a special deal. Craving a nice spaghetti dinner, I allowed myself to be led to a small Italian restaurant. Free drink. I ate my dinner while Isaac waited outside.

I had met Isaac while walking through the city's central plaza on my way to have dinner. He was maybe twelve years old. He was selling postcards but, it being near the end of the trip, I just didn't need any. He tagged along with me anyway, keen to practice his English. But unlike everyone else I had met while traveling who wanted to practice their English on me, Isaac was also intent on teaching me some Spanish. He forgot about his postcards and just steered me to the restaurants while we conversed in halting Anglo-Spanish.

Once the Italian restaurant's clipboard girl had reeled me in I figured Isaac would wander off. But he was waiting for me when I finally emerged after I'd finished eating. We walked together back toward the hotel.

We had a seat on some stone steps and talked. We would point at things and teach each other the word for it in our own language. He asked about the USA. Isaac had also taken an interest in my watch, and my shoes. He asked me if I would give him my watch. I told him I needed it, that a tourist like me had a lot of times to keep track of – departure time, arrival time, lunchtime.

"Okay", he said, pointing at my shoes. "You give me shoes?"

I told Isaac that he was in luck. I just happened to have brought a spare pair of shoes on the trip and, for some reason that I can no longer recall, the spare pair, though practically brand new, had not fit me at all. I told him I would give him the shoes on my last night in Cusco. But, I told him, they were much too big for him. He didn't mind. He said he would give them to his father.

From what I had been able to figure out, Isaac lived in one of the hill neighborhoods, a relatively poor section of Cusco. The old city sat in a flat valley, small houses reaching up the surrounding hills. His father was a laborer of some sort and Isaac chipped in by selling postcards. Whether the shoes fit anyone in the family didn't matter – they could always be sold. I told Isaac I'd be sightseeing outside of Cusco the next day and would look for him when I returned in the afternoon.

The next morning we visited Ollantaytambo, a massive Inca ceremonial site overlooking the confluence of two rivers. A succession of ten-foot-high terraces rose skyward, forming a huge wedding cake mountain. A smaller, human-scale staircase cut through the terraces all the way to the top. I stopped several times on my way up to catch my breath, the altitude still a factor. The Andes provided a spectacular backdrop, towering above the landscape. The Incas were masters of fountains and irrigation and we explored all of the old stonework, still carrying water even now.

Later we stopped at a villa for lunch, featuring a food I had never encountered before – sliced roast alpaca. I couldn't get enough; it tasted like lean roast beef. But I declined an offer of what seems to be Peru's most popular beverage, Inca Kola, a piss-yellow, sickly sweet, bubble-gum-flavored drink. I wanted to save room for more alpaca.

Next we stopped in Pisac, on the way back to Cusco, to visit the outdoor market. The sprawling market had just about anything a tourist could want, including refrigerator magnets for Edith, who we were still dragging around like an anchor. I bought myself an alpaca sweater and an alpaca blanket. It was just an alpaca kind of day.

Back in Cusco by late afternoon, I found Isaac near the plaza and told him I wanted to do some shopping. I told him what I was looking for and he brought me to a covered shopping arcade, a dimly-lit maze of small stalls selling everything from hats to ceramics to batteries. It was like the dollar-store version of the market at Pisac. I could have blundered around in there all day without finding what I wanted, but Isaac led me directly to the stall I needed and translated for me. I thanked him and told him I was going to go off and find dinner. I would look for him again later in the plaza.

After dinner we had another two-way language lesson. I told him I was going to Machu Picchu the next morning. He had heard of Machu Picchu but, not surprisingly, had never seen it, except in the pictures on the postcards he sold.

I had to get up at five-thirty the next morning to catch the six-thirty train to Machu Picchu or, technically, to Aguas Calientes, the town at the foot of Machu Picchu. That early in the morning, Cusco's narrow cobblestone streets, usually crammed with traffic, were completely empty, the city silent and seemingly deserted. But there was action over at the nearby train station.

Boarding the train for the four hour ride, I settled into a left-side window seat. We would be following a river valley for much of the way and the river would be on our left, making that the more scenic side.

The train slowly wound down from Cusco's 11,000 feet, snaking back and forth. Before long we were down in the Sacred Valley of the Incas, the river rushing along as if racing the train, the brown Andes looming over us. The train clattered past Ollantaytambo and at mid-morning pulled in to the station at Aguas Calientes. We walked from the train through a bustling market on our way to a fleet of buses waiting to make the ascent to Machu Picchu. I noticed that there were many hawkers of insect repellant but we had seen hardly any bugs at all in Peru so I ignored them and found a seat on one of the buses.

The road to Machu Picchu is a series of thirteen switchbacks that gradually zigzag their way to the top, eight thousand feet above sea level (but a significant three thousand feet lower than Cusco). There was an entry gate that hid the site's grand views until we passed through. On the other side I stopped and stared.

I had seen Machu Picchu in photographs so many times that my first impression was a mixture of bland familiarity – gee, it looks just like the pictures! – and sheer awe that I was standing there, like walking onto an old movie set only to realize the movie was still going on all around me. Bright green grass grew on descending stone terraces that gave the place the feel of an amphitheater without a stage. A llama sat impassively atop one of the terraces, greeting the new arrivals. Stone buildings stood open to the sky, their thatched roofs having long ago disintegrated. Stone steps led up and down through the terraces and I eventually made my way to the top, the pointed peak of neighboring Huayna Picchu still towering above.

Machu Picchu was built in the mid-1400's and occupied for only a century before it was abandoned. The whole place is constructed of perfectly fitted stones; no mortar was used to glue them together. That it has survived at all in earthquake-prone Peru is a testament to the skill of the builders.

As I stood listening to an explanation of one of the site's features, a strangely crafted rock that served as a sort of calendar, I happened to glance down at the back of my left arm. It was spotted with tiny red dots that left a slight smear when I touched them. A quick check revealed more spots on my other arm, as well as several on both legs. I had been bitten by *something*, and multiple times. I had felt nothing. I suddenly made the connection to the insect repellant being sold down in the market when we arrived.

Machu Picchu is infested with small, biting flies that are almost too small to see and whose bite is painless. I was wearing a white shirt of course, so I began holding my arms out to the side so I wouldn't get blood stains on it. I looked like I was preparing to jump off the top and glide back down.

At this point I was ready to have lunch at the cafeteria-like restaurant sitting next to the ruins, where I used as many wetted napkins as I needed to clean the smears of blood off of myself. Afterward, as I poked around a little more before it was time to take the bus back down, a small thunderstorm blew in. A vivid bolt of lightning crackled directly behind the peak of Huayna Picchu and I ducked back into the cafeteria to wait.

The bus ride back down to Aguas Calientes is a game. The game is played by young boys who run directly down the steep hill, shortcutting the switchbacks so as to meet the bus at every turn, smiling and waving before plunging downhill to meet it again at the next one, and so on down the thirteen switchbacks, all the way to the bottom, where they board the buses and collect a reward of spare change from the delighted passengers.

On my way through the market leading to the train station I bought myself one of those odd-looking wool hats common in Peru, the ones with the ear flaps and pointy tops. Almost twenty years later it remains my favorite winter hat.

Night fell as the train approached Cusco. It would soon be time for one last dinner, this time with Isaac.

Isaac was sitting on the curb in front of the hotel when I arrived back from the train station. I had told him that I would treat him to dinner that night and he already had a place in mind.

As we walked, another boy of about nine seemed to materialize out of nowhere to join us. Isaac introduced me to his brother, Sebastian. So it would be dinner for three tonight. I was just glad that Isaac didn't have a sister, too.

I was brought to an inexpensive-looking, cafeteria-ish establishment with cheap tables and chairs and a front counter where you placed your order and stood waiting for it. At Isaac's request, I ordered the quarter *pollo* – that's chicken to English speakers – dinner, complete with sides, for each of them. That sounded good to me, too, so I ordered three. They seemed familiar with the place and grabbed their favorite table while I waited for the food.

Once I set the food on the table all chatter stopped and Isaac and Sebastian attacked their meals like they hadn't eaten in days. But halfway through they both suddenly stopped eating. Isaac went to the counter and came back with a cardboard box. The two boys carefully packed the rest of their dinners in the box. They were taking the leftovers home to their father, Isaac told me.

After dinner was over, Sebastian took the box and ran home with it while I walked back to the hotel with Isaac. I told him to wait outside while I went in and got the shoes I had promised him.

Isaac was a serious kid. I hadn't seen him smile much and hadn't heard him laugh at all, but his face lit up when I handed him the shoes. I had only come here, far from home, to see the sights, but this turned out to be the best and most unexpected sight of all – the smile of a poor young boy who was just living his life as best he could. Isaac would be about thirty years old now as I write this. I sometimes wonder if *his* son is wandering the plaza now, selling postcards.

The airplane climbed up out of the valley and cleared the Andes. Our second arrival in Lima was thankfully less eventful than the first. This was just a domestic flight, no need for customs nightmares this time. We checked into our hotel and began our whirlwind tour of Lima. It was the last day of the trip.

Our first stop was the Plaza de Armas, the

original center of the city, which was founded in the 1500s by Spanish conquistador Francisco Pizarro. The plaza square is bounded by impressive old palaces, including the Government Palace, as well as the Cathedral of Lima, completed in 1622. The cathedral, originally a simple adobe structure, has been repeatedly expanded and updated, partially destroyed by earthquakes, and repaired numerous times over the centuries. We visited the cathedral mainly to see the last resting place of old Francisco Pizarro himself, his tomb on prominent display.

Pizarro's remains have seen as many changes as the cathedral itself. Buried at first in the original cathedral's courtyard, his body was later exhumed and his head and body reburied in separate boxes beneath the cathedral floor. In 1892 what were thought to be his remains were dug up and put on display in a glass coffin. Eight-five years later, in 1977, Pizarro's actual remains were rediscovered beneath the cathedral. The impostor, whoever he was, was reburied and Pizarro's head and body were reunited at last in the tomb he occupies today.

Two months after my visit to the Plaza de Armas, a neighborhood just a few blocks away was the scene of a major tragedy when a stockpile of fireworks caught fire and exploded. The resulting fire claimed almost three hundred lives.

Next up was the National Museum of Anthropology and Archeology, featuring yet more dead people. The thing I mostly remember about the museum was its collections of skulls, housed in its Human Remains Gallery. There was a collection of misshapen, grossly elongated skulls, a result obtained by binding the skulls of young children as they grew, done to show high status or to achieve some sort of standard of beauty. They look like, and are eagerly claimed to be by UFO aficianados, the skulls of aliens. Also on display was a collection of skulls that had had holes drilled in them, presumably some sort of ancient brain surgery. If you opted for brain surgery in those days, you had to have a hole in your head.

We arrived back at our hotel in the upscale Miraflores district in late afternoon. I decided to walk the eight- or-so blocks to the ocean, watch the sun set over the Pacific, and pick up a couple of bottles of water on the way back. That was the idea. The roads in that area were straight, grid-like, the ocean was west and the hotel east. I couldn't possibly get lost, could I?

I had walked along the coast a short distance before turning around and going back. I must have started back along a different road than I had walked down. The hotel wasn't where I expected to find it. When I had gotten lost in Dublin, and in Saigon, it had been afternoon. There had been helpful people about. But with nightfall here the streets had become empty, the landmarks shadowy.

The regular grid of streets gave me hope. I would just walk up and down one street and then the next until I found the hotel. If all else failed I could always backtrack to the ocean and start over. As I searched, the rising panic I felt wasn't about being lost in Lima. After all, I simply couldn't be *that* lost. What I really feared was missing dinner.

After what seemed too long a time, so long, in fact, that I had begun to doubt my strategy, I turned a corner and there it was, my hotel. I didn't even miss the appetizer.

If you've never had a three-thirty wake-up call, consider yourself fortunate. Feeling chilled, I dressed quickly and made a final, groggy inspection of my room, careful not to leave anything behind. I wouldn't be coming back.

Airport security paranoia had arrived in Lima; my collapsible dollar-store umbrella was deemed a potential weapon and had to be shifted to my checked baggage, a reminder that I was about to return to the land of the free and the home of the very, very frightened.

After clearing Customs in Miami I had to

check in for my next flight and found myself enjoying a couple of hours of the new normal – massive snarls of tired travelers caught in security gridlock, argumentative confusion over what was or wasn't allowed in your carry-on bags, hastily-hired screeners still learning how to use their equipment. I had always considered air travel to be fun. Those days were over.

Chapter Eight: Costa Rica – April 2002

It had snowed lightly the morning I left for Costa Rica. There is no better reason than that to fly south.

I arrived in San Jose on the eve of a presidential election. I arrived well after dark, too late for dinner, too early for bed, so I took a walk around the neighborhood of my hotel. The first thing I noticed was that walking would have to be done carefully – the sidewalks were crooked and buckled in many places, pushed up and cracked by past earthquakes. On first impression San Jose seemed a little nicer than I expected, perhaps just a little cleaner, a little saner. Election posters hung by the hundreds, plastered to every fence, wall, and pole, sometimes twenty copies of the same poster together, like a block of postage stamps. Pacheco or Monge? Conservative or Socialist? This face or that face?

The Presidential election had actually occurred two months prior, but a three-way split had left no candidate with the required 40% of the vote. The top two, Pacheco and Monge, were facing each other in a special run-off election. I had no idea what issues were of concern to the average Costa Rican, but in this, Central America's oldest and most stable democracy, whatever disagreements there might have been were thankfully not accompanied by gunfire.

Pickup trucks full of campaigners cruised the streets, blaring the Spanish equivalent of "vote for Monge!" or "vote for Pacheco!" from loudspeakers. One of the candidates had numerous posters that said "Vote Por Usted". It took me a while to realize that "usted" simply meant "you" in Spanish and that there was no one named Usted running for anything.   I really hadn't made up my mind yet whether to vote for Pacheco, Monge, or myself and, not being eligible to vote anyway, I decided to head back to the hotel and get some sleep.

On the morning of Election Day our tour of San Jose focused on one thing above all else – the city's grand, nineteenth-century opera house, officially known as the Teatro Nacional de Costa Rica. Impressive from the outside, the inside was beautiful and ornate. It was the only building of any real significance that I set foot in during my time in Costa Rica. This trip would be all about nature and wildlife, and volcanoes.

Poas volcano rises just to the north of San Jose. We stopped on its lower slopes to see the coffee being grown there, then continued up to the visitors' center. A paved road and a couple of hiking trails led up from there. I hiked up through the tropical cloud forest, a strange, misty realm of twisted trees, moss covering almost everything.

Tropical cloud forests are found in the tropics' higher elevations, an almost permanent fog keeping them wet and lush, the higher elevation keeping them cool and temperate, creating a unique habitat for plants and animals found nowhere else. At Poas, volcanic gases leaking down the volcano's flanks further impacted the environment, carving out pockets of stunted growth. As I neared the top of the trail I could begin to smell sulfur, the rotten egg smell bubbling up from the crater just ahead.

Emerging from the cloud forest I found myself at the crater's observation area. A wooden platform had been constructed behind it for elevated views but the view from the lower railing was breathtaking enough. The crater spread out to left and right as far as I could see. In the middle was a pale blue lake, Laguna Caliente, thick clouds of steam rising from its edges. Through binoculars I could see bubbles breaking the lake's surface.

Laguna Caliente is one of the world's most acidic lakes. Though the level of acidity varies over time, the lake's water is often more acidic than the acid in your car's battery. There is a layer of liquid sulfur at the bottom. Nothing lives in the lake. Indeed, the volcano has scoured all life from its summit with eruptions and acid rain.

I was fortunate to be visiting when I did. From time to time the park is closed and access to Poas is restricted due to eruptions that can fling out large rocks and poisonous gases. These days visitors to Poas are required to wear helmets and the hiking trails are closed, only the paved road to the top still open. But on that sunny spring day Poas was peacefully venting its sulfurous steam and the lake was bubbling like a hot tub.

After leaving Poas we headed east, dense rainforest on either side of the road, until we came to the La Paz waterfall, one of Costa Rica's most recognizable places, located conveniently close to passing tourists. We all hopped out of the van to admire the effect gravity has on water. Well up the waterfall a couple of hikers stood on a platform jutting out next to the rush of water. It was all very pretty and serene. But a few years later an earthquake rocked this part of Costa Rica and dozens had died in mudslides right here near this waterfall.

We continued north and were driving along

when we suddenly pulled off the road in front of a long, low building. We were essentially just taking a bathroom break but there was an odd combination of things to see inside. On one side of the building was a collection of rusty, antique farming equipment. On the other side were several terrariums containing red and black tarantulas. Out the back window hung a hummingbird feeder around which buzzed half a dozen hummingbirds. We were asked if we'd like to handle the tarantulas.

"Are these pets?", we asked as a man there scooped a red and black tarantula into his hands and brought it out to meet us. No, he said, they were recently captured from the nearby area. Apparently, they kept a fresh supply on hand. Who wants yesterday's tarantula, after all?

I watched as one fellow traveler after another gave the tarantulas a perch on their sleeves. I was content to observe. Spiders are best kept at a safe distance, like a mile or so. Oddly, these would be the only spiders I would see during my time in Costa Rica. I was quite okay with that.

After a while we were told that the tarantulas were getting a little cranky and it was time to put them away. Soon we were on the road again.

The schoolyard was buzzing with activity. We had stopped to watch the election in action, the school having become a polling place for one day. At least a hundred people were lined up to vote, those that had finished flashing purple thumbs as they left. The purple thumbs were from a dye applied when they voted, preventing them from voting again, the Little Jack Horner method of combating voter fraud. We poked around like United Nations inspectors but it didn't take long to see what there was to see. Pacheco or Monge? I wondered who I'd be voting for if I knew what was going on.

Leaving the school, we followed a truck

carrying a load of black bananas. We had seen bananas growing, workers in the fields laboring between the broad green leaves, hacking out bunches of still-green fruit. The bananas in the truck ahead of us were slowly oozing their insides out through splitting black peels. Who would want these bananas, we asked. Perhaps they would be fed to pigs? Where was this truck going with its rotten load?

Pedro, our affable, guitar-strumming guide, gave us the answer.

"They are taking them to the baby food factory".

It was late afternoon when we arrived at the Sarapiqui Rainforest Lodge. Conical, African-looking buildings dotted the grounds, which also included a botanical garden, an archaeological park, and a neighboring rainforest preserve, reached by a suspension bridge. It was hot and humid and hummingbirds were humming everywhere. Bats roosted in the upper reaches of the dining room's high ceiling.

After dinner I spent some time in my room reading, from time to time using the book to swipe at a large palmetto bug that had invaded my room, its wings barely able to lift its bulk as it lurched across the room from wall to wall. It was not even nine o'clock yet but I turned out the light and went to sleep. We had a big day coming up.

The next morning we drove to a clear spot on the banks of the Sarapiqui River to begin our whitewater rafting excursion. There were three rafts for our group, five to a raft, plus one competent Costa Rican "driver" for each. Helmets, life jackets, and paddles were handed out and we were given instruction in the basics of whitewater rafting: the verbal commands for when to paddle and when to stop and the right and wrong things to do if we found ourselves thrown into the water.

For the next two hours we would try to be obedient crew members. We waded into the calm water near shore, flopped into our rafts as gracefully as we could, and we were off.

It was a wonderful ride. The rapids were frequent and fun, never frightening. We operated like a well-oiled machine. Nobody whacked me in the head with a flailing paddle and we all managed to stay in the raft the whole way.

River rafting is one thing; rafting through a tropical rain forest adds another dimension. Toucans swooped through the canopy, a sloth hung from a branch above the water, trees wrapped in parasitic vines struggled to breathe. Halfway through the trip we pulled over to a sandy riverbank beach and got out to check out some of the smaller life – blue-and-red and green-and-black poison dart frogs and a bright green basilisk, otherwise known as a "Jesus Christ" lizard for its ability to scurry across the surface of the water. By the final hour we were all seasoned rafters in search of bigger adventures, and in search of lunch.

Lunch was a picnic of sandwiches near the river and I quickly wolfed mine down and wandered away to explore. I was soon joined by one of the locals who gestured for me to follow him into a wooded area nearby. He wanted to show me some of the local wildlife. We needed to go no farther than a large tree no more than fifty yards from where everyone else was still eating lunch. A large rhinoceros beetle, as big as my fist, clung to the bark. Nearby, still stuck to the tree, were the empty husks of several huge, dead cicadas. The ones still living had been making the most shrill whine that I've ever heard insects make, a constant, insistent whistling that had been our soundtrack all day.

Suddenly scooping something up from the leaf litter on the ground, my new friend gestured for me to hold out my hand. I wisely insisted he show me what was in *his* hand first. It was one of the green and black poison dart frogs we had seen earlier. I quickly checked to make sure I had no cuts on my hand and then allowed him to rest the frog in my palm. Poison dart frogs can excrete extremely toxic substances through their skin but are safe to handle if the toxin has no way to enter a person's bloodstream, such as a cut. And many of the frogs are not toxic at all, mere pretenders. Nevertheless, I made sure to wash my hands thoroughly afterward. Costa Rica is a popular place to retire, not expire.

  Back at the lodge, I was on my way across the grounds to visit the botanical garden when I noticed something moving up a nearby tree trunk. It was a snake, black and yellow, about six feet long. Some other people gathered with me as we watched it climb up into the branches, dangling for a while from the lowest branch before resuming its upward trek. I made sure not to walk under any more trees after that.

  The botanical garden, with its vanilla orchids and other growing spices, was an aromatic delight of the scratch-and-sniff variety. You really had to get your face in it to enjoy the smells. In the garden I found a familiar-looking tree which sported sharp round thorns on its trunk and up and down every branch. It was the same kind of tree that I had seen in Kenya with Derek and Jeanene. I sent them a postcard the next day, telling them that I had found our mystery tree and that, indeed, it had not been native to Africa. It was a young kapok tree and this was its native land.

  The palmetto bug had apparently found its way back out of my room, so I had the room all to myself again as my head hit the pillow well before nine o'clock that night.

  The suspension bridge wobbled and swayed beneath us as we walked across it to the Tirimbina Rainforest Preserve, located on an island in the Sarapiqui River. The bridge spanned the gap from the rainforest lodge to the island. I stopped in the middle to watch some iridescent blue butterflies before continuing to the far end, where a set of spiral stairs led down to the rainforest floor. We set off down a narrow, semi-paved trail and were soon engulfed by a sea of green, the view in any direction limited by the dense vegetation. Our guide, Pedro, told us to wait while he stepped into a small clearing to inspect the leafy plant growing there. He bent down and looked up underneath the folded leaves, then returned to us and told us we should accompany him, one by one, to see what he had found, but that we needed to be as quiet as possible. When it was my turn I crouched below the plant and looked up into the fold of a leaf. Hanging there, upside-down and apparently sleeping peacefully, were several small, white bats. It was the first time I had ever thought of bats as "cute" but there was no denying it. I quietly withdrew so as not disturb their nap.

As I stood near a tree, waiting for everyone else to see the bats, I noticed a large black ant crawling down a branch. The next time Pedro emerged out from under the leaves, I pointed out the ant to him and asked if it was anything dangerous. He nodded seriously.

"Bullet ant. They're called that because the sting is like being shot with a bullet. You'll live but you'll wish you were dead".

He motioned the group to gather around and pointed out the bullet ants, now several of them, and cautioned us not to lean against or even rest a hand on any of the trees.

Somewhere above us howler monkeys barked like dogs and swung through the branches. The barking of howler monkeys would follow us throughout the trip and we watched as this group scurried and played up in the canopy.

The ground here was dotted with golfball-sized holes, the abandoned or still occupied homes of the local tarantulas. I was happy to see only holes and no spiders. I still hadn't seen even one mosquito since arriving in Costa Rica, a fact that boggled my mind. A tropical rainforest without mosquitoes? It was too good to be true but I never did see one there.

        We rattled and bounced our way up the long winding hill to the Bosques de Chachagua Hotel, nestled in a secluded patch of forest. The rocks and ruts that jarred us all the way up the dirt road insured that seclusion. Toucans perched on branches in the surrounding trees. A rainbow of colors was splashed here and there all about the grounds – a brightly painted oxcart rolling past a flower-fringed pond, more flowering plants growing everywhere, Rafael the parrot sitting on his perch just outside the hotel's main office.

        I sat on my room's front porch taking it all in. The porch had enough bench seating for a baseball team. My room was actually more like a house, a whole building to myself, complete with resident geckos and a beautiful shower with a glass wall from waist-level up, no need to take your eyes off the view even there. A large slug oozed across the shower floor, leaving a slimy trail. Such is the lumpy lap of luxury in the tropics.

        We were on our way north to the Rio Frio, near the Nicaraguan border, for a boat trip when we pulled off the road to buy chicken pastries. Nearby, the road crossed a short bridge over a deep gully. Pastry in hand, I walked out onto the bridge and looked over the side, looking down on the tops of trees growing up from far below. The leafy branches were supporting the weight of at least a dozen iguanas. Other iguanas lounged on the bridge supports, sunning themselves. It was a beautiful day to be an iguana in Costa Rica.

        The road ended in a small border town and we walked down to the river to board a waiting boat. A half mile upriver to the right was Nicaragua. We turned left.

        The Rio Frio runs through the most biodiverse region of Costa Rica. Monkeys frolicked in the trees above, birds and butterflies filled the air, and caimans patrolled the waters or sunned themselves on logs. Strings of birds' nests drooped from branches, hanging down to almost touch the river's languid green surface We ate a picnic lunch on the riverbank. If I'm ever asked if the presence of caimans nearby detracts in any way from a nice picnic lunch my answer will be this: "Please pass the chicken".

We made a few stops the next day on our way to the Arenal volcano. We stopped first for a visit to an elementary school. The kids sang the Costa Rican national anthem and then it was our turn. Despite a quick rehearsal on the bus, our rendition of "The Star Spangled Banner" was lackluster at best. Dancing lessons and indoor soccer with an improvised, lopsided ball of cotton fabric followed. We had lunch at a cattle ranch and were treated to a display of calf-roping, then continued on to the town of La Fortuna for ice cream cones and a leisurely stroll around town.

San Juan Bosco Catholic church dominates the view in La Fortuna. It towers over a green, landscaped park, the town's central plaza. Rain was moving in as I snapped a picture, the lower half of a cloud-shrouded mountain visible behind the church. On a clear day I would have seen smoke and ash billowing from the conical peak. The mountain was Arenal.

At that time the Arenal volcano had been erupting more or less continuously for almost thirty-four years, having awakened from dormancy one summer morning in 1968, burying three small towns on its western slopes in lava and hot ash. These days it sometimes huffed and puffed and shot boulders out like popcorn; most of the time it just oozed, little glowing pieces of the mountain sliding down its flanks.

We spent the night at the aptly named Hotel Montana del Fuego – "Mountain of Fire" – in the volcano's shadow. Arenal's summit at night was supposed to be a fireworks show of tumbling, red-hot rock but it was often wreathed in clouds, as it was on this night. We were assured that if the clouds lifted we would be awakened to see the fiery sight, no matter how late it might be.

Walking back to my room after dinner I was stopped in my tracks by something blocking the path. Well, "blocking" is perhaps the wrong word, as I could have easily stepped over them, or on them. But I stopped just the same to watch them as they worked. Soon four or five of us had gathered to watch the little parade.

We were watching a column of leaf-cutter ants as they carried neatly snipped-out bits of green leaves from out of the trees, over a clutter of leaves and small branches, across the wide walkway, and into the bushes on the other side. There were hundreds of them in a steady procession, many more returning the other way empty-handed (empty-jawed?) to get more, still others, the security guards, patrolling up and down the line. And we became another line of defense, warning others who happened along to mind the ants and watch their step. We were all working as a team, humans and ants striving for a common goal.

The clock said 5:05 a.m. when the phone rang in my room. The clouds had lifted from the summit. Get up, sleepyhead, and look at the volcano!

I fumbled my way into shorts and shoes in the dark of my room, wanting to keep my eyes adjusted to the darkness. I pushed open the door of my little cabin and stepped outside. Looking up at Arenal's summit I could see a few faint streaks of red forking down. A glowing red ball rolled a short distance. The glow got dimmer as wisps of cloud floated back in and ten minutes later the peak was again wrapped in the gray gauze of night clouds. Curious about something, I took a short walk.

As I'd suspected, the leaf-cutters were still at it, though their security guards were having coffee and doughnuts. Sorry, I don't think so straight at five in the morning. Perhaps those tiny crullers and little steaming mugs were just in my mind. The raucous barking of howler monkeys was all too real, however. I retreated to my room to escape the racket. Just as I closed the door and got back into bed, a bird slammed hard into the window and dropped to the ground outside my little cabin. In this kill-or-be-killed world of nature, cabin window had prevailed over bird. This time.

The Buena Vista Lodge is located on a sprawling property that is a patchwork of rainforest and arid semi-desert. We had left behind the high humidity of the lowlands for the dry air here on the lower slopes of the Rincon de la Vieja volcano. Steaming water flowed through the ground below us, bubbling up here and there in hot springs. Volcanic mud belched forth as well. The Buena Vista was also a working ranch. Men rode by on horseback, and pickup trucks kicked up dust trails on dirt roads that crisscrossed the land. I was torn between the large square swimming pool and the hammocks strung up near my room. The pool won. This time.

On our first morning at Buena Vista we gathered at the corral to get mounted up for a horseback ride to the nearby volcanic mud bath. It had been many, many years since I had been on a horse and I was quite surprised at how high off the ground I was as I settled into the saddle. A fall from way up here would be quite a significant tumble.

We were given the basic instructions on how to control the horses and then we were off. Constantly adjusting myself to stay balanced atop my steed as we worked our way up, down, and through some tricky terrain, I was beginning to get rather saddle-sore as we mercifully reached the mud baths and dismounted. We all headed for the changing rooms to get into bathing suits, then reconvened at the mud bath.

There is nothing quite as wonderful as volcanic mud. If you've ever used Lava soap you know why it's called that. Volcanic mud is like sandpaper for the skin. We scooped warm mud from a heated pot and rubbed it all over ourselves, faces on down. After giving it a minute to dry we washed it off under a shower. I came out as warm, clean, and smooth as a penny in a washing machine.

After sitting for a few minutes in a volcano-powered steam room, I continued on to the nearby twin swimming pool – one side hot, one side cold, with a narrow connection between them. I went back and forth between them until it was time to go.

Horses were waiting for those who wished to ride back to the lodge. I rubbed my aching backside and opted for a ride on a tractor-pulled cart.

We had a number of options for what to do after lunch. Most of the group opted for the rainforest zipline ride. I was more interested in a nice rainforest hike, as was my fellow group member Judy.

Pedro pointed us in the direction of the hiking trail's beginning, told us there was a small waterfall at the trail's end, and set off with the ziplining crowd. But Judy and I had become a bit confused by Pedro's directions and we set off walking up a dirt road that we expected to lead to the trail to the waterfall. There was dense rainforest to our right and wide open pasture to our left.

We eventually began to believe that we could hear the sound of falling water ahead. We stopped and listened. Yes, that sounds like water, just up ahead and to the right. The trail must be right up there. We continued along the dirt road a while longer until we came to another road. A pickup truck drove by, leaving a dusty trail. We listened again. Do you hear water? I think so. Maybe not.

Forty-five minutes after setting out we decided to turn around. We hadn't found the trail yet and, clearly, we were not going the right way. We started back.

Expecting a walk through shady rainforest, neither of us had thought to bring water. The sun baked us and the dry air dehydrated us. We weren't lost, all we had to do was walk back the way we came, but we both began to feel like we might not make it.

I took my hat off to let the sweat dry. I put it back on to avoid the sun. Back and forth, hat, no hat. I felt dizzy and faint. Judy was feeling it, too. There was no shade in which to rest, nothing to do but keep walking in hopes of reaching the lodge before we both keeled over. And, maddeningly, just on the other side of that wall of rainforest, we could still hear the sounds of falling water.

We staggered on, steps becoming unsteadier. Just a little further, we told each other. I fanned myself with my hat, put it back on. After a while we could see the beginning of the zipline course. We were almost there. We'd been walking for an hour and a half.

When we finally reached the lodge we saw the beginning of the rainforest trail, clearly marked. How could we have missed it? Judy excused herself and went back to her room. I went straight to the outdoor bar.

I ordered a Pepsi and a water, then had a seat at one of the tables. It was mid-afternoon and I was the only one there. I drank the bottle of water in about ten seconds, then sat back and started working on the Pepsi. I felt a little cold and clammy; my body's thermostat was swinging like a pendulum. After half an hour sitting in the shade I began to feel normal again. I still wanted to take the rainforest hike, so I bought another bottle of water and set off down the trail.

The rainforest trail turned out to be worth the effort. It was a forty-five minute round-trip hike on an easy trail with many sights to see on the way, including a tree with huge and fabulously folded buttresses. I found a number of small pits dug by my favorite insect, the ant lion. At the end of the trail there was indeed a waterfall, though a rather scrawny, squat, and unspectacular one. A jumble of boulders lay scattered about a clearing at the trail's end. I was tempted to have a seat and rest a bit before the return trip when I spotted a flash of red and black in my peripheral vision. I looked in time to see a small, foot-long snake disappear beneath one of the boulders. It was bright red with black bands. I am no snake expert but even I could recognize a coral snake, many of which are quite venomous. Pedro later identified it from my description as a Central American coral snake, and it was indeed quite dangerous. I decided I didn't need any rest after all. Half an hour later I was back in the swimming pool, rewarding myself for a difficult day. I even had time for the hammock before dinner.

Fortunately for us, the Mennonites had made it to Costa Rica many years before we had. The Amish-like sect is well known for dairy farming and we pulled into the parking lot of their large store on our way south to the Rio Tarcoles. The place was jam-packed with milk and cheese and butter. It might well have been the best cheese available from Amarillo to Argentina. But we weren't there for the cheese. We were there for the milkshakes.

One very important thing for any tourist to understand before taking a group tour is this: the itinerary doesn't tell the whole story. It merely lists a schedule of highlights, the most popular sights a tourist might want to see. It never mentions the milkshakes. It never mentions the unexpected detours, the sunsets, the chance encounters, the iguanas in the trees – all the things you will remember most. You can't just close your eyes and take a nap between points A and B. That's where the real action is. And the milkshakes. Mine was chocolate and my biggest regret of the entire trip was that we didn't have time to stay for a second one.

We watched the sun set that evening over the Pacific Ocean, while Pedro strummed his guitar and shots of coffee liqueur were passed around. Then we took turns looking at the full moon through a telescope Pedro had set up. There was nothing in the itinerary about that either.

Costa Rica lies between the Pacific Ocean to the west and the Caribbean to the east. It's about 170 miles at its widest, the ocean never more than about eighty-five miles away and usually much closer. Nonetheless, today would be our first visit to a Costa Rican beach.

A short boat trip across the Gulf of Nicoya from Puntarenas took us to a small private beach at Punta Coral. We were to spend the day lounging, lunching, playing horseshoes, and, if all the leisure became overwhelming, swimming or hiking. Palm trees leaned at odd angles over the water. A sandy beach led to a calm finger of water reaching in from the gulf. But this finger was an extension of the Pacific Ocean's long reach and the ocean is not a toy, not a plaything. It is a savage soup of hidden horrors.

But how bad could this little out-of-the-way lagoon be? I decided to chance it. As some of us were getting ready to go for a swim, Pedro gave us one little warning.

Apparently, quite a few jellyfish tentacles had been washing up on this beach. Not whole jellyfish, just tentacles. But they could still deliver a nasty sting.

I waded out into the water anyway and spent some time floating in the salty water. But it was no good. I was too apprehensive to enjoy the water and soon got out again.

But there was another option for water fun. A number of sea kayaks lay on the shore waiting for someone to take them out on the water. Half a dozen of us decided to try them out. We rowed toward a spiky rock sticking out of the water that looked to be a mile away but was probably only half that. We were warned not to veer too far from shore, as we could be swept out into the ocean by the currents. With that new apprehension in mind, I set out.

Halfway to the spiky rock I realized something important – I don't enjoy kayaking. My arms were aching and the ocean was just drooling at the chance to see how long I'd survive in its choppy waves. I turned around and rowed back, arms and shoulders burning with the effort. It was hammock time.

We drove back to San Jose on our final day in Costa Rica. As we approached a road bridge ahead we saw that a number of people had pulled their cars off the road and were now standing on the bridge, looking over the side. This was the well-known Crocodile Bridge.

We parked by the side of the road and joined the other people on the bridge. We were looking down on a sandy beach at a bend in the Rio Tarcoles. At least a dozen crocodiles lay on the beach or partially in the water. And these were massive American crocodiles, which regularly grow to over twenty feet in length. They were soaking up the sun, side by side, like strips of bacon in a frying pan. It was a beautiful day to be a crocodile in Costa Rica.

San Jose was still there when we got back. I wandered a pedestrian avenue in downtown San Jose lined with stores of all kinds. I found a place to have lunch and topped it off with a milkshake. It wasn't a Mennonite milkshake but it wasn't half bad.

I would be flying home the next morning. I hoped that the snow we'd had on the morning of my departure would be long gone, with the spring well underway. But April in Albany can bring any kind of weather. It could be this, it could be that. I would just have to wait and see how Mother Nature voted.

I won't leave you hanging – Abel Pacheco was elected President of Costa Rica with 58% of the vote and served one four-year term.

Chapter Nine: Argentina and Antarctica – November and December 2003

  I was doing what I always do on Thanksgiving Day – eating turkey and watching football. But this was no ordinary Thanksgiving. I was eating my dinner in the international terminal at Dulles airport in Virginia, waiting for my overnight flight to Buenos Aires. It turned out that Thanksgiving was a great day to travel – everyone was already where they needed to be and I had the entire terminal practically to myself. A uniformed man pushed a broom down the massive terminal until he had become just a speck. The stores and concessions were closed. I parked myself in front of one of the terminal's TVs and watched the Miami Dolphins beat the Dallas Cowboys as I ate my turkey sandwiches. It was kind of lonely and weird, but traveling alone is always lonely and weird.

  It was the first time I had ever been away from family and friends at Thanksgiving, but my mother had not let me go without Thanksgiving dinner – she had cooked a small turkey breast and made me sandwiches. Some chocolate chip cookies rounded out the feast. There was no place open from which to buy a drink, so I slurped a bit of warmish water from a drinking fountain to wash it all down. As the game ended, the terminal had finally begun to receive a trickle of travelers, soon to be a steady flow. Life had returned to the terminal. I sat and watched the coming and going of an international mix of people, here now to board overnight flights, east to Europe or south to South America. My own flight would depart at ten.

    I arrived the next morning in Buenos Aires but I still had another flight to go. I needed to take an hour-long bus ride to the domestic airport on the other side of the city. The bus cut right through the heart of the city and so Buenos Aires is the only city in the world that I have seen strictly through the window of a bus. It looked nice enough and I thought I might come back again one day to visit it properly. But right now I was on my way to Ushuaia.

    Ushuaia, Argentina is the world's southernmost city, and almost the last permanently inhabited place of any kind. It's so far south that it's not even on the continent of South America, but on the island of Tierra del Fuego. There are a couple of large ranches on another island just to the south, but that's it. After that it's ocean all the way to Antarctica.

    The flight south from Buenos Aires took me over Patagonia. From the window of the plane, six miles up, it was brown, flat, and nearly featureless. It was the single least interesting place I've ever flown over, just countless miles of brown with the occasional straight line of a little-traveled road. But by the time we approached Ushuaia, mountains had sprung up, the very tail end of the Andes. We flew over snow-capped peaks that surrounded the town on three sides, and dropped down into the bowl they formed. The ocean was Ushuaia's other border.

The weather was unusually warm for Ushuaia in November, a balmy sixty-five degree day in what for them was late spring. By the time I reached my hotel it was nearly dinnertime. I had opted for an assigned roommate for this trip, as a single cabin on the cruise would have been prohibitively expensive. When I opened the door to my room, three Filipino men rose from one of the beds to greet me. They were three relatives traveling together. One was my roommate; the other two were sharing the room next door. Those arrangements would be the same on the cruise. We decided to have dinner together in the dining room of our hotel, the Hotel Albatros, before turning in for the evening

The massive Hotel Albatros dominates the city's center, overlooking the port. The city is spread out along the water; going inland, one is soon climbing a hill. The city thins out with each block climbed and you are soon in the foothills of the Andes.

After breakfast the next morning I took a walk around. The port was directly across the street from the hotel and I could see the ship I would be sailing on, the *MV Lyubov Orlova*, waiting in its slip. The weather had returned to normal – the temperature struggled to reach the mid-fifties and a brisk and steady wind blew in from the ocean. Flags whipped and snapped on their lines.

Ushuaia is home to a truly weird mix of architecture, a seemingly random assortment of odd shapes and vivid colors. Snowy mountains surrounded the city, giving it the feel of a Colorado ski resort. Blasts of polar wind continued to sweep in from the south, their passage unobstructed by the six hundred miles of ocean between Antarctica and Tierra del Fuego.

The city's motto is "fin del mundo, principio de todo", which translates as "end of the world, beginning of everything". It all depends on which way you're headed. But, as it turns out, the world doesn't end there after all. There's one more place at the bottom of the world. Still, the signs all around town proclaiming "fin del mundo" gave Ushuaia something of an apocalyptic feel, like a doomsday preacher shouting "the end is near" in Times Square.

Checkout time at the hotel was eleven a.m. and the cruise didn't depart until late afternoon, so the hotel was allowing cruise passengers the use of its lounge. I would go out exploring for an hour or so and then return to the hotel for some rest and hot chocolate, then go out again. Too cold to stay out, too boring to stay in. Eventually I'd seen everything I could see within walking distance. I got one last hot chocolate, found a seat in a corner of the hotel lounge, and read a book until we were summoned to board the bus for the quarter-mile drive to the ship.

By the time I had settled into my room and reported to my station on deck for the mandatory lifeboat drill, we were already beginning to pull away from Ushuaia. I stood on deck for awhile, watching the little city, nestled in its encircling mountains, fade into the distance as we made our way into the Beagle Channel.

The *MV Lyubov Orlova* was a Russian ship specially outfitted for polar cruising. If the word "cruise" makes you think of swimming pools, deck chairs, sunny ports of call, shuffleboard, gluttony, and inebriation, then you've got the wrong idea about polar cruising. The *Orlova* was comfortable and cozy. There was a lounge with a bar at one end and a reading area/library, stocked with books about Antarctica, at the other. Photographs of the ship's namesake, the Russian actress Lyubov Orlova, adorned the lounge's walls. There was one dining room, where there was a buffet breakfast each morning and amazingly fancy dishes served for lunch and dinner. The evening entertainment was a movie, shown in the ship's meeting area. There was a lecture or two presented each day. The subjects included penguins and snowflakes. There were views to be had from the ship's decks, which were connected by a grand spiral staircase. There was no shuffleboard.

The *Orlova* was carrying about a hundred passengers (from at least fifteen different countries) and almost as many crew. There was the regular ship's crew (mostly Russian and Ukrainian), who kept everything afloat, made our beds, and kept us fed, and there was the expedition crew, the polar experts who would be leading us ashore and answering our questions. But before we could go ashore, we had to get there, and that meant crossing the Drake Passage.

The Drake Passage is the border area between the southern Atlantic and southern Pacific oceans, and extends five hundred miles south from Tierra del Fuego into the Southern Ocean. It is notorious for having some of the roughest seas anywhere on the planet. It would take a day and a half to make the crossing – departing in the evening, we would spend the entire next day and night at sea, arriving in the relatively calm waters of the South Shetland Islands the following morning. We weren't expected to enter the rough part until after midnight.

I woke up the next morning to the bucking bronco ride the cruise had now become. The first item on my schedule was to get dressed and go to the dining room for breakfast. Getting dressed while standing up was not an option. I rolled out of bed onto the floor and crawled to the dresser. Clothes in hand, I stood just long enough to topple back onto the bed. Once I was dressed, my hands were free to steady myself as I lurched up the hallway toward the dining room.

We had been instructed the evening before on the correct and incorrect methods of staggering about the ship like drunken sailors. Rule #1 was to not grab an open doorway for support – if the door suddenly slammed shut you'd be picking your fingers up off the floor. Walking had become much like surfing – keep your center of gravity low and hands up and at the ready. It got a little easier with practice, but not much.

The dining room, which the night before had been the scene of a sedate and lovely dinner, now resembled a roller derby rink. Passengers struggled to load their plates with bacon and eggs and such at the buffet table with a minimum of flailing. Getting back to their seat at a table was the next challenge as random human cannonballs hurtled past them. Any loose items on the table had to be watched carefully to keep them from flying off. Coffee cups spilled coffee into saucers whenever we tilted too far. Flat food was good. Round food was a problem.

For all the up and down and back and forth, I wasn't feeling any seasickness as we gathered in the lounge that morning for a lecture on the different kinds of snowflakes. The talk was just ending and I was about to congratulate myself on my seaworthiness when the feeling started to come over me. I careened as quickly as I could through the rolling ship to get back to my room. I made it into the tiny bathroom just in time. But the good news was that I only had this one bout of seasickness and felt fine thereafter. Nonetheless, I decided to spend the rest of the day in bed.

Feet up, head down. Head up, feet down. Rinse and repeat. I could see gray splotches of water splashing against the tiny porthole every time the roll of the ship brought me head up, feet down. Prone inactivity helped keep the nausea at bay. I got up only to stumble to lunch and dinner. I knew that by the next morning we'd be in calm waters again.

It was nice to enjoy a good, perfectly horizontal breakfast the next morning. Afterward, I went out and stood on deck. We would soon be approaching the South Shetland Islands, about ninety miles north of the Antarctic continent. This was the point at which we would begin to see icebergs floating by as we continued south. Everyone was on deck, wanting to be the first to spot an iceberg.

The first iceberg was spotted and a cheer went up. We had arrived in the Antarctic. Soon we were passing dozens of icebergs to left and right. There were a few impressively big ones, some medium ones, and some little chunks of ice that could only pretend to the title of "iceberg". Most were flat-topped, especially the larger ones, their sides carved into fantastic shapes by the water. Groups of penguins rode aboard some of them. They were out cruising just like we were.

Our first shore excursion would be after lunch on one of the Aitcho Islands. The South Shetland Islands lie about ninety miles north of the actual continent of Antarctica. They include a sub-group of small islands known as the Aitcho Islands (a literal pronunciation of "H.O.", after the Hydrographic Office of the British Royal Admiralty, which surveyed the area in the 1930s). Only recently have I discovered that the island we landed on has its own individual name as well – Barrientos Island. It would be my first chance to get dressed up in my cold-weather clothes, most bought or borrowed specifically for this trip.

The weather was actually not that cold; it would be in the upper twenties every day, the same temperature as Albany at that time of year. But we would be out in it for a couple of hours or more on each landing, walking in snow. Also, as there were no docking facilities on these uninhabited islands, the Zodiacs would get us as close to shore as possible, where we would have to step out into foot-deep icy water, often with large chunks of ice floating in it, before wading ashore.

So I was in my room, getting ready for our first landing, putting on the full array of recommended clothing for the first time. This included my regular clothes (t-shirt, jeans, underwear, and socks) plus the following:

> waterproof pants (put on first, then roll legs up)

        wool socks
        waterproof knee-high wading boots (put on, fasten, pull waterproof pant legs back down over boots, covering them, not tucked into them)
        wool sweater
        waist-length winter coat (bright red or yellow for visibility; mine was red)
        light nylon inner gloves
        winter gloves
        wool hat (the one I bought at Machu Picchu)
        sunglasses

    By the time I got everything on I was overheated and couldn't wait to get out into the cold air. But, thankfully, the process of dressing would get easier and quicker each time.

    I joined the back of a line of people waiting to descend the ship's narrow outer stairs to the waiting Zodiacs, which were ferrying people ashore before coming back for more. Dressed as I was, the cold air was a relief. Within a few minutes almost a hundred passengers had been deposited on the chilly beach of Barrientos Island.

    Brown circles a little larger than baseball pitcher's mounds dotted the snow all over near our landing site. Each contained dozens of penguins, the random motions of which had worn the snow away in a circle. A lecture we had had on the different types of penguins enabled us to identify all the kinds we found – Adelie, Gentoo, Macaroni, and Chinstrap penguins, though almost never mixed together. The most easily identifiable were the Macaronis, with the spiky yellow tufts coming out of their heads, and the Chinstraps, with the black line across their throats which looked like, well, a chinstrap. None of them were more than two feet tall.

Here and there were narrow penguin "roads", grooves the penguins had worn in the slopes leading down to the ocean, where their food was.

Penguins are, quite simply, fun to watch. Within the penguin circles were individual nests built of small stones. The penguins were constantly stealing rocks from each others' nests to add to their own. Others were going this way and that all around us, ignoring us completely. Penguins waddled until suddenly deciding that sliding would be more effective, then shot past us down their little penguin bobsled runs. They looked like a bunch of children enjoying a snow day off from school.

A little further inland the penguin colonies thinned out and the stark black and white Antarctic scenery came into full view: the bare black rock jutting out of the snow in spires, the icebergs floating offshore in water that was sometimes steely gray, sometimes vivid blue (the only color to be seen, except for the red and yellow of our coats and the yellow tufts of the Macaronis), the snow clinging to black mountains, the tuxedoed guardians of this desolate place hopping and skidding past us as we ignored them and gazed into the distance at snow and rock, ice and water, and the black and white *Orlova* waiting patiently for our return.

Our next stop was Livingston Island, home to more penguins (every place in the South Shetlands is home to more penguins) and enormous elephant seals. The beach was crowded with elephant seals, some of the males weighing three or four tons. Most were just lying on the beach like sausages, but it was breeding season and some of the males were snorting and grunting, throwing themselves at each other, chest-bumping, like unarmed gladiators. It was best to watch from a safe distance.

The next day found us approaching

Deception Island, the circular peak of a mostly underwater volcano, still very much active. The volcanic cone formed an almost perfect circle of rock, a ring island. But there was an opening in the circle, a gap about 250 yards wide, just enough for the sea to pour in and flood the interior, and just wide enough for a ship to pass through. It was the most protected harbor in the Antarctic and had been used in the previous century as a whaling station. Captured whales were brought there to be slaughtered. Rusted equipment from those days still stood, half-buried in snow and ash. Penguins walked the beach like vacationers.

The island had the same black and white color scheme as the rest of the Antarctic, but with a thousand shades of gray as well from the volcanic ash that had settled on the snowy slopes that ringed the island.

One of the expedition leaders was digging a hole in the black sand of the beach. As he dug, hot water bubbled up from below, filling the little pool. Soon it was ready for those who wished to do a little Antarctic bathing. It was another reminder that we were standing within the caldera of an active volcano. I preferred to watch, not relishing the idea of emerging again from the hot water into the freezing air.

I stomped around the island, checking out the ruins, until the battery in my camera went dead from the cold. I was ready for some hot chocolate.

The lounge on the *Orlova* served cookies, coffee, and hot chocolate every day in late afternoon. We would usually just be returning from a shore excursion so, after a quick stop at my room to shed three-quarters of my clothes, I would go there to luxuriate in a soft chair and a warm drink, and maybe a cookie or two. But I didn't want to spoil my appetite. Dinner would not be far off.

The word from the expedition crew was that the *Orlova* served the best food in the Antarctic. It was easy to believe them. It was like eating lunch and dinner at a five-star restaurant every day. The logistics of it confounded me; I couldn't even imagine where that much food would be stored, much less how such magic could be made with it day after day.

    The expedition crew was also a special treat. One had once been chief magistrate of the British Antarctic Territory, presiding over the rare instances of crime, and the less rare cases of grievances, that arose in this land that belongs to no country, despite the British territorial claim (and the claims of other countries). He told us all about it at dinner one evening, at least the ones of us who were randomly seated with him that night.

    Another member of the expedition crew was a cinematographer, based on the remote Norwegian island of Svalbard, who specialized in filming polar bears. A few months before the cruise I had been captivated by a sequence in a nature documentary I had seen on TV, which showed a polar bear attempting to pull a beluga whale from a watery breathing hole in the ice where a pod of them had become trapped. The whales could not escape, but they continued to elude the grasp of the bear. The standoff had lasted for hours, a portion of which made it to the TV screen. The man sitting across the table from me at lunch one day was that cinematographer, and he told the story of how he had come to be there filming the scene.

    He had been at home in Spitsbergen, on twenty-four hour call for the BBC. The documentary's producers had been scouting from the air, flying over the barren polar regions in search of wildlife in action, when they had spotted the whale/bear drama unfolding. My lunch companion had gotten the call and within the hour was on a plane to the trackless wilderness of northern Canada, along with a sound man, where he arrived in time to film the sequence that I had found so memorable.

    Despite his extensive experience in the

Arctic, this was the cinematographer's first visit to Antarctica, and he was just as excited about it as I was. Now that we had explored the South Shetlands, it was time for us to cover the remaining ninety-mile distance to the Antarctic Peninsula.

The Antarctic Peninsula is a narrow finger of land reaching north toward South America, the northernmost reach of the southernmost continent. We would be sailing south along the peninsula as far as Vernadsky Base, the Ukrainian research station, before turning around and coming back. Our next landing would be on the continent itself, at a place called Neko Harbor.

A harbor in Antarctica is simply a sheltered nook along the rocky shore, and a bit of flat shoreline to step onto. But that step would put me on my sixth continent. If I ever make it to Australia I'll have all seven.

I stepped out of the Zodiac into a foot of water. Basketball-sized chunks of ice banged against my ankles as I waded ashore at Neko Harbor. A tiny, decrepit hut stood in the snow, surrounded by a few penguins. They looked like they were waiting in line to use an outhouse. The land sloped uphill, so I kept closer to shore. There was nothing there, really. The view wasn't anything out of the ordinary. Except for the outhouse penguins there was no life around. But we were *on the continent*. It was our one and only chance to actually stand on the continent of Antarctica, a thing impossible to do throughout most of human history. As it turned out, we had almost missed our chance.

After only a few minutes ashore, an alarm was sounded and we were ordered to return to the landing site. The wind had shifted and was now pushing more and more ice in toward the harbor. Zodiacs raced to ferry everyone back to the *Orlova* before the massing ice made it impossible. Anyone who didn't make it back in time would be stranded ashore until the wind changed again, possibly hours, possibly longer.

It was a bumpy ride on the Zodiac as we rode over the thickening soup of water and ice back to the ship. But everyone made it and we were soon headed south again, looking for another way to spend the extra time we now had.

Once again we climbed down the ship's metal outer steps to the waiting Zodiacs. We had found an ice-free bay a little farther south. When I say "ice-free" I mean that it wasn't clogged with chunks of ice. There was no good landing spot here, so the plan was to just cruise around in the Zodiacs, taking a look at some of the larger and weirder ice formations floating in the bay.

There were ice cream cones of snow and ice reaching up from the water, flipped-over icebergs now showing their sea-carved undersides, loops and arches anchored to masses of ice that floated just below the surface. There was one huge arch, large enough for all the Zodiacs to pass beneath side by side. But that was too risky to do, in case the arch should suddenly collapse. Though mostly a spectacle in white, the ice also displayed a range of vivid, bright blues, especially at or just below the surface of the very clear water. As it had afforded us this opportunity, I was happy to have had my continental landing cut short. I had stepped there and that was enough. But this ninety-minute spin around the bay had been spectacular. We finished with a landing of a different kind.

Closer to shore we came across a small, round ice floe, just a flat piece of snow-topped ice floating in the ocean, its shape rounded by the surrounding water. It was about half the size of a football field. I watched as a Zodiac sped toward it and plowed up and over its edge. Another Zodiac did the same. My Zodiac took aim at the floe and followed suit, launching us out of the water and up onto the ice. We hopped out and took pictures of each other as we stood on this slab of ice adrift in the ocean. It was the perfect prelude to another late afternoon spent in an easy chair sipping hot chocolate.

      That evening I stood on deck, grimacing at the wind chill, as we threaded our way through the Lemaire Channel, considered one of the most scenically spectacular passages in the Antarctic. This far south, the late spring sun wouldn't set until after midnight, so there was plenty of light for the seven-mile traverse. Cutting a pathway between the peninsula and Booth Island, the Lemaire Channel is like sailing in a canyon. Walls of rock and snow towered on both sides of the mile-wide passage. A dull orange sun hung low in the sky in front of us as we sailed west through the channel.

      As we finally emerged into a wider sea at the channel's end, and with my face going numb, I made my way back to my room. My Filipino roommate and his companions were in the room next door drinking. That's where they usually were when they weren't in the bar. They tried to wave me in to join them but it was late and I'm not much of a drinker. I told them I'd see them at breakfast and said goodnight.

      The next day we reached the southernmost point of our travels – Vernadsky Base, the Ukrainian research station. It was where the south-polar hole in the atmosphere's ozone layer was first discovered. That hole meant that ultraviolet radiation levels here in the Antarctic were very high – sunburn is a serious concern for anyone spending significant time in this part of the world.

      Vernadsky had three things that are quite uncommon in the Antarctic – a semi-resident population, a post office, and a bar. It was time for me to mail the fistful of postcards I wanted to send, which would arrive back home stamped with a truly unusual and exotic postmark, and with a Ukrainian stamp attached.

      We had a brief tour of the base, just a few

ramshackle buildings in the snow. It was part office space, part monitoring equipment, part living space. We were advised not to wander off, as leopard seals had been coming threateningly close in recent weeks.

This was as far as we were going – it was now time to turn around and return to the civilized world. Our first stop on the return would be on Petermann Island, just a little north of Vernadsky.

Petermann Island was a playground for penguins. Different species had worn away their own campsites. The land rose away from shore, steep but climbable, and just a little way up the view was spectacular – penguins in the snow, the exposed black and brown rock of Petermann, the *Orlova* out at sea, the black and white of snowy mountains beyond it, blocky icebergs floating near it, a Zodiac cutting a line from shore to ship, ferrying some people back. By the shore icicles hung beneath sheets of ice and slabs of rock.

This would be our next-to-last landing. We returned through the Lemaire Channel and continued northeast to our final shore landing. Another island, another penguin breeding colony. But this time we came across something we hadn't seen yet – there was a leopard seal sunbathing in the snow. We gave this dangerous predator a wide berth and kept a careful eye on him, but he seemed content to dream away his afternoon. This was his equivalent of an easy chair and hot chocolate. We left him to his sweet dreams (probably of devouring penguins, but, hey, everyone's gotta dream, right?).

That night the crew had the fun idea of serving dinner on deck. What could be better than eating a hot meal in the freezing cold? A steady breeze added to the enjoyment. I hurried to eat before icicles could form on my fork and before my cheeks got too numb to tell if I was even chewing anymore. I weighed the prospect of dessert against the possibility of freezing to death. Dessert went down to defeat. I cruised the lounge in search of a stray cookie on my way back to my cabin.

Sunsets here were more like sun-lowerings, but they still produced some marvelously pastel skies of yellow, purple, and red clouds. We were bumping and banging through seas littered with ice, but the ice began to thin as we bypassed the South Shetlands and headed back into the dreaded washing machine of the Drake Passage.

But the ocean was calmer on the return trip and we didn't suffer the constant rolling of our first passage. With a day and a half of nothing but ocean to look at outside, we turned our attention again to fancy meals and nightly movies. The bar was busier than ever. It still seemed like another world, but I would actually be home in a couple of days. This adventure was nearly over.

We were standing on deck, approaching one of the most famous points of land anywhere in the world – Cape Horn, part of Chile, where Atlantic and Pacific Oceans meet. A few small buildings sat up on a grassy expanse well above the water. A memorial sculpture had also been erected on a high point, dedicated to the sailors who had lost their lives here over the centuries in these unforgiving waters. We could see a couple of men up there. They waved. We waved back and sailed on by.

We arrived back in Ushuaia in early afternoon. Southern summer was just a couple of weeks away and the snow on the mountains ringing the city had melted away significantly since we had left eight days ago. I puttered around Ushuaia one last time, killing a couple of hours until it became time to take a taxi to the airport and begin the journey home.

Thunder and lightning crackled as I sat in an airport lounge in Buenos Aires, watching the storm through a tall window as it lashed the runways with sheets of rain. It was not the best weather for flying, but I would encounter much worse when I got back to Albany.

The ground was white when my plane touched down at Albany Airport – a foot and a half of snow had fallen just two days before. I had left Antarctica to come home to a colder, snowier world.

Around the time that my flight was landing, less than ten miles away at the Port of Albany a cargo ship rolled over in the icy Hudson River while being loaded. Three Russian crewmen died in the mishap. The deep snow, the icy water, the ship with its Russian crew...had I really returned home or was I still in my cabin on the *Orlova*, dreaming?

In 2016 a Canadian rock band called Billy Talent released a song titled "Ghost Ship of Cannibal Rats". It was based on the very strange fate of the *MV Lyubov Orlova*.

In November of 2006 the *Orlova* had become grounded on Deception Island while attempting to negotiate the narrow passage into the bay. It had been freed by another ship and, with the damage being minimal, had made it safely back to Ushuaia. Otherwise, the *Orlova* continued in service without incident, carrying passengers to both the Arctic and Antarctic for several more years. But the ship's fortunes began to turn sour in September of 2010.

After sailing into the port of St. John's, Newfoundland, the *Orlova* became enmeshed in a dispute that arose between the ship's Russian owners and a tour company that had paid to charter it. The owners had failed to maintain the ship adequately and now owed the charter company a refund due to a canceled cruise. The ship's crew had also not been paid in months and were financially destitute, without a way to get home. In the end, the ship was seized by the creditors and the crew were put up in a hotel in St. John's, where they remained for three months until arrangements could be made for their return home.

At that point the ship's Russian owners decided to simply abandon the ship to the creditors and walked away from the whole mess. And so the *Orlova* sat for the next year and a half in the port of St. John's until an offer was finally made for it by a ship-scrapping operation.

The plan was to tow the *Orlova* down to the Dominican Republic, where it would be broken up. But first a team of people had to go aboard and make sure the ship's engines were still operational, and that the boat would float once out on the ocean.

The initial inspection deemed the *Orlova* seaworthy, but the team refused to return for further inspection, citing the presence of a large population of rats aboard the ship.

An essentially abandoned ship sitting in port for eighteen months is an attractive home for rats. There must have been plenty of food still aboard, and plenty of opportunities to come and go from the ship. Clearly, these were tourist rats and they were enjoying the finest a cruise ship has to offer.

The ship remained in port for a few more months while plans for moving it were finalized, and in January of 2013 the *Orlova* was finally underway again, a tugboat pulling it out of the harbor of St. John's and into the open ocean, heading south for the Caribbean.

By the next day rough seas had caused the towline to fail and the *Orlova* began to drift free in the North Atlantic, off the Canadian coast. Fearing the *Orlova* might drift into offshore oil platforms, a week later another boat found it and regained control, towing it farther out to sea. Yet another ship was contracted by the Canadian government to go out and bring the *Orlova* back to St. John's. But once again the towline broke and the *Orlova* began drifting northeast, out into international waters. No longer fearing for the safety of its coastal oil installations, the Canadian government gave up its efforts to recapture the ship, citing the fact that the *Orlova* was now in international waters and, therefore, not their problem anymore.

And so it continued to float, and drift, somewhere in the vastness of the North Atlantic. Now cut off from the port, and probably running low on food aboard ship, it was speculated that the hundreds (or possibly thousands) of rats on the *Orlova* had most likely turned cannibal, with only each other left to eat, unless they had somehow learned to fish. There were reports of sightings of the *Orlova* as far east as a few hundred miles from the Irish coast, where some feared the ship might go aground and spill its cargo of mutant, zombie rats.

Beacon signals from the ship continued to be received until March 2013, when it is speculated that the *Orlova* probably sank to the bottom of the North Atlantic. But no one is really sure exactly what happened to the *MV Lyubov Orlova*. It might still be floating around somewhere among the icebergs of the North Atlantic, the Ghost Ship of Cannibal Rats.

But whether it's still drifting or resting gently at the bottom of the ocean, it's nice to think that the *Orlova* I remember is at least still intact, and not disassembled. There might even still be one cookie left in the lounge that the rats overlooked.

Chapter Ten: China – June 2005

Hot. Oh my god, it was hot. I was in a bad mood and I didn't know why. Maybe it was the heat. Did I mention it was hot?

My flight from Chicago to Beijing had been delayed six hours, my hotel room overlooked a noisy school playground, and my left eye felt like it had sand in it. Maybe those played into the bad mood. Also, did I mention it was hot?

Summer had not yet officially begun but much of China was melting in a heat wave and the humidity was turned up pretty high as well. My assigned roommate had suffered some sort of passport snafu and had been unable to make the trip, so I found myself enjoying a single room. But for some reason I was not feeling engaged with this trip. In fact, I felt like I wanted a divorce. Twenty days, I told myself, and just nineteen more after today. What was wrong with me? I was in *China*. I should have been like a kid on Christmas morning, but I just didn't feel like opening my presents.

Maybe it was my mother. This was the first trip I had taken since she passed away. She had been the one who encouraged me to travel in the beginning, and she was the one most interested in hearing about my travels when I returned home. It wouldn't be the same anymore.

Maybe it was Beijing. Just like every massive Chinese city, Beijing was too big, too chaotic, and in many ways too *familiar*. China was a lot like the USA – cities of gleaming glass cubes separated by vast expanses of farmland, with mountains and desert in the west, mighty rivers cutting through the heartland, cold in the north, hot in the south, regional cuisine, sophisticated cities dotting its east coast. The only thing it was lacking was a west coast – we have Venice Beach, they have Mongolia.

Maybe it was the gritty feeling in my left eye, and the way it reflexively closed in bright sunlight.

Or maybe it was the heat. Did I mention it was hot?

We had four days to spend in Beijing. We drove here, we drove there, but I never got any sense of the full scope of the city, never had any feel for where in the city we were at any given time. It was just too big.

We started off our sightseeing with an old favorite, and I mean *old* – the Forbidden City, forbidden no longer. This was in the heart of central Beijing. A little bit of construction was going on a little way in from the entrance. A wooden wall surrounded the area. A sign on the wall said "The ancient building is renovating. Excuse me for bringing trouble to you". But, really, it was no trouble at all. I was happy to see the old place getting a facelift.

Built in the early 1400s as the seat of imperial power, the Forbidden City consists of nearly a thousand buildings on a square-ish island surrounded by a moat, reachable by a number of short bridges. The chief building material was wood, and the primary color red. There is an outer court surrounding an inner court. One passes through layer after layer of buildings, separated by vast open squares, as one approaches the innermost area. Statuary stands on guard everywhere – lions, dragons, turtles, phoenixes. This home of emperors used to be like a Chinese Vatican. Now it feels more like a Chinese Disneyland, complete with souvenir hawkers. You could fit the entire Vatican City, plus the Kremlin, into its sprawling grounds, with room left over for Trafalgar Square. It's a grand but coldly formal place, built to dazzle and dismay those who dared seek an audience with the emperor, or to impress his adversaries with the vastness of its scale. It was meant to be not just forbidden, but forbidding.

The nearby Tiananmen Square was next, another exercise in Chinese hugeness. One of the world's largest urban public squares, Tiananmen is so vast that the farthest parts seem to disappear beyond the horizon. Walking out into the square is like sailing away to sea in a little rowboat. Though only half the area of the Forbidden City, Tiananmen Square's open emptiness makes it feel larger.

This, of course, was the site of anti-government protests in the spring of 1989. After a couple of months of growing demonstrations in Beijing and other major Chinese cities, and the occupation of Tiananmen by student protestors, the Chinese government had finally sent the tanks rolling in. Estimates vary, but it's likely that over a thousand people died in the ensuing lopsided battle for control of central Beijing. Those deaths had occurred in the area leading to and near Tiananmen, but not on the actual square where I now stood. Looking at the immense space around me, I couldn't help but wonder what the government had expected. If you build a space big enough for thousands to gather, thousands will gather.

For all the people crammed into Beijing, there are still plenty of places to find peace, quiet, and some semblance of solitude, like our next destination, the Summer Palace. Originally an imperial retreat, the Summer Palace is actually several palaces set among gardens and lakes on the western fringes of Beijing. There are ornate bridges, temples, and pavilions. It's the Forbidden City's laid back country cousin. It was all so very photogenically Chinese.

North and west of the Summer Palace, Beijing finally begins to give way to rugged, forested hills, the line of a wall clearly visible along the ridge lines. We would be paying two visits to the Great Wall today. First would be a visit to a wild section of the Wall.

We pulled into a small parking area already occupied by two cars. Four or five people were exploring the Wall. Other than that, we had the place to ourselves.

This so-called "wild" section of the Wall appeared to be just that – little visited and lacking maintenance, some sections were deteriorated to the point of collapse. Here the Wall rose and fell with the mountain ridges, stone steps leading up and down. It was a strenuous climb, but only because I was trying to go quickly. Also, did I mention it was hot?

I stopped at the top of one rise and looked out over the hazy hills. The view went on for miles – more sections of wall cresting more low peaks, all the way to the horizon and beyond. A stiff breeze blew, providing some welcome relief from the heat. It was June 12th, my mother's birthday, and I took a moment to commemorate it. In one of my last conversations with her she had asked me where I planned to travel next. I had told her that China was a likely possibility. She had been pleased about that.

The part of the Wall that everyone is familiar with is near Badaling. This is the huge, wide, renovated section of the Wall that celebrities and visiting dignitaries come to look at, along with thousands of regular tourists every day. It was hot (did I mention?), there were more steps to climb, and the Wall was crowded. Having already visited a much more authentic part of the Wall, I opted to skip it and spend the time souvenir shopping instead, then looked for a cold Coke and some shady rest. I still wasn't enjoying myself much but my eye was feeling a little better.

I had developed a theory. As we drove from place to place my left eye would gradually feel worse, until I could hardly bear to open it in bright light. Whenever we got out of the bus to visit a place, it would slowly begin to feel better. I theorized that the bus's air conditioning, working overtime against the heat and humidity, was drying out my eye. Why only the left one, and not the right? I always sat on the left side of the bus. Perhaps the cool air was coming down from above along the window. I never bothered to sit on the right side to test my theory. I am a failure as a scientist.

Back in Beijing we continued to make the rounds, visiting the artisans laboring to turn out exquisite objects in porcelain, or cloisonne, or silk. We spent some time with the kids at an opera school. Chinese opera isn't about fat ladies and high notes. The kids were training in voice, movement, even some rather martial-looking arts. We visited an herbal market, where an exotic assortment of dead plants and animals was on display, including stacks of flattened lizards, piles of coiled snakes, and sacks of small, dried scorpions. We also visited one of Beijing's rapidly vanishing old, original neighborhoods.

Beijing's old neighborhoods are gradually being cleared to make way for new high-rise offices, new apartment buildings, new roads ringing the city, new hotels for foreign visitors, new metal-and-glass architectural extravaganzas. The old, one-story, tile-roofed residential neighborhoods could never accommodate the ever-increasing millions of Chinese packed into Beijing. In the few such neighborhoods remaining, one could still find the older, slower, more traditional world.

We were gathered in a small room by a courtyard, listening to stories about the old way of life, when the storm hit. It was over in five minutes. But in that five minutes a torrential hailstorm had dropped from the sky, the hailstones making a deafening racket as they landed on the tile roofs. The sloping roofs funneled all the hailstones into the courtyard, where they ricocheted like bullets, some of the stones shooting like shrapnel into the room where we were sitting. Afterward, a small woman with a broom swept the stones into piles. They looked like piles of diamonds glittering in the newly-returned sunshine.

      If you've never been to China, you've never eaten Chinese food. A Chinese restaurant in the USA is about as authentically Chinese as a pizza parlor. Orange chicken, crab rangoon, and fortune cookies are as Chinese as a cheeseburger.

      Most of our meals were served communally around large round tables with a rotating center, fifteen or twenty different dishes circling past us like horses on a merry-go-round. There was rice, of course, and noodles. Vegetables of all colors were prominent in the mix, while my carnivore tendencies were satisfied by the fish and all the small scraps of meat I could find. I practiced picking up peanuts with chopsticks, as I had become adept at doing in Vietnam. Lotus root soaked in orange juice was an unexpected treat, a bit like sweet pineapple. Some of us turned our teacups right-side-up to be filled. Others, like me, with no taste for tea, left ours upside-down, opting instead for China's other traditional drink – Coca Cola (face it folks, Coke, like the cockroach, is *everywhere*. After bottled water, it must be the most universally available drink on the planet).

      There were some special dinners as well, like Peking duck one night, and twenty courses of dumplings on another (I thought it would be easy to eat twenty dumplings. Around dumpling number twelve I realized I was wrong). The dessert was always watermelon, the regular red or a yellow variety I had never seen before.

      But what you won't find in China is dairy –

milk, butter, and, to my greatest chagrin, cheese. There were a few rare exceptions to this, and in Tibet it would all be different, but by mid-trip I found my nightly dreams invaded by talking cheeseburgers and flying pizzas.

We would be taking an overnight train from Beijing to Xi'an. I had just settled into my cabin and stretched out on the bed when my cabin-mate arrived. She was a young Chinese girl, about sixteen or seventeen. She sat down on the bed across from mine and burst into tears.

For the next five minutes she just sat there sobbing. Oh, good grief. While I was sympathetic to whatever her sadness might be – boyfriend trouble, homesickness, the unavailability of cheese – I did not relish the thought of spending the night as an extra in her soap opera. But after a few minutes she gathered her things, got up, and left. I never saw her again. A short time later a young Chinese man, who appeared to be a college student, took her place and quickly fell asleep. Sobs had been replaced by snores. I could handle that.

I woke up the next morning and looked out of my cabin's window. Nondescript farmland flashed by. We were on the outskirts of Xi'an.

With a population of just over five million, Xi'an is China's fourteenth largest city. Let that sink in. In the USA there is only one city larger than that – New York City. Our third and fourth largest cities, Chicago and Houston, have a combined population less than that of Xi'an. (There are many different figures given for populations of cities, both in China and the USA, depending on how strictly a "city" is defined. I have seen a figure of over twelve million for Xi'an under a more expansive definition. Here I'm using the most restrictive definition.)

Chinese cities are simply too big to try to take in all at once. The best we could do was carve out a few small chunks and visit those. And it was even hotter in Xi'an than it had been in Beijing, so we would be taking those chunks slowly.

My hotel in Xi'an was nestled in garden-like grounds just a short walk from the Giant Wild Goose Pagoda (not to be confused with the Small Wild Goose Pagoda, also in Xi'an). Built in the year 652, the Giant Wild Goose Pagoda was built like a brick wedding cake, currently with seven tiers. I say "currently" because the wedding cake has grown and shrunk over time. Originally five tiers when first constructed, it was renovated fifty years later and expanded to ten levels. An earthquake almost a millennium later reduced it to its current seven. You could say the pagoda has had its ups and downs. *I* wouldn't say it, but *you* could.

On the walk over to the pagoda I passed through a sculpture garden and then came upon a small grassy square with a sign posted in the middle that read "please take pity on lush and green grass". It did look rather pitifully lush, so I walked around it to reach the dancing waters on the other side. I had come for the evening show.

Out in front of the Giant Wild Goose Pagoda was one of those huge, open, concrete expanses that the Chinese seemed to love. Despite China being packed with over a billion people, it never felt crowded to me. In fact, it often felt quite empty. And these huge public squares could hold hundreds, thousands, and still feel spacious. But here there was something a bit different. Sections of long, low seating alternated with rows of spotlit fountain jets. Hundreds of people, mostly locals, came for the nightly show, sitting among the lights and spray as music played and water fountained up here and there, pulsed squirts popping up in front of and behind us as we sat and watched, the water reflecting the reds, blues, and greens of the lights, the pagoda looming over the festivities. It had a certain Fourth of July flavor to it. It was another instance of feeling that China was very much like the USA. Replace the pagoda with the Washington Monument and it was almost like home.

Xi'an is an ancient city, at least three thousand years old, with evidence of occupation extending back even further. It was China's capital for many centuries and was once the largest city in the world. It was the beginning point (or end, going the other way) of the famed Silk Road, the ancient trading route between East and West, along which spread, in both directions, goods, ideas, religions, and even the plague.

I stood atop Xi'an's massive city wall, built in the 1300s on top of existing fortifications, which runs for over eight and a half miles in a rough square around central Xi'an. The walkway on top of the wall is long and wide enough to hold drag races (they don't!). Once again I found myself in a mostly empty, wide open space here in this country of a billion or more people. Of course, "empty" is a relative term on a walkway fifty feet wide, and the wall felt more like a path from one side of the city to the other than a barrier between them, more a highway than a hindrance. The wall being too long to circumnavigate on foot, bicyclists flashed past me on rented bikes, the only way to make it all the way around in a reasonable amount of time. Cars streamed by below, outside the wall, and I looked down on rooftops and lines of laundry hanging out to dry. The sun was burning overhead as I ducked under a parapet for shade. I had wandered this wide sea of bricks long enough. I was ready for lunch and then a visit to what I knew would be a highlight of this or any other trip.

In the scrubby farmland to the northeast of Xi'an can be found some holes in the ground filled with broken stuff. That's a lot like saying that in the rolling countryside of England one can find some rocks standing in the grass. Or that China in June can be slightly warm.

In the mid-1970s local farmers began unearthing pieces of what turned out to be one of the greatest archeological finds of all time, the Terracotta Army of Xi'an. Consisting of thousands of life-size warriors, horses, and chariots all fashioned from clay, the Army, constructed around 200 BC, was buried with the Emperor Qin Shi Huang, to be his guardians in the afterlife. At least eight thousand individual statues have been found in the areas excavated so far, which represent just a small fraction of the entire site, which is believed to extend for many square miles. With the exception of one figure found completely intact, everything uncovered was in a jumble of fragments. In the thirty years that had passed since their discovery, a couple of thousand figures had been painstakingly reassembled and now stood in rows and columns in the earthen pits in which they were found, surrounded by countless more shards scattered about, still waiting to be pieced back together in what was an ongoing project that would last for decades more.

    An airplane hangar-sized building had been constructed over the main pit to keep out the elements and inside, down on the floor of the pit, ancient soldiers stood like troops being inspected. Their ranks stretched from one side of the pit to the other, and went far back until they thinned out into unreconstructed rubble piles. Each individual warrior was unique, with a variety of different facial features and expressions. They were once brightly painted but that had all flaked away, leaving them a solemn grayish-brown.

    Though broken and faded, they were still a remarkable sight. And the work that had gone into restoring them, and was still going on, was as impressive a thing as the Army itself.

    A few of the tourists leaning against the railing, gazing into the pit, seemed disappointed that the Army hadn't been found intact, in mint condition, as they had perhaps envisioned. They seemed to have no appreciation of what they were looking at. Intelligent travelers have a word for these people. They are called "idiots".

    We had one stop to make on our way to the

farming village – the local market, overflowing with fruits, vegetables, and other things we could not categorize. We had each been handed about a dollar in Chinese yuan and we fanned out to see what we could find, and how far we could bargain a dollar into stretching. We would be presenting our purchases to our hosts for the evening.

I soon found myself haggling over how many potatoes I could get for a Chinese buck, outraged by how badly (I guessed) I was being gouged.

"Only five potatoes? *Seven* yuan? Outrageous! I'm never coming back *here* again!", I said, which was true. There were smiles all around, numbers scratched on notepads, potatoes held in an old Chinese woman's grimy hands like they were diamonds, nodded heads. A deal was struck. The Chinese economy lurched forward imperceptibly. I returned to the minibus with a sack of spuds.

It was time for the always fun, always awkward, home stay. We arrived in a small farming village east of Xi'an in mid-afternoon and were soon divided up, two or three of us sent off to stay with one of several families in the village.

Our tour guide dropped us off with a quick introduction to the lady of the house, who spoke no English whatsoever. She was home alone, her husband out in the fields, her son away at school. The three of us – myself and my tour companions, who my lack of memory will call Bob and Jane, from Iowa maybe? – were invited to have a seat in the living room. Our hostess left us for a few minutes and then returned with three glasses and a metal pitcher of water, giving us a broad smile as she sat down across from us. The three of us each poured a glass of water for ourselves, noting that it was scalding hot. We politely sipped our glasses of near-boiling water, smiling and nodding at our hostess, making yum-yum faces. Mmmhmm, that's some good water, boy! A few syllables were uttered back and forth, all of them stuck on their own side of an impenetrable language barrier. But I'm pretty sure now that I know what our hostess was saying.

She was probably saying something like "Don't drink that yet, you morons, let it cool down first". It was later explained to us that the water had been presented to us that way in order to show that it had been boiled and was therefore safe to drink. We were supposed to drink it later, after it cooled off. Our hostess must have thought that either we were insane or we came from a country where *everyone* was insane.

Intelligent travelers have a word for people like us. We are called "idiots".

The man of the house had returned from working in the fields and now five of us sat around a table eating dinner. Being a picky eater hadn't been a problem up until now in China, most of our meals having consisted of a large array of different dishes that I could either take or leave as I desired. But here on the farm there was one item on the nightly menu, and it was whatever this stuff on my plate was. I did my best. I rearranged food on my plate to make it look like less, I yawned (so, sleepy, hope I can last until dessert!), I looked below the table hoping to find a hungry family dog there. The summer sun was still well above the horizon. May I be excused so I can go out and play? Even Bob and Jane from Iowa were struggling. I ate a few more bites and hoped I'd been polite enough. I was excused to go out and play.

It was almost sunset and over by the school an international soccer match was going on. It was American tourists vs. little Chinese kids and the kids seemed to have the game well in hand. I joined the fun for a while but, with daylight still remaining, I suddenly felt a bony hand clutch my arm from behind. It was my Chinese mom, and I was being told that it was my bedtime. My hosts were apparently the early-to-bed type.

This was not unusual for a farm community, but none of the other adult kids were being hauled off to bed by their figurative earlobes yet. I gave the ball one last sullen kick and allowed myself to be dragged home.

Bob and Jane from Iowa were already settled into their room, wondering what to do with themselves until it got dark enough to sleep. I stretched out on my bed and rested my head on the beaded pillow. I was already dreading breakfast. I was pretty sure we wouldn't be having Cocoa Puffs.

Feigning a queasy stomach was a far easier task than eating whatever the hell was staring back at me from my plate at breakfast the next morning. Bob and Jane from Iowa looked well rested as they pushed pieces of this and that around their plates, raising excruciatingly tiny bites to their lips experimentally, probably wishing they'd thought of the stomach ache excuse before I did. We all heaved a sigh of relief when our guide poked her head in the front door and asked if we were almost ready to leave.

We gifted our gracious hostess with exotic T-shirts from our far-off homeland (Iowa Hawkeyes from Bob and Jane, the New York City subway system from me), hopped on the bus, and were soon on our way to the airport for a flight to Wuhan. I was hoping the airline would feed me some lunch. I was getting pretty hungry.

The airport for Wuhan was quite a distance from the city. As our bus pulled out onto the highway we could see the skyline of Wuhan in the distance, like the Emerald City in The Wizard of Oz. A vibrant city of over seven million, to a tourist it was just another Chinese mega-city, nothing to see there, and our next destination took us in the opposite direction, toward Yichang. So long, Wuhan! It was nice to (almost) see ya!

The four hour bus ride from Wuhan to the Three Gorges Dam was long enough to aggravate my eye again, and the scenery was more drab than picturesque, so for the last couple of hours I napped. Damn air conditioning. I was eager to get out into the humid air again, with a little spray from the dam as a bonus.

The Three Gorges Dam is one of the most ambitious engineering projects in human history, the world's largest hydroelectric dam. Built chiefly to control regular and devastating flooding along the Yangtze River, the dam has been nothing if not controversial.

The Three Gorges of the Yangtze form one of China's most scenic attractions, and riverboats cruise up and down between Yichang and Chongqing, a trip of four or five days, depending on whether you're going upriver or down. The land rises steeply on both sides of the river, from steep, rocky cliffs to forested slopes, the river cutting a narrow channel through it. Small tributaries cut smaller gorges of their own before adding their flow to the Yangtze here and there.

I can tell you what it looked like when I was there, but it's all different now.

The positive side of the dam was that it would allow China to control the often catastrophic flooding that plagued the lower Yangtze below the area of the dam, with the added benefit of generating a considerable amount of electrical power. The dam would allow for a huge reservoir to be created just upriver, the water of which could then be released downriver in a controlled manner.

The negative side of the dam project was that it would cause the level of the river upstream to rise by about three hundred feet, drowning archeological sites, villages, towns, and cities all along the length of the river, and detracting from the scenic spectacle. The Chinese government was in the process of relocating at least a million and a quarter people from their homes and land to new government-built towns and cities. Much of what I saw would soon be underwater. It was a visit that I could not put off until the future.

The dam itself was an impressive sight, a massive project still under construction. There was much more to building the dam than just pouring concrete. The course of the river itself had to be altered to direct the flow of water exactly where needed, locks had to be constructed to allow ships to get up and down. The dam had already been under construction for a decade and would require almost another decade to complete. The dam was coming on line in stages and there was already gushing water and whirring turbines, trucks full of crushed rock making dusty tracks in the areas under construction.

But now it was time to see what would soon be unseeable, to visit what would soon be unvisitable. We made the short drive to where our riverboat was docked, eager for our five days cruising to begin, upriver to Chongqing (which we formerly called Chungking).

I remember almost nothing about our riverboat other than that my room had a door leading out to a narrow balcony where I sometimes sat, and that I spent most of my time sitting on the front deck looking at where we were going or sitting on the back deck looking at where we had just been. The view was pretty much the same either way – a ribbon of water snaking between mountains. But those "mountains" were just the walls of the gorge. At the top the land spread away from the river in flat, fertile plains.

High up on the walls of the gorges we could see numbers that had been affixed there, indicating, in meters, the height the water would reach once the dam project was completed and the area flooded. As we passed beneath a bridge spanning the gorge we could see numbers on the walls above it. The bridge would be completely submerged eventually, as would several other bridges we passed under.

A humid haze hung above the river, muting the colors and blurring the focus, leaving us sailing through a misty land that time would soon forget, already wearing its funeral shroud.

In places the gorges' walls rose nearly vertically from the river. In other places the land rose gently in a wide valley of terraced farms, towns, and, higher up, shiny new cities waiting to be populated. We passed plenty of other boats headed downriver – the Yangtze was a major thoroughfare for shipping – and quite a few other riverboats.

At one point we boarded some smaller boats and took a side trip up a tributary to the Lesser Three Gorges. It was pretty much the same, but narrower. A man walked a goat fifty feet above us along a trail that hugged the wall of the gorge. I imagined that somewhere along the way another, smaller tributary must branch off, leading to the Even More Lesser Three Gorges. A few more branchings would certainly lead us to the Mini Three Gorges and, inevitably, the Micro Three Gorges, an inch-wide river running through someone's muddy footprints. Clearly, all the river cruising was giving me too much time to think. We eventually returned to our riverboat and continued toward Chongqing.

Have you ever wondered what it would be like to wake up one morning and find everyone else gone? I mean gone, vanished without a trace, leaving you the only person left on Earth? Visiting the new city was just like that.

Still well short of Chongqing, we had been deposited on the north bank of the Yangtze and were now making our way through a small farm, dodging chickens, to begin the climb up to the new city, situated well above what would one day be the river's new level. We would be visiting a typical resident of this fair new city in his typical apartment.

And this man, formerly a farmer, was indeed a typical resident, in the sense that he seemed to be the *only* resident in what appeared to be a city with a capacity to be home to a hundred thousand or more, newly built by the Chinese government for the displaced people of the river. Apartment buildings stood on a tree-lined grid of streets, streetlamps stood ready to light the night, sidewalks were paved and waiting for the crowds to mingle on humid summer evenings. But I wouldn't have been surprised to see tumbleweeds rolling down the empty streets. Except for this one man and this one apartment, the city was uninhabited and dead quiet. Once again, here in crowded, crowded China, there was plenty of space, and hardly a soul around. It would have been a great place to film a post-apocalypse movie.

He gave us the required speech about being very happy in his new place, which, for some reason, was on the third floor of his building. Cracks were already showing in the concrete of the staircase, and a dribble of condensation from the air conditioner ran down the wall. Our host smiled weakly as he looked around his brand new apartment, already a leaky dump, and sighed that yes, he did miss his farm. I hoped he would at least have a few neighbors soon, someone to reminisce with about the good old days. Our footsteps echoed down the empty streets as we returned to the boat.

We left the boat for good in Chongqing, another Chinese mega-city of eight and a half million, where we had just enough time for a visit to the Joseph Stilwell Museum before a four hour drive that would bring us to Chengdu, as far as we could go by land. West of Chengdu rugged mountains began, continuing all the way to Tibet and beyond.

The Joseph Stilwell Museum, named for the American general who was commander of US forces in China during World War II, was a celebration of how the USA and its

Chinese buddies kicked the crap out of the Japanese in that war. The walls were hung with photographs of American and Chinese military commanders meeting, planning, and plotting together against the vile Japanese menace. These days we plot and plan with the Japanese to keep the Chinese menace at bay. One day the two of them will unite against *us* and that'll be it. Sayonara.

As we boarded the minibus for the long drive to Chengdu, I realized my eye was no longer bothering me. Five days on the humid Yangtze had done it good. Now I could watch the nondescript scenery flashing by as we drove. I knew China was full of scenic wonders. I had seen them in National Geographic. I had seen them on postcards. We had just floated through some. But we never seemed to *drive* past anything worth skipping a nap to see.

Chengdu is a cozy little town of about ten million or so. That said, it actually does feel a bit more walkable than most Chinese cities, with a slower pace and plenty of open space. But arriving in mid-afternoon, with a morning flight to Lhasa the next day, left little time for exploration. Instead, I spent the half hour before dinner exploring Chinese TV.

There seem to be three main types of programming on China's many TV channels – historical costume dramas, silly game shows, and news and documentaries, ranging from chipper news readers to eye-glazing reports on concrete production and mining quotas. Before long I was just sticking to CNN Asia, in wonderfully comprehensible English. If I was patient enough I could sometimes catch the score of the latest Red Sox game.

I stepped out of Lhasa's airport into a delightfully temperate breeze. Our guide advised us to bundle up against the cold. It was about sixty-eight degrees and it felt wonderful. I didn't even notice the change in altitude yet.

The Chinese must be expecting Lhasa to

grow into another Chinese mega-city. There is no other reason to build its airport so far out of town. Snow-capped mountains ringed the horizon as we made the long and scenic drive into the city. We passed over rivers that flowed through the brown and green high plateau of Tibet. We had left Chinese Buddhism, with its formal and almost clandestine nature, behind and were now about to experience the more overt and exuberant spectacle of Tibetan Buddhism. Colorful prayer flags flapped in the breeze. We stopped at the Nietang Buddha, a seven hundred year-old stone Buddha, colored a vivid orange and blue, carved out of the base of a mountain, thirty feet high and looking almost brand new. Other Buddhas were painted on the rock wall next to it. Everything was draped in pieces of gauzy white fabric, thrown there by worshipers showing their respects, trying to throw their offerings as high as possible to ensure the best of fortunes. It looked unfortunately like streamers of toilet paper the morning after Halloween. A yak stood nearby, ignoring the Buddhas and the worshipers and the tourists. What is any of that to a yak?

  A new four-lane highway now connects Lhasa with the airport, cutting this scenic drive in half. It hadn't been built yet when I was there and that's a good thing. I was happy to have the extra time to see Tibet's countryside, to meet a roadside yak or two, to let it sink in that these mountains I was looking at were the *Himalayas*.

  We drove through Lhasa's brief and dusty outskirts and into the city, past the Potala Palace looming above us on our left, and soon reached our hotel, located within steps of the Barkhor Bazaar. Lhasa was a city made for walking.

  Lhasa sits at an altitude just a little higher than Cusco, Peru, about 11,800 feet, but here there was no coca leaf tea awaiting us when we arrived at the hotel. While I had acclimated quickly to the altitude in Peru and had slept well, the same would not be true in Lhasa. I slept fitfully every night in Lhasa, and had strange and vivid dreams. I blame it on the absence of coca and recommend the Chinese government institute a program to either grow or import some.

After checking in to the hotel I was looking forward to exploring the Barkhor Bazaar, just half a block away. The cool, mountain-clean, spring-like air had re-energized me, and Lhasa was considerably smaller and easier to negotiate than the Chinese mega-cities. With a population of less than half a million, Lhasa was just a little hick town, like Mayberry or Hooterville. Shucks, tweren't nothin' to it at all, really.

As I headed for the front door I heard my guide suggest I take a coat, or at least a sweater. I ignored her and walked out into a beautiful day.

To visit the Barkhor Bazaar is to walk in a rough circle around the Jokhang Temple, always in a clockwise direction. To walk in the other direction is both rude and counterproductive, a bit like trying to swim upstream like a salmon. I joined the pedestrian flow and began my first circuit. An assortment of Tibetan goodies for sale were on display, including prayer wheels, singing bowls, and huge slabs of yak butter. Maroon-robed Buddhist monks made up a significant portion of the crowd. The *crowd*! Here, in by far the smallest city we would visit, there was a feeling of crowdedness that I had not experienced anywhere else in China except the Beijing subway. There were tourists, yes, but many locals as well, many spinning hand-held prayer wheels as they walked. I bought myself one and walked on, spinning it merrily.

Climbing the three flights of stairs to the hotel's roof was a three-part process – climb one flight, rest, try to breathe normally again, repeat. But the view from the rooftop was worth it. The Potala Palace, home to Dalai Lamas past, sat majestically on its hill in the near distance, almost seeming to float in the air. We would be saving our visit to the Potala for last.

Today we were to listen to a talk about Tibetan culture while sipping yak butter tea, then walk around the Barkhor, with a visit to the Jokhang Temple, then visit a Buddhist monastery and an orphanage. Lhasa was quickly becoming my favorite "Chinese" city.

I put "Chinese" in quotes because Lhasa is not really a Chinese city, it's Tibetan. China has controlled Tibet since the 1950s but the only thing Chinese about Lhasa is the population, swelling from an influx of Chinese encouraged by the government to resettle there as a means of exerting its control.

We learned a bit about Tibetan history as we were given cups of yak butter tea. I had read many times that yak butter tea is a so-called acquired taste, another way of saying that it's downright horrible. But to me it tasted like nothing more than melted butter and I enjoyed it enough to finish it. I noticed a few half-finished cups around the table – it seemed not everyone had my taste for liquid fat.

Out on Barkhor Street again, we wound our way clockwise until we reached the front of the Jokhang Temple. Buddhist pilgrims lay on the ground in front of the temple on mats that they had unrolled for the purpose, inching closer and closer to the temple while sprawled face down on the ground.

The Jokhang Temple, dating back to the seventh century, is Tibet's most sacred site and pilgrims make the journey here from all over huge but sparsely-populated Tibet. Sellers of yak butter were doing a brisk business nearby – many of the pilgrims purchased it as an offering.

Inside the temple, pilgrims lit yak butter candles as the crowd circled around clockwise, holding them or leaving them in offering. It was dark, the darkness punctuated by all the candles, and crowdedly narrow, hot and stuffy. It was good to finally emerge from a stairway onto the roof, looking out over Barkhor Square. A gentle drizzle had begun and the huge square's paving stones were wet and glistening. I took in the view for a while before leaving the temple.

Out in front of the temple was what looked like a concrete bunker set into the ground. I stepped down and into it. Inside, in near-total darkness, row upon row of candles were flickering, each a little thimble of burning yak butter, hundreds of them in neat rows all around the bunker. The smoke drove me out again after a minute or two.

Emerging from the bunker, I was approached by two Tibetan men, pilgrims from somewhere out in the countryside, here to visit the big city. They were tourists just as much as I was. They were marveling at my height – six feet, three inches, not abnormal for an American but a giant among the Tibetans – and asked me if I would pose for pictures with them. It may have been their first time in the big city and they were marveling at all the exotic sights. I had come halfway around the world to be one of those sights, The Giant Pale Man From Far Away.

The centuries-old Sera Monastery is located on Lhasa's northern outskirts and is home to hundreds of Buddhist monks, always easily recognizable by their maroon robes. We paid a visit to the monastery's courtyard to watch the monks debating. The debates were over points of Buddhist teachings and featured much shouting and loud, almost violent, hand clapping. Questioners stood and fired questions at other monks seated on the ground, stomping their feet and crashing their hands together to punctuate their queries. Dozens of monks were scattered all over in groups, taking no notice of me as I wandered around among them. I felt like a hologram, a projection from somewhere far away intruding into their world without actually touching it. At our next stop we would be intruders again, ghosts passing through another very real world. But this time we would not be ignored.

The children of the orphanage, boys and

girls mostly six through twelve, stood in rows and columns as we entered the outdoor courtyard, greeting us with a song or two under the supervision of the orphanage staff. Then we were each singled out by two or three children, who took us by the hands and led us on a tour of their insular little world behind the orphanage's walls, the classrooms, the cinderblock bedrooms, their artworks and games. We sat on the beds, three boys smiling at me as I took their picture. We kicked a ball around. At the risk of sounding cynical, they were working hard for the donations that would be asked of us when we departed. I didn't mind. If anyone's got a better reason to ask me for money I'd like to hear it.

As we were about to leave, a young girl motioned for me to bend down so she could tell me something. She placed her hands on my cheeks, looked up at me, and said "goodbye".

Goodbye, kid. Hope you get out of there someday.

We returned to the minibus, where a bottle of hand sanitizer made the rounds. If that sounds harsh, it's not meant to. Visiting a place like Tibet is like going to see the tigers at the zoo. The full immersive experience could be hazardous to your health. Sometimes it's necessary to remain behind a safe barrier. You don't stick your head in the tiger cage and you don't take disease lightly in Lhasa. You don't know where those orphans' hands have been.

The postcard wonder of the sights and views in Lhasa can be a Disneyland veneer that lulls one into forgetting the unsafe tap water, the iffy sewage system, the yak urine running down the gutters of the street outside your window. Okay, I probably made up the part about the yak urine, but not really. There was *something* running in the gutters, and it wasn't milk and honey. The point is, when in Lhasa boil your water and wash your hands. And wear a sweater when you go out. You don't want to catch a cold, do you?

Just outside of Lhasa we paid a visit to a small village to see the daily life away from the big city. Here, as elsewhere around Tibet, the yak was everything. At least a thousand yak dung patties sat drying on top of a stone wall, soon to fuel the fires for cooking and heat. Another wall was a piled-up jumble of rocks and yak patties, with a yak skull or two sitting on top. A few living, breathing yaks stood around, nosing the ground, chewing, ready to produce more fuel.

I had been enjoying my first experiences of eating yak. Dinner one night had featured yak steak, lunch the following day had been a nice, juicy yakburger. The yak butter tea hadn't made me gag. Yes sir, right about then I was considering opening a Tibetan restaurant when I got back home, Dave's House of Yak, or maybe The Yak Hut, or better yet, Chez Yaques.

It was finally time to visit the Potala Palace, which had been looming over us from its hilltop perch for the past couple of days like a fairytale castle in the clouds. There were a lot of broad steps to climb and I was still feeling the altitude, so there was much resting for breath on the way up.

Construction of the Potala Palace was begun in the mid-1600s and it served as the winter palace of the Dalai Lamas until the current one fled the country in 1959. The palace is enormous, with thirteen stories, over a thousand rooms, ten thousand shrines, and two hundred thousand statues. It looks like a huge white fortress with another red one sitting on it, sort of like a sundae with a cherry on top.

We climbed all the way to the top, which, at an altitude of over 12,100 feet, would be, and still remains, the highest point above sea level that I have ever reached. Standing on the Potala's roof, which is now off-limits to tourists, I could see all of Lhasa spread out on the valley floor, ringed by mountains, snow capping the ones on the horizon.

Inside, the Potala was dimly lit, hot and stuffy. We passed huge shrines to Dalai Lamas of the past, set well back behind screens and railings, a massive collection of statuary. Paper money from all over the world lay strewn where it had been tossed in offering – it collected between railings and screens and littered the floor everywhere. There was currency from Afghanistan, Malaysia, Laos, India, and many other countries. No photographs are allowed inside, so all I have is my memory, and I do remember feeling quite relieved when I finally came out again into sunshine, fresh air, and a cool breeze. We would be headed back to stiflingly hot China in the morning. I let the cool air blow across me as I stood on the Potala's roof again and took in one last view of Lhasa.

We were back in Chengdu again, another quick hit and run. In the morning we would pay a quick visit to the nearby panda sanctuary before catching our flight to Hong Kong. I was ready to see some pandas, see Hong Kong, and go home. It had been a long trip.

Pandas are fun to watch. They're awkward and tend to fall over rather easily. And the panda sanctuary had given them plenty of things to play on and fall off of – trees, ladders, bamboo platforms, each other. It was like watching the world's most uncoordinated acrobatic troupe. The much smaller red pandas seemed embarrassed by the oafishness of their black and white cousins and kept to themselves.

We could have watched pandas tumble over all day but our flight to Hong Kong wouldn't wait. That was just as well. I was ready to go home and eat some cheese.

What can I say? I like cheese. The Chinese don't. They seem to eat everything else, but lactose intolerance is widespread in China, so you'll hardly see a glass of milk, a pat of butter, or a slice of cheese outside of tourist hotel breakfast buffets. There had been a bit of a break from non-dairy in Lhasa, where they drink melted yak butter out of teacups and think nothing of throwing a little yak cheese on a yakburger if requested. Maybe worldly, metropolitan Hong Kong would offer a few tasty varieties.

As we approached Hong Kong I could see large clusters of high-rise buildings sticking up toward the sky like hypodermic needles. Ah, there's Hong Kong, one thinks, look at all the skyscrapers! Then it ends, there's a little bit of water, and a new cluster begins. This is just the outskirts, the suburbs of Hong Kong. Island after island packed with skyscrapers flashed by below. I had never seen such a collection of tall buildings, not even in New York City. Like a fireworks display reaching its grand finale, the real heart of Hong Kong finally exploded into view, wrapped around the city's grand harbor. And "fireworks" is an appropriate word to use – Hong Kong provides an ever-changing light show every night.

On our way in from the airport we could see that Hong Kong looked less like the other Chinese cities and more like a Chinese-British amalgamation, which made sense given the territory's ownership history. The Brits had only handed Hong Kong back to the Chinese a few years earlier. The horse-racing track we passed could have been a piece of England transported there. Hong Kong's bustling Tsim Sha Tsui area, where our hotel was located, could have passed for Piccadilly.

I checked my watch as we neared the hotel. Good, I was only a little late in arriving. I'd hate to keep Steve waiting.

I knew Steve through mutual friends back home. He was American, living with his Japanese wife and their daughter in Hong Kong, where he was a teacher. Hong Kong was a perfectly international home for such an international family. We had made long-distance plans to meet at my hotel on the afternoon of my arrival. I was only a little late, but so was Steve. Just a few minutes after I checked in we met in the hotel's lobby and were soon strolling down Nathan Street, dodging the drips.

The road cut through the heart of Tsim Sha Tsui's skyscraper jungle and almost every window of every building, all the way up to the thousandth floor, had an air conditioner in it, cranked to the maximum to ward off Hong Kong's heat and humidity. And they were all constantly dripping water, so that a stroll down Nathan Street required an umbrella even on a sunny day. Umbrella-less, we dodged and weaved our way through the dense pedestrian crowd, avoiding the heaviest waterfalls. The view down each cross street we passed was a dense forest of signage, competing for our attention like trees competing for sunlight.

We soon came to the first stop on what would be an international evening in China's least Chinese city. It was, of course, an Irish pub.

From there we walked past restaurants of all nationalities and decided on an Italian one. An hour later, full of Guinness and lasagna (with, be still my heart, *cheese*), our final stop was an Australian jazz club called Ned Kelly's Last Stand, which featured an American jazz band. I felt like I'd left China for a while and gone on a brief world tour.

Much of our conversation concerned my travels in China, what I had liked the most, which of those places Steve had also been, and which ones he still hadn't visited but wanted to. I enjoyed an evening of feeling more like a local than a tourist, like someone who actually belonged there.

I would see Steve again a few months later on his next visit to the USA. I would have a big head start on him – I would be going home in just a couple more days.

The next morning I began to realize that I

had brought more back with me from Lhasa than a prayer wheel and a singing bowl. I found myself more in need of a bowl that *didn't* sing. Stomach churning, I somehow managed to make it through the day's activities but I was dreading the flight home if I wasn't feeling better by then.

    Hong Kong's high-rise buildings also rise with the land as it slopes upward from its magnificent harbor, but down in the depths of the skyscraper canyons things look decidedly more Chinese. Lively markets sell everything from oranges to snakes. At the Man Mo Temple giant incense coils that looked like huge lampshades burned slowly, taking a couple of weeks each to burn all the way down, filling the temple with smoke so dense that it drove me back outside after a couple of minutes. If the incense had any medicinal properties I didn't feel them. My guts still felt like a hot lava cake ready to erupt.

    No visit to Hong Kong is complete without taking in the view from Victoria Peak at night. There is a light show every night along the harbor, and many of the city's tallest buildings are part of the show, with lights pulsing and strobing in all different colors, like smokeless fireworks. From the Peak, all of that is laid out before you, below you. I told my guts to behave for awhile as I ate an ice cream cone and watched the show.

    Later, back at the hotel, I was given a precious gift by one of the teachers. There were two women in my tour group, teachers from Chicago, who were traveling together. One of them, knowing my intestinal plight, knocked on my door that evening and offered me some anti-diarrheal pills she had with her. I accepted them gratefully and they did wonders. By the next afternoon I was feeling fine again. The flight home would not be a nightmare.

    We were on our own for lunch on the last day and I was feeling well enough to go out and see if I could find any cheese to make a sandwich. Even in Hong Kong, international

Hong Kong, cosmopolitan Hong Kong, formerly-British Hong Kong, lasagna and ice cream-eating Hong Kong, I still could not find any decent cheese in any market. In one small grocery store I found, and settled for, a small package of what was advertised as cheddar. It had apparently been aged for about three seconds and tasted about the same as the plastic it came packaged in. No problem. I was going home the next morning.

       For the first time on my travels, my mother was not at the airport to pick me up when I arrived back in Albany. I took a cab home. The cabdriver couldn't have cared less where I had just been, what I had just done. I rode along, bursting with stories I had no one to tell.

       And perhaps that's why I decided to write this book. All travels are stories and stories need to be told.

Chapter Eleven: Turkey – June 2006

I woke up, looked down, and saw Bulgaria. That probably needs some explaining.

On a foreign trip, one of the drawbacks to living in Albany is that I always have to fly to an international departure city first. Any trip out of the country requires at least two flights. And one of the drawbacks to booking flights through a tour company is that they will give me the cheapest flights, regardless of what curious routing that may involve. And so my air itinerary to Istanbul had an odd kink in it: I would have to fly to Washington's National Airport, then fly from there back north to JFK in New York, then fly out of New York non-stop to Istanbul. And the extra flight had backed up my departure time from Albany to an unreasonably early six a.m.

Being a night owl by nature, I decided my best strategy would be to stay up all night before the flight and leave for the airport at about four in the morning. I could, I reasoned, sleep all I wanted on the plane.

It worked perfectly. By the time I finally

reached JFK I was dead tired. Buckled into my seat and waiting for takeoff, all I had to do was lean my head back and I was gone, out, instantly asleep.

I missed the safety instructions. I missed taxiing out to the runway. I missed two hours of sitting on a sweltering runway waiting for clearance to take off. I missed the takeoff. I missed the Atlantic Ocean, most of Europe, the in-flight movies, and all the snacks, drinks, and meals.

I woke up, looked down, and saw Bulgaria, but I didn't know right away that those rolling fields were Bulgaria. If I had awakened in a dark room I may have been a bit disoriented for a few minutes. But my surroundings jolted me into instant awareness. I looked at the flight map imbedded in the seatback in front of me, which showed where the flight was from minute to minute. I was amazed to see that we were somewhere over southern Bulgaria, fast approaching the Turkish border. The ground below was a patchwork of farmland, all greens and golds. Flight attendants were passing out immigration forms. A few minutes later the pilot announced that we were about to begin our final approach to Istanbul. It had been by far the easiest flight of my life. And to make it even better, it was morning in Istanbul. Despite the eight-hour time difference, I was waking up in the morning, just as I should be, ready for a brand new day to begin.

Istanbul is surrounded by water, and the water is surrounded by Istanbul. The Bosphorus connects the Sea of Marmara with the Black Sea to the north. Bridges span the Bosphorus, connecting the European side of the city with the Asian side to the east. Fingers of water reach into the European side – more bridges are needed to stitch up Europe.

On our way in from the airport we drove along the Sea of Marmara on a sunny summer morning. Just before the Bosphorus begins, cutting the city in half, a small, last piece of Europe juts out into the water, the continent's last southeastern gasp. This small area was the center of ancient Byzantium and is now the location of Istanbul's three most famous sites – the Blue Mosque, the Topkapi Museum, and the Hagia Sophia. It was also the location of our hotel.

We were welcomed with glasses of cherry juice on arrival at the hotel. In many of the countries I've visited there seems to be one particular beverage, rare or unknown at home, that is on offer absolutely everywhere. In Kenya it was passion fruit juice. In Peru it was Inca Kola. In Tibet it was yak butter tea. Here in Turkey it was cherry juice. I came to learn that Turkey is the world's leading cherry producing nation. I sipped my cherry juice and watched the boats on the water from my outdoor table, the Blue Mosque looming over my shoulder behind me. I was well rested and ready to see the sights.

Just up a short and winding road from the hotel stood the Blue Mosque, our logical first stop. First, let me just say that Istanbul is a spectacularly old city, a museum of antiquity on top of which they have just kept building, right up to the present day. To say that a certain building is five hundred years old is to say that it's relatively new. The Blue Mosque, built in the early 1600s, is more than a thousand years younger than the neighboring Hagia Sophia, which was built in the 530s.

To start from the beginning, Byzantium was founded in the 7th century BC by Greeks spreading east from the home country. After being largely destroyed in the 2nd century AD, it was rebuilt and renamed Constantinople, becoming the new capital of the Roman Empire in 330 AD. By the time the massive Hagia Sophia cathedral was built in the 530s, it was the center of the Greek Orthodox Church and the Hagia Sophia was the world's largest building. In 1453 AD the Ottomans took control, bringing Islam to the city and sweeping away most of the Christian influences.

The Ottoman Empire backed the wrong side

in World War One, leading quickly to its demise, and the new Republic of Turkey was born in 1923. The sultans were out, a new, secular government was in, and the city had a new name yet again – Istanbul.

The Blue Mosque is a functioning mosque, not a museum, so we wandered around inside with soft footsteps and hushed voices. The interior was a wide open space and, not surprisingly, blue was the dominant color. It sparkled and dazzled with hundreds of stained glass windows, tiled mosaics, and hanging lamps. Women said their prayers in a separate room, behind a screen. From the outside, the Blue Mosque was just as impressive, with multiple domes and six huge minarets surrounding it, looking a bit like rockets waiting for liftoff.

Not far away stood the Hagia Sophia. Almost fifteen hundred years old, the Hagia Sophia had been a Greek Orthodox cathedral until the Ottomans took control of the city in 1453. All of the Christian iconography had been covered up, stripped away, or simply defaced and the Hagia Sophia was converted into a mosque, which it remained until 1931, when it became a museum and tourist attraction. Turkey's frequent devastating earthquakes make the building even more remarkable. Anything less structurally sound would have been a rubble pile by now.

The interior of the Hagia Sophia was showing its age a bit. But I can only hope to look half as good when I'm 1500 years old. Wandering around the second floor, I rested on a marble parapet, overlooking the main floor below. I had found the graffiti.

I had been surprised to learn that back in the 9th century there had been Vikings in Istanbul. One of them had apparently carved his name into the marble like a naughty schoolboy. It basically said "Halvdan was here". During the 10th and 11th centuries, while some Norsemen were sailing west to ultimately discover North America, the Ottoman emperor's personal guard was made up mostly of mercenary Vikings. And, silly me, I had always pictured Vikings as being entrenched in Scandinavia, sitting around on tree stumps in the snow, sharpening their axes. But they were travelers, too. In that I felt a kindred connection, though I resisted carving my name next to Halvdan's.

There is currently a proposal being seriously considered to make the Hagia Sophia a mosque again. That would be a shame and, to me, rather redundant, with the huge Blue Mosque sitting just a few hundred yards away.

Next down the line was the Topkapi Museum, built in the 15th century as the palatial home of the Ottoman sultans. Featuring the usual mix of gold, jewels, weapons, artworks, and other antiquities, the museum also held a glass case within which were purported to be the right hand and forearm of John the Baptist. Maybe it is, maybe it isn't. I myself was unable to make a positive identification. There are several other places that claim to have old John's arm bones in a case, or a box. If they're all telling the truth, John the Baptist would have had to be half man, half octopus.

The next day we decided to spice things up by going to, naturally, the spice market. But this was no ordinary market. Istanbul's Spice Bazaar is roughly 350 years old. The shrink-wrapping machines were of a little more recent date, as were the electric lights and the occasional New York Yankees baseball cap in the crowd. Seller after seller had similar colorful displays of a rainbow of spices. There were the reds of chili pepper and sumac, the yellow of saffron, the oranges and browns of paprika, cinnamon, and curry. There were heaps of dried fruits and nuts, teas, dried caviar, and candies, including a multi-colored array of Turkish Delight. I had been requested by someone at home to bring back some fresh cinnamon. They were all offering more or less the same product, so I picked one of the vendors at random and did the haggling dance (no, not a literal dance, don't be silly), then watched him shrink-wrap my purchase until it formed a plastic package as hard and dense as a baseball. That cinnamon would stay fresh for a thousand years.

The Black Death arrived in Constantinople in 1347. Just add it to the list, along with the conquests and the earthquakes. Just another rough patch in a long, long history. Life went on, and to prove it the Galata Tower was constructed the following year, 1348.

The 220-foot stone tower, cylindrical, with a pointy cap on top, was constructed as an observation tower to watch over the harbor and was later used as a watchtower for fires that might break out around the city. These days it's considered the best place for a panoramic view of Istanbul.

And what a view it was! Except for about twenty rather rowdy Turkish grade-school field-trippers running around and begging to be photographed, Istanbul's twelve million inhabitants were all out there somewhere in the vast sprawl of the city, which extended from horizon to horizon and beyond. Waterways converged below us, the Galata Bridge conveying a swarm of traffic from one side to the other. Minarets punctured the skyline by the dozens. Far to the left of my view the Asian side beckoned us to explore another continent. We would be flying well into Asian Turkey the next morning.

Kayseri, Turkey is a city of over a million people. I've never been there, but I've used its airport. Kayseri is the air gateway to Cappadocia.

The Cappadocia region occupies a plateau in central Turkey that was flooded with lava and ash from volcanic eruptions about three million years ago. Harder rock settled on top of lighter and over the ensuing millennia the lighter, underlying rock has eroded away. The result is thousands of what are called fairy chimneys – tall spires of rock, most with flat slabs of the less eroded, harder rock still resting on top like oversized hats. And the process is ongoing – we found rock formations in various stages of spire-production. In places there were rows of fairy chimneys still connected to each other by rock not yet eroded away. In other places there were what looked like sand dunes but which were rolling hills of frozen lava. Gentle folds in those hard dunes were the very beginnings of the fairy chimneys of the future.

    In places where the rock had formed fatter, rounder formations there had been dwellings carved out of the soft stone. Beginning in about 300 AD people had hollowed out homes, granaries, and churches all through the rock, building several stories up into the spires and especially down below ground level. The area was in regular political and military turmoil and the cave dwellings made an excellent refuge for those wishing to avoid the various conflicts of the day. Thousands of people made their homes there over many centuries, and people are still living in hollowed out caves in the area to this day. You can book a room at an old, hollowed out hotel if you like. Personally, I preferred the hotel where we were staying, near Nevsehir. It had something most caves simply don't have – a swimming pool.

    On our first day in Cappadocia we had visited the old cave dwellings and hiked among the fairy chimneys. It was June and the weather was full-on summer. I spent the late afternoon in the pool, wondering what could be better than this. The answer popped into my head when I realized it was time to dry off and have a fabulous buffet dinner in the dining room next to the pool. Oh, the hardships of travel!

    Actually though, sacrifices do sometimes have to be made in the pursuit of travel memories. I would have to rise at 4 o'clock the next morning but it would turn out to be one of my favorite and most memorable days spent anywhere. I set the alarm for that ungodly hour and got to sleep as early as I could.

There's something a little weird about getting up at four in the morning. The world is chilly and dark and sensible people are sleeping. It's hard to believe I'm not one of them, hard to believe that I have things to do and places to be in the pre-dawn darkness of central Turkey. It feels like a secret mission.

Our little group boards a minibus in the gloom and we are soon on our way. The office of the hot-air balloon company is just a few miles away. There we are given cookies and coffee while we wait for mysterious hot-air balloon logistics to be sorted out. My group are not the only people there. Ballooning in Cappadocia is very popular; it is considered one of the finest places in the world for it due to both the wind conditions and the dramatic scenery. Soon everyone has been loaded into minibuses and the whole convoy heads out to the staging area.

At least a dozen balloons are lying on their sides in a field, being inflated by hot jets of flame. Dawn is approaching and the darkness has already begun to give way to murky morning light. Grazing horses stand nearby as the balloons, one by one, begin to take full shape and rise erect above the wicker baskets that will soon be dangling beneath them. Each basket has several compartments around the outside, with the pilot and his flame in the center. There is room for about three people per compartment, about eighteen passengers per balloon. With a supporting boost from helping hands, we climb into the basket and arrange ourselves evenly. A few photographs of the balloons and the horses have brought me to the end of a roll of film. I stand in the basket putting a new roll in my camera. I click the camera's cover shut and look up. We are thirty feet off the ground. I hadn't even noticed when we lifted off.

As we rise higher we can see the sun just

coming into view from behind the mountains to the east. The village we are now floating above is still shrouded in darkness. The sun will have to rise a little higher before its rays will reach the valley floor. We hear the faint barking of a dog. A minute or two later we hear a rooster crowing below us, the sound just piercing enough to reach us. Otherwise, the world is even quieter than before; the only sound we hear is the whoosh of the flames rushing up into the balloon, keeping us aloft as we rise even higher.

There are other balloons in the air around us, blobs of color suspended in the sky. We rise high to take in the full landscape, fields, villages, and rock formations spread out below us. We descend to skim just above the tops of the fairy chimneys. There is hardly any sensation of motion; it is the land that rolls away below us, the land that approaches or recedes.

After ninety minutes aloft we drop lower and lower. The sun paints the shadow of our balloon on the frozen dunes as we skim above them. A flatbed truck races to meet us as our big balloon shadow darkens the field just below us. We land with hardly a thud and immediately there are men there to grab the basket, holding it steady as we climb out. The flame goes out; the balloon slowly deflates as the men detach the basket and load it onto the flatbed.

By the time I'm standing on the ground again there is a table waiting for us next to the flatbed, complete with a bright red tablecloth. There are wine glasses, champagne, and, of course, cherry juice. We drink a toast to our safe return from the sky and get back aboard our minibus to return to the hotel. It has been an eventful day already and we haven't even had breakfast yet.

The hotel's breakfast buffet was the kind that people take photographs of, that poets write odes to. It was magnificent. It had everything in the known breakfast universe.

There were eggs, of course, and sausage and bacon. There were potatoes, noodles, breads and pastries, pancakes and french toast, fruits, juices, syrups, sauces. There were plain donuts sitting next to a vat of warm chocolate to dip them in. My table overflowed with plates and glasses. If I'd been wearing a belt it would have cut me in half.

After breakfast we got back aboard the minibus, its tires groaning under our breakfast-laden weight, and headed back out to see more rocks, more cave dwellings, and the fortress town of Uchisar.

Uchisar can be seen from anywhere in the region. Amidst all the shapes and jumbles of rock there is one massive chunk rising nearly two hundred feet above the surrounding land, a rounded hump of hollowed-out stone. At the top there is an ancient castle, and a flag flying from a pole. All the way down through the rock there are living spaces carved out, some now even used as hotel rooms. The village of Uchisar clings to the lower slopes.

I stood at the top, resting against the flagpole and taking in the view.   Depending on what direction I looked, the landscape was either brown and green with sparse farmland, or a moonscape of brown and gray rock. Blue humps of weathered mountains marked the horizon. It had been a hot and dusty climb to the top of the citadel of stone. Despite my breakfast gluttony I was ready to climb back down and go to lunch.

We drove through a forest of fairy chimneys, making a couple of photo stops. At one stop there was a police station directly across the road. It had been carved out of a large glob of rock, of course. I half-expected to run into Fred Flintstone somewhere along the way.

We stopped for a simple lunch of Turkish pizza and cherry juice. Turkish pizza is a very thin, crusty pizza topped with crushed tomato and spices. There is no cheese, but ground lamb is often added for us non-vegetarians. It was quick and light and absolutely perfect.

We returned to our hotel by mid-afternoon and I was able to catch up a little on my sleep shortfall, lounging in a deck chair next to the beautiful pool when I wasn't actually floating in it, beating the heat. And that, gloriously, was all I did until dinner.

And dinner was another exercise in buffet excess. I might just have exploded for real if we hadn't had a schedule to keep. But we couldn't linger over dinner. We had an evening out to get ready for.

Group touring tends to be an early-to-bed, early-to-rise way of life. An evening out is a rarity unless you're up for it on your own. But tonight we were going out to see a whirling dervish ceremony. It was about a half-hour's drive away.

The ceremony was being conducted in a 13th century caravanserai. Caravanserais were the motels of the old trade routes, safe havens on the dangerous road, places to get something to eat and a place to sleep for yourself and your camels before continuing on your way. We were ushered in and shown to our seats. A central stage was surrounded on three sides by seats a few rows deep. We were given a printed description of what we would be seeing and what it all meant. We were told that what we would be witnessing was a religious ceremony and not just entertainment. We were asked to remain silent and to refrain from photography and from applauding at any time before, during, or after the ritual performance.

The whirling dervish ceremony is a practice of the Sufi offshoot of Islam, a mystical branch somewhat akin to Buddhist monks, pursuing inner spiritualism rather than worldly things. Accompanied by minimal music, first one dervish, then two, and eventually four at a time spun like tops, their snow-white frocks ballooning around them, making them look like flower petals or perhaps badminton birdies. While spinning, the right hand is raised to form a connection with the heavens, the left is lowered to offer that connection to the lowly world down here on Earth. For the better part of an hour they spun and spun and spun. The effect was hypnotic and, combined with having gotten out of bed at four o'clock that morning, I soon found myself slipping in and out of consciousness, drifting in circular dreams.

The practice of spinning derives from a central belief that everything in the universe is spinning, that spinning is simply the natural order of reality. This belief was extraordinarily ahead of its time, originating long before science showed us that yes, indeed, everything from subatomic particles to galaxies is in fact going around and around and, moreover, can't help but go around and around forever. Even our trip was forming a circle, as we would next drive back west and south, then north again, eventually returning to Istanbul, where we would be able to swallow our own tail.

It was the end of a very long and eventful day, that morning's balloon ride already seeming so long ago. In the morning we would leave Cappadocia and drive west to Konya, then on to Lake Beysehir. We had no choice but to complete the circle.

On the way to Konya we stopped to see how silk is produced, from the steaming of the silkworm cocoons to kill the pupa inside, to the unraveling of the cocoons, the separation of the fibers, and the winding of silk thread. And, of course, there were carpets being woven, and finished ones for sale. A woman took a silkworm cocoon, about the size of a very large peanut, out of a wicker basket and handed it to me as a souvenir. I still have it, although it has gotten a little fuzzy with the passage of time, some of the outer surface having unraveled a bit in puffs of soft, silky fur. If I shake it I can hear the dead, dry would-be-moth pupa rattling around inside.

Silkworms produce a liquid from their salivary glands that instantly hardens into a silk fiber. A silkworm cocoon actually consists of just a single strand of silk up to a mile long that must be carefully unraveled. Several strands together make a silk thread. Next time you luxuriate in the feel of silk just remember that it's nothing more than caterpillar spit.

Later that day our minibus pulled over to the side of the road and parked next to a field of white flowers on tall stalks. Our guide, Yigit, hopped off the bus, decapitated one of the flowers, and got back aboard with his trophy. The flowers were opium poppies, the source of opium, codeine, morphine, and ultimately heroin, as well as poppy seeds. Yigit explained that the government allowed for a certain amount of poppy farming for the production of poppy seeds, with Turkey being the world's second-biggest producer. But at this stage of the flower's life it was full of sap. Yigit used a knife to cut open the bulbous seed pod under the flower. A thick white sap oozed out through the cut like liquid rubber. This was what all the fuss was about, what opium and the other drugs was processed from. Yigit passed the oozing bulb around inside the bus so we could all get a good look. After being passed around, the bulb ended up back with me. I kept it with me until we had to fly from Izmir to Istanbul. I figured it probably wouldn't be a good idea to get on a plane in Turkey with raw heroin in my pocket. I'd seen *Midnight Express*, and *that* was only hashish.

We reached Lake Beysehir in late afternoon and were welcomed by the farm family with whom we would be spending the night. Several of us took a walk down to the lake shore to have a look. Lake Beysehir is the focal point of a Turkish national park. I have since read quite a bit about what a beautiful lake it is, the flowers, the birds, its lovely turquoise water. None of that was on display in this part of the lake.

The water looked still and brackish, a couple

of rusty canoes sat on the shore like discarded tin cans, and something didn't smell quite right, although that could have been the nearby cows. We walked back to the farmhouse for dinner with the family.

Dinner featured what I had come to think of as Turkey's Big Three of foods, as they seemed to be present at every meal – lamb, yogurt, and cherry juice. Dinner conversation was limited, as our hosts spoke very little English and no one in my group had mastered Turkish yet. There was much passing around of dishes, smiling, nodding, and yum-yum pantomiming. Stepping outside for an after-dinner smoke, I had a gesture-filled conversation with a member of our host family, primarily about how much snow we each got in the winter, chopping at our legs to indicate how high the snow would accumulate. Night had fallen on the farm and cows were sleeping in the nearby pasture. I decided to call it a night and join them in slumber.

Most farmhouses don't have a dozen bedrooms and this one was no exception, so layers of blankets had been laid on the floors of several rooms to accommodate the fourteen of us in my group, plus Yigit and our driver. I chose a good spot and stretched out on the blankets, pulling another over me. A few minutes later Abe crawled onto the "bed" next to mine.

To save a few bucks, on this trip I had opted to have an assigned roommate. They gave me Abe.

Abe was a Jewish New Yorker. He looked like a diminutive version of Bernie Sanders. Abe was not a bad roommate, but he liked to turn out the lights and go to sleep much earlier than I did. This was the first time I had beaten him to bed. I decided that I deserved a room to myself on all future travels, as I didn't much enjoy reading my book-before-bedtime while sitting in the bathroom with the door closed.

Morning came and we left Lake Beysehir

behind us, destination Antalya, on the Mediterranean coast.

Antalya served mainly as a base from which to explore some very impressive nearby Roman ruins. Actually, the Greeks and Romans lived side-by-side and left ruins that are often intermingled, with most of the old Roman ruins sitting on top of Greek ruins that sit on top of the ruins of whoever came before the Greeks. It's a layer cake of antiquity.

We wandered down the broad avenues of Perge, its broken columns lining the route. We visited the ruins of Aspendos, and its remarkably well-preserved amphitheatre, built by the Romans in the 2nd century AD, though designed by a Greek, which could seat up to 15,000 people and which still hosts performances to this day, having remained in good enough shape to renovate.

Driving west along the coast toward Fethiye we came next to the town of Demre, the very new name of the ancient Greek city of Myra. It has to be one of the oddest tourist traps I've ever visited.

Back in the 3rd and 4th centuries AD, this town was the home of St. Nicholas, the Christian bishop of Myra, on whom Santa Claus is originally based. After visiting the ancient and crumbling Church of St. Nicholas we wandered through the town in search of lunch.

It is impossible to miss the big statue of Santa Claus that looms over the town square from atop his concrete pedestal, bell in one hand and sack of goodies tossed over his other shoulder. He seems more than a little out of place in a town that is almost entirely Muslim. I walked down the street past a vast array of Santa Claus trinkets for sale. Fat little Santa figurines hung by strings like executed prisoners. As I sat and ate lunch outside a small cafe, a rosy-cheeked Santa beamed at me from the wall he'd been painted on. It was late June and eighty degrees outside. I wondered what the real St. Nicholas would have thought.

Fethiye was the starting point for the next phase of the trip. We boarded a *gulet*, a wooden yacht that would be our hotel, our restaurant, and our transportation for the next five days as we slowly meandered west along the coast. On the bluffs above us were to be found an assortment of leftovers from olden days, more remnants of the Greeks and Romans, what was left of fortresses, amphitheatres, aqueducts, buildings, houses, and harbors. There were cliff dwellings hollowed out of the hills, long abandoned. Along the coast were towns with harbors swarming with boats, mostly pleasure craft, shiny new sailboats and yachts as big as ours.

Each day we would spend a couple of hours in the morning, and a couple in the afternoon, walking the trails above the shore, our chocolate-brown yacht often visible below us through the trees as it drifted on the strikingly turquoise water to meet us at the end of the hike. Among the ruins one day we encountered a group of Turkish girls picnicking among gnarled olive trees. The days were sunny and warm and the pace was leisurely. The few small islands we could see offshore belonged to Greece, a country I have still not yet visited.

Except for the hikes there wasn't much to do but sit in the sun on deck reading a book, nap in the shade to the sounds of gentle waves, and linger over meals. I could have climbed down a ladder and gone for a swim in the warm waters of the Mediterranean, but I was suspicious of that very salty sea. The Mediterranean is a long finger extending from the hand of the Atlantic Ocean. A variety of sharks, including great whites, can be found there, lurking beneath the dark surface, just waiting for a lamb-fed, cherry-flavored morsel like me to float by.

Lamb-fed. Yes, indeed. Lunch aboard the yacht was usually lamburgers, or Turkish pizza with lamb. At dinner one night back in Antalya I had been served one of the strangest dishes I've ever eaten. It started with a bed of potato sticks – you know, those crunchy, matchstick-shaped potato shards that come in a can – which was topped with yogurt and chunks of lamb, with tomato sauce on top. I'm not sure where that rates on the scale of culinary finesse, but it was absolutely delicious.

And one afternoon I had been walking in Antalya when a sheep came charging out of a side street and nearly ran me down. How could I resist? They were practically throwing their tasty selves at me.

All the napping had one serious drawback – I had trouble sleeping at night. I was simply too well rested, perhaps more sated with sleep than I have ever been. So I often left Abe snoring in our cabin and stumbled out on to the pitch-dark deck to lie on my back and watch the stars.

Not all of the ruins along the coast were ancient. One day we walked through some Greek ruins of much more recent vintage.

Asia Minor, the southwest Asian peninsula that Turkey occupies, has always been at the crossroads between Asia, Africa, and Europe. Wedged between the Greeks and Romans to the west, the Egyptians and Arabs to the south, and the Persians and others to the east, the region has always been fought over, with one group displacing another throughout history, as well as coexisting side-by-side at times . In the early 20th century the area was a contentious mess, with the Turks at extreme odds with the Greeks and Armenians. Genocidal purges were commonplace. Hundreds of thousands were systematically exterminated.

After World War One I the Ottoman Empire was carved up, the Sultanate was abolished, and the piece of the empire that became modern day Turkey was established with a secular government. But it was agreed that Greeks living in Turkey would be relocated to Greece and Turks in Greece would be relocated to Turkey. That said, the real division was Christianity versus Islam. Any of the few Turkish Christians or Greek Muslims were allowed to remain in place. About a million and a half people were relocated in total.

One result of these upheavals was that some abandoned Greek villages in Turkey were never reoccupied. We explored one of these ghost towns, empty for eighty years, walking its broken streets, passing by its crumbling, now roofless stone houses. We visited the church, its beautifully ornate interior now flaking away. I doubted it would last two thousand years, like so many of the other ruins had.

We spent our last night aboard the yacht in the harbor of Marmaris. The partying lasted almost until dawn.

To be clear, there was no party taking place aboard our yacht. But the bay was ringed with nightclubs, the main harborside avenue of Marmaris teeming with vacationers enjoying the nightlife. Many of the boats anchored nearby were also pulsing with music and lights. Abe fell asleep right away despite the revelry but he snored to the beat all night long.

We left the yacht behind and had some time to wander about Marmaris in its morning-after hangover haze. We didn't wander too far and soon it was time to board the bus for the final drive to Kusadasi. We knew that Marmaris could be a little hazardous – what drew the vacationers, the chance to go nuts and make some noise, also drew Kurdish terrorists from time to time to do the same. We had no desire to linger there. A few weeks later a tourist bus was bombed in Marmaris. This came as no surprise.

What did come as a bit more of a surprise was the bombing in Antalya, which killed three people. And the bombings have continued, in Antalya, Marmaris, and all over Turkey. The lapping of the turquoise waves, the peacefulness of the olive groves, the silence of the ruins were all very much like the tranquil hush that I noticed on the African savannah – that tranquility could last all day, or could be shattered in an instant by a pouncing lion. In Turkey the lions planted bombs.

Kusadasi was the base for our visit to Ephesus, perhaps the best-preserved of all the ruined Greco-Roman cities, and the location of the Temple of Artemis, one of the Seven Wonders of the Ancient World.

Kusadasi itself sat across a bay from our hotel. The bay was crowded with a steady traffic of huge cruise ships, all here to dump their cargo of tourists into the fractured avenues of Ephesus. We would make our visit in the morning, hoping to beat the disembarking crowds.

I walked down to the hotel's beautiful swimming pool and went just past it to find a short path leading down to the water, a narrow finger of the Aegean Sea. I wanted to see how easily I would float in its very salty water. I would only be a few feet from shore, in just four feet of water. That was enough to quell my terror of the ocean.

I floated like a styrofoam cup. I was so buoyant that it was hard to force my legs below the water when I wanted to stand up. I could remain floating there or I could get out and go to the pool. The Aegean had saltiness and sharks. The pool had jacuzzi jets. Guess which one won out.

Early the next morning we were off to Ephesus, racing against the convoy of buses that would be coming in from the port. Built by the Greeks in the 10th century BC, by the turn of the millennium it was a thriving Roman port city. With its harbor slowly silting up, Ephesus eventually lost its access to the sea and with it its standing as an important trading city. By the end of the 14th century it had been finally and completely abandoned.

There were as many ruins at this one site as we had seen at all our other stops put together. We walked down long avenues between the often surprisingly intact remains of buildings, arches, statuary, columns, carvings, mosaics. Inscriptions in the marble told the names and dates of people and events long gone. We visited a communal men's room. Around the room's stone walls were marble benches with holes spaced a few feet apart, trenches running in front of them to carry clean water . We all picked a hole to sit on, getting the feel of things, closing our eyes and imagining taking a dump in ancient Ephesus.

At the far end of the city we came to Ephesus's huge amphitheatre, twice the size of the one at Aspendos. To climb its steps looked akin to climbing a mountain. It is believed that gladiators once fought in that stadium. These days the only fighting was between tourists trying to get the perfect photograph.

A short drive from Ephesus took us to Selçuk, where the remains of the Temple of Artemis can be found. Built in the 6th century BC, destroyed and rebuilt more than once, and ultimately burned to the ground for good in the 3rd century AD, all that's left now are some of the foundation stones and a single surviving column.

We had lunch in Selçuk and had a little time for shopping on this our last full day in Turkey. Among the shops selling T-shirts, key chains, and sunglasses was one with a sign in front advertising "genuine fake watches". They probably came with a real useless guarantee.

We drove to Izmir to catch a flight back to Istanbul. I knew I would have to endure my crazy flight itinerary in reverse – after landing in New York I would have to fly to Washington before I could get back to Albany. And this time I would be wide awake for the whole trip.

Not long after takeoff from Istanbul lunch was served aboard the flight. The flight attendants pushed their carts down the aisles, handing out a special treat to the passengers, who were mostly Americans. If we were expecting one last meal of lamb and cherry juice, we were wrong. Instead we were served something that they just don't normally eat in Turkey, and Turkish Airlines showed that they have a sense of humor.

        They served us turkey.

Chapter Twelve: Indonesia – April and May 2019

      Eight hours is a long time to spend waiting but it affords plenty of time to notice both the big trends and the small details. Five hours into an eight-hour wait between flights at Los Angeles International Airport I had seen the late afternoon rush and the evening lull, and now I could tell that traffic was picking up again for the overnight flights across the Pacific, many of which departed at midnight or soon after, like mine. I kept an eye out for any celebrities who might be passing through LAX that evening, but they were all traveling incognito. I checked the departure board now and then but it still wasn't showing my flight information, my departure gate. And then I noticed my shoes.

      Sitting there in a randomly chosen departure lounge I looked down and noticed that the bottom was starting to peel off from one of my shoes. Disbelief vied with indignation in my mind. These shoes were brand new! Today was the first time I had worn them! They at least needed to last for the next three weeks in Indonesia. Sure, I only paid thirteen dollars for them at Walmart and, yes, I know, you get what you pay for. But even thirteen dollar shoes should last three weeks. These were only hours old and fading fast. And I hadn't exactly been putting them through a torture test. I'd just been sitting around all day.

Thirteen years after my last foreign adventure I had knocked the cobwebs off my luggage, dug my recently renewed passport out of a drawer, and decided to go traveling again now that I was retired and financially secure. And it had to be Indonesia, tops on my wish list for many years. But it was a daunting trip for the travel-rusty, requiring four flights and forty-three grueling hours of alternately sitting and waiting and sitting and flying. It was almost too much to bear the thought of until I arrived at Albany Airport on departure morning, checked my luggage, and got my boarding passes. From that point on I was just cargo being shifted. I surrendered myself to the air travel System and was swallowed into the great belly of that beast.

You can go around the world in the System without ever seeing anything but the Earth from seven miles up. Having been given aisle seat after aisle seat, I hadn't even had *that* view. Between flights you're like a blood cell squirting through the veins of our interconnected world. Wherever you are you walk through the same gates, corridors, tubes, and lounges, and ride an endless moving walkway that spans the globe. The languages change but the ever-present English translations are the same. Gate C52 is Gate C52 no matter where in the world you are.

In the System there are no beds, no hammocks, no patios, no pools, no gentle breezes. There are no mealtimes. You eat and drink when fed, regardless what your watch says. There is no day and no night. Time is measured only in minutes and hours, elapsed or yet to go.

First I had to fly to Newark, then from Newark to Los Angeles. After eight hours in LA I would board a trans-Pacific flight to Taipei, arriving fourteen hours later. I would have a few hours there to splash a little water on my face and wonder what time it *really* was, having crossed a dozen time zones and the International Date Line. Forget the time, I wouldn't be sure what *day* it was. Then I would board a flight to Jakarta, a final four and a half hours in the air. I would have to clear customs before the System would finally spit me out onto the streets of Jakarta.

But right now I had a problem. I wandered down the shopping mall that is the backbone of all modern airports until I found the newsstand. I was hoping they might have some Super Glue. I was in luck. There amidst the international newspapers and the I Heart LA t-shirts I found a tube.

I didn't use it right away. Being a bit concerned that my flight still hadn't appeared on the departures board, I decided to poke around a bit and soon discovered that I was in the wrong terminal. I followed the arrows directing me to the correct terminal, figuring that this would lead to some sort of train or shuttle, but ended up walking for forty-five minutes. Let's just say LAX is not one of my favorite airports.

Once upon a time, in a time zone far away, my fourteen hour flight finally landed. Now sitting in a windowless basement departure lounge in Taipei, I resolved to attempt to repair my troublesome shoe. To make a long story a little shorter, the glue fixed my shoe but I had gotten some glue on two of the fingers of my left hand. Immediate action was needed to keep from having two fingers glued together for the entire trip. I raced into a nearby men's room and tried my best to wash off the glue. I was partially successful – my fingers remained separated but I had hardened glue residue on my fingers for several days.

The Customs area on arrival in Jakarta was hot and humid, hundreds of people in two snaking lines, one for

Indonesians coming home, one for foreigners. The heat was a reminder that I had traded April in Albany for tropical temperatures. I wouldn't have minded sweating a little if I hadn't been wearing the same clothes for the past two days.

Passing out of Customs I was greeted by a driver from my tour company, there to pick up just me and drive me to the hotel an hour away. Others in the group had arrived on other flights, or had already started their trip with an optional pre-tour visit to Borneo.

I got my first look at Jakarta on the way in from the airport. Traffic drove on the left side, the first and most immediately noticeable hint of the exotic. We passed unreadable signs in Indonesian as a light rain fell. The famously fearsome traffic was flowing easily. The rain had stopped by the time we reached the hotel. I was looking forward to a change of clothes and a chance to just be motionless for a little while, no longer in the System.

My room was on the 14th floor of the Santika Premiere Hayam Wuruk Hotel and the view of Jakarta from my window was spectacular. Jakarta is one of the world's largest cities, with a population of over ten million (and a metropolitan area of thirty million, second only to Tokyo). Skyscrapers filled the view but down below them the city's old traditions played out while motorbikes flooded the avenues like rushing water. I decided resting could wait. I couldn't wait to go out and explore. It was four o'clock in the afternoon and there wouldn't be much daylight left here near the equator. I changed my clothes and took the elevator down to the front desk. I just needed some money.

I had changed a hundred dollars at the airport but had been given nothing but 100,000 rupiah bills, worth about seven dollars each. I need to break that down into smaller bills, a process that would continue to be problematic throughout the trip. Imagine buying a pack of gum at a gas station and handing them a $100 bill. It was often like that in Indonesia. Even the front desk at this 22-story modern hotel in the heart of Jakarta couldn't make change for me. I waited while they sent someone out to break down a couple of bills for me.

While I was waiting at the front desk the tour guide for this trip, Jumena, introduced himself. Maria, our local Jakarta guide, was with him. Jumena informed me that a free buffet dinner was being served up on the 22nd floor until eight p.m. But right now he and Maria were going to lead a little walk around the area for anyone interested.

About six of the sixteen people in my group came along for the walk. Maria led us out of the hotel, around a corner, and up the adjacent avenue. We had gone barely a hundred yards when she stopped to show us something.

Next to the sidewalk stood a wooden box with wire mesh sides and top, and some small plastic chairs. Inside the box were several dozen cobras available for purchase. A couple of young men stood behind the box.

Maria explained that they were selling the cobras for meat but that they also made a supposedly medicinal cocktail from the blood of the snakes. The blood would be mixed in a cup with snake bile, honey, and rice wine. It was a good-for-what-ails-ya kind of drink. Maria was intent on purchasing a cobra to have for dinner that night. She asked if any of us wished to try the drink.

I had barely met my fellow travelers who had come on the walk but was a little surprised when they all seemed reluctant. I hadn't come halfway around the world to say "no thank you". I was sure they hadn't either. Someone had to get the party started. My hand shot up.

"I'll try it!", I said.

One of the men removed a cobra from the tangle of them in the box and neatly snipped its head off with what resembled a cigar cutter. He held the cobra vertically over a cup as the blood drained out, helping it along with a few gentle squeezes. He reached into the snake and fished out the gall bladder, adding its few drops of liquid to the cup. He continued to skin the snake as the other man mixed honey and rice wine into the cup, while the cobra's head continued to writhe on top of the box's wire mesh. With one swish of the cup I was handed my cocktail. I took a sip.

It tasted mostly of the rice wine, with the blood adding a certain earthy grittiness to the mixture. It wasn't bad, it wasn't good. I offered a taste to my fellow travelers. A couple of them tried it hesitantly. I considered that a small victory.

While Maria waited for her cobra meat, I couldn't help noticing the durian for sale a few feet away. In fact, we *all* couldn't help noticing. It smelled like an open sewer. Maria, now holding a bag of cleaned cobra meat, asked if we'd like to try some durian next. More reluctant glances.

"Absolutely!", I exclaimed. And so Maria bought us a durian to try.

I had encountered durian before in my travels. I had seen then growing in Vietnam and had seen notices in a number of hotel rooms there advising that durian was strictly prohibited in the hotel. That's because it will make your room smell like someone died there. A week ago.

Despite an odor that has been variously described as rotting garbage, decomposing corpses, or even old gym socks, durian supposedly tasted just fine. It was, in fact, very popular. After seeing them growing in Vietnam I had forgotten all about them for years. But now here they were, just feet away. Of course I had to try it.

Maria purchased one of the green, spiky, five-pound fruits and we cut it in half. Even a skunk might have fainted at the aroma.

Inside was the part you eat, a bulbous wad

of slimy yellow goo, more than enough for all of us.

We were given latex gloves to put on to keep the smell of sewage off our hands while we ate. I reached in and scooped out a few fingers' worth of goo and raised it to my mouth.

"Hey, wait a minute", I said. "If this stuff will make my hands stink, what will it do to my *breath*?"

I was assured that my breath would remain cobra-fresh. It was time to take the plunge. I stuck two latex fingers full of yellow mush in my mouth and licked them clean. The taste and texture were about halfway between lemon custard and vanilla pudding, but a little slimier. It wasn't bad at all. We were all taking tastes, smiling, nodding, and remarking on how not-awful it was. I took a few more tastes. But, even though it tasted good at first, I found myself liking it less and less with each bite, so much so that I couldn't bring myself to lick the last of the goo from my glove. I peeled it off and dropped it in a trash can. I had checked durian off of my to-do list. I wouldn't be seeking it out again.

I was just finishing dinner while taking in the view of Jakarta at night from the 22nd floor when Maria walked in to the dining room carrying a small tray. She had had the cobra diced and cooked and was now offering us samples. It tasted like chewy, gristly pork. There's a joke in there somewhere about a man eating snake.

The lights of Jakarta blinked and blazed through the windows of my room. I pulled the curtains closed. After sleeping sitting up the past two "nights", I had really been looking forward to stretching out on my bed and luxuriating in the sheer horizontalness. Morning arrived what seemed like seconds later.

Looking out the window, I watched the

schoolgirls in bonnets bicycling around spacious Fatahillah Square as I ate lunch at the Cafe Batavia. The bicycles, mainly pink and light blue, with matching bonnets, stood in rows to rent. The square itself was a nugget of Indonesia's colonial DNA, bounded on all sides by old Dutch Colonial buildings from the days when the city was known as Batavia. These buildings now mainly housed museums, including the puppet museum we would be visiting after lunch. Though it was just an ordinary Thursday, there was a festive air around the square and the girls in their hats kept bumping their bicycles over the paving stones.

When lunch was over I decided to use the men's room at the Cafe Batavia. The dining room walls had been covered with celebrity photographs, both old and new, in frames. As I wandered out of the dining room, along a hallway, and down the stairs, I was kept company by even more framed celebrities. They seemed to cover every wall in the place. As I entered the men's room I noticed that the photos just continued. And here, in the bathroom stall I was now standing in, Paul Simon leered from his spot on the wall, about crotch-high. I wondered who he had offended to have been given such a special place in that establishment. I put my hand over his eyes and did my business.

Post-colonial Indonesia has had an intermittently tumultuous history – fits and spasms of violence, the scars of which can be seen in the still burned-out shells of buildings, many just windowless facades, in some Chinese sections of Jakarta, have plagued the country throughout its political upheavals. We drove past some of those ruined buildings several times in our jaunts around the city. That evening we would have the chance to hear from someone who had been there in 1998 when riots raged and Chinese shops were looted and burned.

We were ushered into a small meeting room on the ground floor of the hotel. The doors would remain closed while the man representing the local Chinese community spoke to us about the riots that wracked Jakarta, and much of the rest of the country, in May of 1998. It was a touchy subject still and our meeting would remain private.

    The rioting had begun as anti-government demonstrations (and the government *would* fall and be replaced as a result) but soon devolved into vandalism, looting, arson, rape, and murder directed at the city's numerous Chinese-owned establishments. As many as five thousand deaths would result nationwide, although not all the casualties were Chinese, as many looters were among the victims, sometimes trapped in the burning buildings they were plundering.

    An uneasy coexistence had returned afterward, but twenty years is too short a time to just forget such things. And so the door remained closed and guarded throughout the meeting so that our guest could speak freely. The next evening we would be meeting a woman who would have similar stories to tell about another troubled time in the country's history. That, too, would be a closed-door affair.

    Our short morning flight to Yogyakarta arrived in time for us to have lunch at our hotel. After lunch we were greeted by a squadron of motorbikes.

    Indonesian traffic had reminded me a bit of Vietnamese traffic, though a bit less chaotic and intense. Motorbikes ruled the road, or at least tried to. With nearly one hundred million on the road, they were easily the most popular and convenient way to get around, especially in the urban traffic nightmare of Jakarta, and there were always swarms of them in any populated area. From my usual minibus seat I often watched them weave and dart between cars as they took advantage of any space available. I was happy to be on the bus and not caught up in that frenzied chaos. And now I was about to climb on the back of one and go roaring around Yogyakarta.

    I have set only a few rules for myself in life

and one of them was "stay the hell off motorcycles". I had never been on a motorcycle, a motorbike, or even a moped. Now here I was, strapping on a black helmet and straddling a motorbike behind what I hoped would be a sane and sensible rider.

I found it easier than I expected. The ride was smooth and my usually terrible sense of balance was not a factor. We zoomed when we could, threaded our way through traffic when necessary, and buzzed along with the other bike traffic like a swarm of bees. I started out with a death grip on my pilot's waist but soon found myself enjoying the breeze and snapping pictures. We made a couple of stops on our ride around Yogyakarta before eventually returning to the hotel. I returned my helmet to my driver, along with a well-deserved tip for not getting me killed. The first thing I said when the ride was over was "I want one". Fortunately, I don't always indulge such impulses. There is no motorbike purchase looming in my future.

Yogjakarta (pronounced "Jogjakarta", or simple "Jogja") has the odd distinction of being a monarchy within a democracy. The city is the heart of the special administrative region of Yogyakarta but, uniquely in Indonesia, the region was allowed to remain a sultanate when it became part of Indonesia in 1950. So Jogja's local government is ruled by a hereditary line of sultans while the rest of the country holds local elections.

That evening we gathered at the hotel, again in a secure room to ensure privacy, to hear an old woman's personal account of the purge of 1965-66.

In 1965 the madness had erupted all over the country, but especially here in eastern Java and also Bali. It is far beyond the scope of this book to detail exactly what happened, but here's the short version: Indonesia's Communist Party had been a significant force in the nation's politics, but when a Communist-led coup attempt failed, the country's government and military began a violent purge of Communist Party members, encouraging the local population to assist them in rooting out that enemy. The result was essentially a civil war between segments of the military loyal to each side. Ethnic Chinese were targeted as well, perhaps due to their perceived connection to Communist China, but also due to the same anti-Chinese sentiments that led to the 1998 riots. Between executions of captured Party members by the government and slaughters committed by regular locals, usually using nothing but machetes, knives, icepicks, or blunt objects, it is estimated that at least half a million people were killed during a period lasting about six months. At the end of it the country transitioned to a new, authoritarian regime that would last for the next three decades, until the events of 1998.

The old woman, whose family had been Communist Party members, told her story of the terror, the killings, the disappearances. Jumena kept a close watch on the closed door.

But here is the most frightening thing of all – Indonesia was the friendliest country I had ever visited. The Irish have a reputation for friendliness and indeed they are some of the sweetest people anywhere. But, as a whole, I had found Indonesians to be the most unwaveringly pleasant, helpful, generous, and welcoming people I had ever met. And yet these were the sons and daughters, in some cases the very people themselves, who had participated in the horrors of 1965 and 1998. It would seem that civility is a thin veneer masking the latent savagery beneath it, and I believe that to be true at all times and in all places. We are a violent and territorial species.

I had begun to notice that hotel rooms in Indonesia all have one thing in common – there is always an arrow in one corner of the ceiling. In predominantly Muslim Indonesia, the arrow is essential, as it points in the direction of Mecca, the direction to be faced during prayers. Even in Bali, which is over eighty percent Hindu, there were still arrows in every room. If there were arrows in hotels in the USA they would probably be pointing to the dining room.

And speaking of the dining room, not counting my snacks of cobra and durian, I had been enjoying the food on this trip very much and would continue to do so. The breakfast buffets always offered a choice of fruit juices. My favorites were kiwi juice and strawberry juice. The food reminded me somewhat of Vietnamese food – plenty of plain white rice, hot sauce, fish, pork, and chicken. Missing were Vietnam's ubiquitous french fries and watermelon. The hot sauce was minced hot chiles instead and the meat was often served satay style (with peanut sauce). To my surprise, strawberries were the main dessert fruit.

The meals were more than enough and yet I found that buying snacks, often at the CocoMart grocery chain, was almost a necessity. It was the only way to break down my huge supply of 100,000 rupiah notes so that I would have smaller change with which to tip the hotel staff. Breaking bills became almost a sport in our tour group as we traveled from place to place. Sometimes it came down to who could get to the cash register before the small bills ran out.

Indonesia is filled with artisans, which is a word meaning "someone much better at crafts than you". One day in Jogja we were given the chance to try our hands at the art of batik.

The batik process involves drawing on fabric with hot wax. The cloth is then dyed, with the waxed parts remaining the original color. The process is repeated multiple times until the desired patterns, images, and colors are achieved.

The wax is heated in a bucket and a special device is used to apply the wax to the cloth. The device resembles a corncob pipe. When dipped into the bucket, the pipe's bowl fills with melted wax. A narrow stem protruding from the bottom of the bowl allows the wax to be applied as if you were writing with a pen.

We were each given a small piece of cloth with a pre-printed pattern to trace in wax. We wore newspaper in our laps in the event of a spill.

The headline on the newspaper in *my* lap said "Dave Sucks At Batik", with a subheadline of "Tries Anyway". I traced the outline of a turtle on my scrap of cloth as best I could, dribbling unwanted globs of quick-hardening wax here and there. Nearby, an expert worked on her morning project. Hers looked like the work of an adult, mine like the product of a three-year-old. After it had been dyed, though, my turtle *did* somewhat resemble one of Picasso's. Maybe there is hope for me yet in the arts.

One of our days in Jogja was largely given to a visit to Prambanan Temple, another to a visit to Borobudur. These two stunning sites (and sights!) are cousins of a sort, about the same age and built from the same dark stone.

The Hindu Prambanan Temple and the Buddhist Borobudur Temple, the largest Buddhist structure in the world, were both built between the 8th and 9th centuries, roughly thirty miles apart, from what seem to be the same blocks of black volcanic rock. Prambanan features a pointy central temple surrounded by over a dozen slightly smaller ones, carvings of gods, birds, dragons, monkeys, and so on adorning every bit of them from dusty ground to pointy tops. Largely destroyed by earthquakes over the centuries, it lay concealed in dense overgrowth until being rediscovered and reassembled in the 20th century. The approaches to the central temple complex are littered with piles and scatterings of stone blocks, representing the wreckage of a couple hundred more temples that have yet to be restored and which may never be. Java being as prone as it is to massive earthquakes, there is no guarantee that the reconstructed Prambanan will survive any longer than the original did, so if you intend to visit you should probably go soon.

At Prambanan I realized that there had been a major change in the way people around the world view photography since I had last traveled in 2006. Back then it was a good idea to ask permission before photographing people. Many, especially in more rural regions or smaller towns, were uncomfortable with being photographed. In Morocco a man had shooed me away vehemently, with angry gestures and flying spittle, from his little fruit stand, where I had taken a picture of the massive pile of dates he was selling. But these days it seemed that everyone from ten years old up had a cell phone, and therefore a camera. It was simply impossible to avoid being photographed anymore and even the Moroccan date seller had probably given up and given in to it by now. And it went beyond the fact that no one seemed to mind having their picture taken anymore. *They* were now keen to have their photo taken with *you*. Troops of Indonesian kids were touring the temple complex while I was there and many of them came up to me as I sat and rested in the heat and humidity and asked if they could take a picture with me.

So now the shoe is on the other foot. It is we the tourists who are stalked by the local paparazzi and asked for permission. I suppose I could have shooed them away, gesturing and spitting, but I have to admit I liked the attention.

The next day we drove north to visit Borobudur. Like Prambanan, Borobudur had also fallen victim to centuries of earthquakes, volcanoes, and neglect and had sat half-forgotten beneath volcanic ash and dense vegetation until being uncovered and rehabilitated in recent times. Borobudur, squat and square like a six-layer wedding cake, had fared better over the years than the more spindly temples of Prambanan and had needed much less reconstruction.

As one winds their way up and around the wedding cake tiers, the story of Buddhism plays out in stone relief on every wall. Carvings in the rock depict Buddhas and monkeys, men and women, all of it telling the story of the Buddha's life and his teachings.

Atop the six main tiers are three smaller, circular levels, home to six dozen stone enclosures that look like latticed birdcages. Stone Buddhas, some now headless, inhabit these birdcages, although some are now empty. At the center of the very top the structure comes to a peak, which these days is adorned by a lightning rod to prevent a reoccurrence of a previous lightning strike that damaged the top.

The view from the top was spectacular. A lush green park surrounding the temple gave way to all sorts of tropical trees that led to rolling mountains and the menacing silhouette of Mt. Merapi, Indonesia's most active volcano.

Back at ground level I wiped the sweat from my face with the hand towel that was my constant companion. It was the hottest and stickiest day of the trip. Jumena was handing out bottles of water and I was already thinking of Bali, of beaches and swimming pools. We would be there in time for lunch the next day.

The parking lot by the airport in Denpasar was full of motorcycles, hundreds of them, not a single car among them. I didn't see a parking lot for cars at all. Our morning flight from Jogja had brought us to Bali and the differences between this island and Java were obvious, immediate, and overwhelming, even before we'd left the airport.

Bali was aggressively ornate, like a fully lit and decorated Christmas tree standing next to the unadorned forest pine that was Java. Every square inch of residential Bali was decorated until your eyes hurt from it. Flowers, fruits, fabrics, carvings, statues, incense. Reds, yellows, oranges, blues, greens, gold. And more gold. It started inside the airport terminal and extended to every corner of the island. The difference between

Java's relatively austere Islam and Bali's exuberant Hindu-hybrid religion was on full display everywhere. Bali was nearly eighty-five percent Hindu. Statuary elephants festooned with strands of flowers stood with sticks of smoldering incense rammed up their trunks. Hindu gods grinned and grimaced, frozen in stone. A thirsty shopper had to step over a scattering of flowers and burning incense on its doorstep just to enter a CocoMart to buy a Coke (or a Pepsi).

By the way, if you ever wake up in some foreign country with no memory of how you got there, here's a handy-dandy way to tell if you're in a sleek and shiny, sanitized, industrialized, capitalized, democratized First World country, an undeveloped, short-life-span, civil war-torn, backwater Third World country, or somewhere in between, the vast Second World:

> In the First World Coke and Pepsi are not your only choices.
> In the Second World both Coke and Pepsi are available.
> In the underprivileged Third World you can only find Coke.

Meanwhile, back in Bali, also to be seen in many decorative places was that cringe-evoking Hindu symbol, the swastika.

Of course, it's not *their* fault that some Austrian lunatic made it *his* symbol as well. They had it first, and for a long time. It looks nice in the proper context, though it still takes a little getting used to.

Leaving Denpasar, we drove past rice paddies on our way to a small village. We walked down a street of low walls, all riotously decorated. Behind the walls were communal courtyards, shared spaces between the small, one-story homes that were hidden away within those compounds. We entered through a gap in the wall to pay a visit to a school of Balinese dance.

The students were all about eight to twelve years old and wore costumes so colorful they would have put a peacock to shame, though here in Bali their costumes were almost camouflage against the decorative background. A few men sat behind the dancers, playing various percussive instruments. We watched them perform a few dances while their teacher explained the nuances and were then invited to try it for ourselves. I learned long ago that dancing is not my thing, so while some in the group tried earnestly, I soon gave up and hung out near the back, just trying to stay out of the way. Next we were invited to play the instruments. I was seated at a *gangsa*, a sort of metal xylophone. Each metal bar was numbered and all I had to do was hit the proper bar with my mallet as the numbers were called out – "five one three five one three five one seven two two one". Let's just say I'll probably never be a professional *gangsa* player, but at least I could do it sitting down.

Bali is full of artisans and craftspeople and we would visit several of them during our time on the island – weavers, puppet makers, mask makers. These were skills beyond our abilities to even attempt, and so we were not asked to try. It's just as well. When it comes to making things with my hands all I seem to be able to make are messes and excuses.

We arrived mid-afternoon at our hotel, the Alila Manggis Hotel in Candidasa, a beautiful property on Bali's east coast, Indian Ocean waves whooshing and crashing on a narrow beach just a hundred feet from a large, square swimming pool. Just outside the sliding glass doors of my room was a patio with a couch, two chairs, and a table. The pool was a thirty second walk away and I had nothing better to do until dinnertime.

The beach here was just a thin strip of brown sand littered with the unfortunately ubiquitous debris that now seems to cover the whole world. Every ten seconds or so waves would break with a loud rushing thump on the beach, a sound that could be heard quite clearly from the open-walled dining room where I sat the next morning eating my eggs Benedict and watching a large ship gliding by out on the ocean, the view framed by palm trees. I felt that I could be happy just staying here forever – the patio, the pool, the ocean, the eggs Benedict, the pineapple juice in an Erlenmeyer flask with a fat bamboo straw, a book, a nap. But even Paradise gets boring eventually (no it doesn't). It would soon be time to move on.

       The beautifully conical volcano Mt. Agung rising menacingly off to our right, we drove past flooded rice paddies and eventually passed by drier fields where workers were bringing in the rice harvest. We hopped out to watch and lend a hand.

       The rice was fully grown, and was now being cut and threshed. The workers, men and women, were beating bundles of rice plants against wooden boards to loosen the grain. We were handed some bundles and began beating them like dusty carpets. Small bits flew out and added to the growing piles on the ground. It was all good fun until it started to rain lightly. That was our cue to knock off work early. We said our goodbyes and continued down the road.

       Mt. Agung continued to dominate the scenery to our right. The 10,000 foot cone is Bali's highest peak and one of its most dangerously active volcanoes. It had last erupted just the previous July and its next eruption would come just three weeks after we drove past it. We'd found a sweet spot in time.

       Turning east again we found our way back to the coast and stopped to see how sea salt is harvested. The salt farmer waded into the surf carrying two large cloth bags balanced at either end of a pole carried across his back. He dipped the bags in the ocean and walked back up the beach, dumping the water onto a flat patch of sand that had been leveled for this purpose. The water would soon evaporate, leaving a salty crust on the surface of the sand. After the salt was skimmed from the sand it was then mixed with more seawater and poured into shallow wooden troughs to evaporate. Pure white sea salt could then be scraped out of the troughs with a scoop that looked like (and probably was) a piece of coconut shell. This would be sold directly to local buyers.

I posed for a salt-scooping photo-op, scraping up piles of wet salt as I smiled at the camera. It was fun to be a salt farmer for ten minutes, perhaps not so much fun as a career choice, although some might find it appealing to have a job that lets them hang out on a beach all day.

We had lunch next to a very nice royal garden. Who the royalty had been exactly was a mystery to me and I really didn't care. They had left a very nice garden behind. It was like Bali concentrate, a super-dense, super-lush version of the usual over-the-top ornamentation. Goldfish the size of small dogs swam in large groups in the garden's several pools, statuary sprouted from the water, water spouted from the statuary, a fountain shaped like a pagoda circulated gushes of water. People walked on the ponds among the statues on concrete lily pads. Stone bridges spanned the various sections. Flowers bloomed in every color. We all emerged feeling just a bit more regal after strolling those grounds.

As we continued on our way towards Ubud I noticed that my plastic watch band had developed a huge crack. It would probably break clean through soon. This was a problem. On a trip such as this it was essential to know what time it was. We ate, departed, arrived, and regrouped at specified times. Sunsets were always around 5:45 in the late afternoon and I tried never to miss one. A watch in your pocket still tells the time but takes a deliberate effort to check. Having the time available at a glance made me feel just so much more in synch with my surroundings.

The dark cloud that had descended on my falling-apart shoes in Los Angeles now showed its silver lining. Because of that emergency repair, I had with me a tube of Super Glue that I wouldn't otherwise have had (and that particular product didn't seem to be available in Indonesia – out of curiosity I looked for it in stores). The watch band was fixed in the time it took to glue two fingers together. Later in the trip I noticed that the outer pouch of my carry-on bag, where I normally kept my passport, plane tickets, etc., had come apart at the seams at one end, allowing whatever was in there to spill out if the bag was tilted. Super Glue to the rescue again! I have now decided that a tube of the stuff is an essential item when packing for all future trips.

We arrived in Ubud around mid-afternoon. The entrance to our hotel, the Plataran Ubud, was right on the busy main road through Ubud, a narrow strip constantly buzzing with motorbikes. A bar and lounge area sat just inside the entrance. A little farther in was the reception area. Going farther back, down a set of steps and up another, I walked along a narrow path with flowers and statuary, the sounds of the street already having faded to nothing behind me. Up ahead was a beautiful small swimming pool and to the right were extensive rice paddies. My room was in a building on the left side, my room's balcony overlooking the pool. Continuing along I passed the dining room, then another, much larger swimming pool. Beyond that there were walking trails, little bridges, flowing streams. It was hard to believe that this haven of tranquility lay hidden behind the main road's busy facade. We would be here for three nights, my room was a forty-five second walk, including elevator ride, from the small pool below my balcony and from the dining room. Who could ask for more?

Crossing the road, even a narrow (though busy) one like Ubud's main road, was a careful process. In Vietnam it had simply been a matter of wading into traffic and hoping it flowed around you like a river. Here it was a bit more demonstrative. You took a step or two into the road and put a hand up as if to say "Halt! Show your papers!". If traffic stopped, you crossed. If it didn't, you tried again. In Jakarta that might get you killed. In Ubud it usually worked.

Ubud is well inland, miles from the coast. Promoted as an artists' community, the town of 75,000 is inundated with over three million tourists annually. The main road is packed shoulder-to-shoulder with hotels, bars, clubs, restaurants, and currency exchanges. But for all of that, tradition was still maintained – there was still the usual pile of flowers and smoldering incense on the doorstep of the CocoMart.

The Monkey Forest occupies an area within the town, well within walking distance of my hotel although we drove over to it. Arriving at the Monkey Forest we were first greeted by a visitors' center complete with the customary pools, fountains, and statues, many with water gushing out of their mouths or other, naughtier body parts. Beyond that we entered the Forest.

The first thing I noticed was the enormous banyan tree that the path had to branch around. Just beyond it I began to see monkeys.

Depending on the source, anywhere from five hundred to over a thousand Balinese macaques inhabit the small forest. There is nothing fencing them in. The busy town outside the forest discourages them from leaving and the regular feedings from the staff encourage them to stay. The macaques were everywhere – on the paths, in the trees, perched on rocks – but were especially numerous near the main feeding station. Babies clung to mothers or explored on their own nearby. There were also Hindu temples on the grounds, and more banyan trees and hanging vines, giving the forest a rather vertical feel. We had been well warned not to bring food into the forest unless we wanted to be accosted by the macaques and I saw no signs of aggression from them while I was there.

Having mostly concluded my exploration of the Monkey Forest, I sat on a low stone wall near the feeding station waiting for the rest of the group to gather. Just then a couple of members of the staff arrived to put out some food for the macaques. As they did, dozens of macaques came charging out of the woods, then dozens more, racing to the feeding station like soldiers storming the beaches of Normandy. If you come from a very large family you've probably experienced this for yourself at dinnertime.

Mt. Batur is an active volcano north of Ubud, erupting as recently as the year 2000. Below its summit lies Lake Batur, a water filled caldera of the volcano. The isolated village of Trunyan has sat on the eastern shore of the lake for well over a millennium, perhaps two, perhaps many more.

Trunyan is home to a group of *Bali Mula*, the old indigenous people of Bali. What sets them apart from most of the rest of the Balinese is their isolationism. And what sets them apart from other scattered groups of *Bali Mula* is one odd practice of theirs in particular, which I will describe shortly. Until recently the village of about six hundred people was accessible only by boat and they have a reputation for not being the most welcoming of hosts. We were going there anyway.

A half-hour motorboat ride brought us to Trunyan's dock. The village was spread out along the lake, the land rising steeply above the village. At least a dozen pagodas rose above the single-story houses. We stepped from the dock into the village and I immediately noticed the spiders, the only spiders I saw anywhere in Indonesia. The village was home to many palm-spanning spiders, their webs thankfully built high, beneath the eaves of the houses or up in the big satellite dish that stood right by the dock. So much for isolationism. Television is like electronic Coke.

These were the only unsmiling Indonesians I encountered and they went about their daily business, watching us warily as we wandered their narrow streets. A Hindu-looking temple was the town's most attractive feature, that and the rather Buddhist-looking pagodas. But these people's beliefs long predate the arrival of those major religions on Bali and they have little use for them.

We climbed a bit until we were above and behind the village. It was another perfect postcard moment – Lake Batur, framed by pagodas, the volcano rising behind it. We had seen life in the village. Now it was time to see death.

We returned to our boats and motored a little farther along the lake shore until we came to a place that could only be reached by this water route – Trunyan's cemetery.

The village's odd custom that I previously mentioned was their method of burial. The dead are not buried underground. Instead they are laid out above ground, with a tent-like bamboo cage constructed over them, a few of their possessions left with them for the afterlife. A nearby banyan tree is said to counteract the smell of decay with its own sweet smell. In fact, the name "Trunyan" is derived from a mash-up of words meaning "sweet-smelling tree".

The first thing I saw on arrival was a low stone wall topped with about forty skulls, previous residents of the bamboo tents. Just to the left and up a short incline stood the cemetery's current tenants -- six bamboo tents each held a body, all of them in different states of decay. In the tent on the far left lay what was pretty much just a skeleton now. His skull would soon be ready for the wall. The banyan tree was working overtime – there was absolutely no foul smell at all. I could imagine there being a sign at the entrance to the graveyard saying "no durian allowed".

While the skulls were clearly venerated, the rest of the body did not appear to be valued at all. Once a body was down to just bones, and the skull had been placed on the wall, it seemed that the rest of the bones were left to slide slowly down the hill and end up wherever, ultimately in the lake I would imagine. Near the cages were a few overturned bowls and dishes. Farther down the hill there was a scattering of human bones laying amid sticks and leaves and a variety of debris, mostly the remnants of the possessions they had been laid to rest with. There were a pair of drinking glasses, two ceramic bowls, a partially-full plastic water bottle, a metal spoon, a wicker basket, four flip-flops, two of them apparently a matched set, and a small glass Coke bottle gone foggy. I told you that you can find Coke everywhere!

The next day we set out for the rice terraces in a flotilla of bright orange or yellow Volkswagen "Things", a model that was briefly seen on US roads in the early 70s. Looking a bit like Jeeps, and spectacularly uncomfortable, they added an unnecessary splash of color to the Balinese countryside. For all of Bali's riotous color, shades of green still dominated the landscape between villages and we were heading for the greenest of green, the Jatiluwih rice terraces.

I had chosen the perfect time of year to visit Indonesia. I arrived at the end of the rainy season. The rains had mostly ended – we saw rain on maybe three days – but the landscape was still lush and green. And this was on full display at Jatiluwih.

With the ever-present volcanoes on the horizon, the terraces descended the slopes and followed the contours of the land. None of Bali's gaudy decorations could have improved the sheer perfection of green on green on green. We walked through the rice fields and saw the remarkable irrigation system that keeps water flowing everywhere it's needed. It is strange but true that the typical tourist will show a keen interest in things that would bore them silly back at home, like farming techniques. We're an easy audience to please.

It was another hot day and rice provides no shade. I was grateful for the bottle of cold water I was given by the driver when I arrived back at our "Thing" and I sat down to drink it in the shadows of a small pavilion.

One thing I appreciated about Indonesia was that, so far, almost no one had pursued me to buy their trinkets or to beg for a handout. That air of financial desperation was not to be seen in Indonesia, at least not where I'd been. There was also a lack of any obvious police or military presence. There were inherent dangers in Indonesia just as surely as there were cobras in the rice fields, but they thankfully remained hidden from me.

This was just the halfway point of the trip but it felt like I'd been in Indonesia for weeks already, in a good way. Each day was so full that it felt like two or three. I was feeling refreshed by the time the rest of the group emerged from the terraces. We had lunch there and then climbed back into our "Things" for the drive to Lovina, on Bali's north coast.

I had arrived about half an hour early for dinner and sat at a table in the hotel's outdoor dining area, about twenty feet from the ocean, a strip of black sand beach between me and the Bali Sea. The sea was dead calm and remained quite shallow a good way from shore. Coral spiked the sea floor and several men were wading through it a hundred yards out in the water, fishing or collecting whatever goodies they could find out there. The sun was beginning to set over the ocean behind a mass of dark cumulus clouds, burning orange holes through them in places. The western sky was going from orange to red as the sun dropped toward the horizon, peeking out from under the clouds as it reached the water. There would be no chance for the reds to turn to purples. Here near the equator the sun set quickly, the whole display lasting no more than fifteen minutes. As full darkness descended and dinner began, I watched the silhouettes of the fishermen, still prying through the coral, now with flashlights or headlamps. This was Lovina, my home for the next two nights.

We made a quick stop at a local market the next morning on our way to spend the better part of the day in a typical Balinese village. We were greeted by the village shaman, shown the village's various crops, and got a look at their usual everyday activities, which involved making things (they seemed to be churning out baskets and bowls), the usual mundane chores of cleaning and food preparation, or the work of planting, tending, and harvesting. When it was time for lunch we handed the items we had bought in the market over to our hosts and together set about helping to prepare lunch, which roaming chickens later helped us eat whenever we dropped something on the ground.

After lunch we were shown the process of making brown sugar and palm wine, which derived from the same source, palm sap. We watched how sap is drawn out of the tree and saw how it makes the transformation to sugar and wine. A bowl of brown sugar chunks was passed around for us to try and cups of palm wine were poured. The wine tasted like rice wine, never a favorite of mine. But the still half-full bowl of brown sugar drew me back to it again and again for "just one more taste".

We were back in Lovina in time to take a walk along the beach as far as Kalibukuk, where an enormous statue of a dolphin, wearing a crown and ringed by several smaller dolphins at its base, dominates a public square. We returned to the hotel in time for another gorgeous sunset. There's nothing quite like watching the sun go down over the ocean. Unless, of course, it's watching the sun *come up* over the ocean.

I was standing on the little strip of black sand

beach early the next morning, watching the sun come up in reds and oranges, the Bali Sea a calm mirror to the fireworks in the sky. We were about to take outrigger canoes across the flat water to a point where the ocean deepened and dolphins could often be spotted. We had been told that some mornings there are plenty to be seen, some mornings few if any. We need not have worried.

Before long groups of a dozen dolphins or more were swimming nearby, breaking the surface and plunging back in. Here and there a lone dolphin would come pirouetting out of the sea, spinning higher and higher before falling back into the water. We had come on one of their most active of days. They were putting on a grand show, without a trainer in sight.

The sun had risen a bit higher by the time we returned to shore. We had only been out about a mile or so and soon thick knots of coral could be seen below the boat in the shallow water. After breakfast on the beach we were on our way again, headed back south.

Bali is not a large island. The drive from Lovina on the north coast to Sanur on the south coast takes only three and a half hours if done in one shot. We broke up our trip with a visit to the splendid Beratan Temple.

More of a park than anything else, the lakeside temple complex has several multi-tiered temple structures rising from knobs of land jutting out into the lake, which is ringed with forested hills. A mosque sits on a hill overlooking the temple complex, like Indonesia's Islam overshadows its little Hindu brother. There are flowers growing in the full spectrum of colors and brightly painted statues of dragons, tigers, at least one owl and one frog. And over there, just beyond the owl, is the revered likeness of SpongeBob SquarePants, holding an "exit" sign with an arrow showing the way out. At this point you say to yourself "yup, looks like I've seen everything now, out I go". And so out I went.

On the extreme southern tip of Bali stands Uluwatu, the Cliffside Temple. Here the land drops straight down into the sea, waves crashing against the high, rocky cliffs, and the small temple stands right at the edge. While there is a path leading directly to the temple, there is another hugging the cliff's edge curving to the right, leading to the best place to view the temple, the cliffs, and the wild sprays of breaking water. But this is also where the monkeys hang out.

The macaques at Uluwatu were much more aggressive than the ones at the Monkey Forest in Ubud. They were daring thieves.

We had been warned not to leave our possessions at risk. We were advised to leave behind hats, sunglasses, and jewelry. I had removed my watch and was being appropriately paranoid about my camera, removing it from my pocket only for the occasional quick shot and only after furtively checking for any macaques nearby. But they were sneaky and fast.

I heard Jumena calling out to a member of my group, Chuck. It was a warning but Chuck was oblivious. Chuck was wearing the sunglasses he had bought just the day before, but not for long. A macaque suddenly jumped onto the wall near where Chuck was standing and in a flash had snatched the sunglasses from his face. Within seconds the glasses had been broken up, with pieces being distributed to several other macaques. Chuck was uninjured and I was not the only member of the group who enjoyed the show with a hearty chuckle.

In my personal experience I have often found Chinese tourists to be loud, rude, and a bit disrespectful, like rules don't pertain to them. But in this case they should have listened. I saw two Chinese teenage girls lose their cell phones to the macaques, the shiny innards of the devices soon strewn on the walkway. I even saw a macaque bounding into the trees with a laptop tucked under its arm, temple security giving chase. I wasn't about to let the monkeys have even a twenty dollar watch. I strapped it back onto my wrist when the visit was over.

Sanur was the perfect place to find dinner on my own that night. The neighborhood around the hotel provided anything a hungry traveler might need. It was jam-packed with both tourists and restaurants, and there was a CocoMart within easy walking distance as well. I settled on a nice-looking Italian restaurant and took a seat outside. Spaghetti and meatballs and a little chocolate ice cream were just the break I needed from rice and satay.

After dinner I wandered up to the CocoMart with buying a snack the excuse to try to break down another 100,000 rupiah bill. As I perused the supermarket (an activity as revealing as watching local TV in my opinion) I came across some one dozen-size cartons of eggs labeled "functional eggs". I have asked many people and even searched the internet, but I can find no one who knows what the term means. If anybody out there knows the answer, give me a call.

We spent another day in the area, visiting Denpasar to join the crowds who had come out for early morning exercise, from jogging to boxing. We visited a beautiful Buddhist temple. I spent more time in and near the hotel's swimming pool. For seven of our group of sixteen the trip would end here – they would fly home from Denpasar in the morning. But nine of us would be continuing on the trip's optional extension to Flores and Komodo. We were just killing time before the final leg of the adventure.

The runway at Labuan Bajo wasn't quite flat, wasn't quite level. The plane shimmied from side to side as we landed and rolled to a stop. We had hopped over a couple of islands to get from Bali to Flores. All the Hindu garishness of Bali was now replaced with purely natural beauty on this island with a Roman Catholic majority.

Arriving in the port town of Labuan Bajo we could see the harbor below us, boats of all sizes dotting the blue water, piers and docks jutting out to meet them. It was another postcard moment.

We still had that glorious view through the windows of the Blue Marlin, a small eatery along L.B.'s main road, where my lunch consisted of the best fish and chips I've ever had. The secret was the fish — instead of the usual boring cod, this featured grouper. It was like eating a big toasted marshmallow made of fish, if that makes any sense.

Labuan Bajo's main road is strictly one-way, so we drove through town in order to circle back and drive to our hotel, the Bintang Flores, about five minutes out of town and on its own beach. The main road runs right along the harbor; the ocean was a deep blue and filled with boats of all kinds — tour boats, dive boats, small personal yachts, and most of all, fishing boats.

Labuan Bajo is all about two things, mostly — fishing and Komodo. Any fish you eat in L.B. was caught that same day. And L.B.'s harbor is the beginning point for visits to the mysterious island of Komodo. There be dragons.

The Bintang Flores had perhaps the best setting of all our accommodations in Indonesia, and the prettiest pool. A debris-free white sand beach began just feet from the pool and the west-facing beach provided the best sunsets of the whole trip. I would be at the pool every afternoon at five thirty to watch the fifteen minutes of atmospheric fireworks. But on this our first night on Flores we would be taking a short drive for a different vantage point (and what would be the trip's ultimate postcard moment).

A short distance out of town we pulled off the road at what was clearly a frequently used viewing spot. Looking west across the water we saw the sun sinking behind a large bump on the horizon, a twin-peaked volcano whose double puffs of dust and ash were silhouetted against the blazing yellow sky. The bright flash of sun just above the volcano, fading to a burnt orange haze all around, gave the impression of an eruption, a cataclysm that would wash us from this viewing spot with a huge tsunami. But the sun descended quickly through its yellows, reds, and oranges and the dark, quiet night soon took its place. The stars came out.

The stars – oh, the stars here were different! Here near the equator some familiar constellations could still be seen, but they were all off, tilted in ways I never see at home. Orion lying on his side, apparently sound asleep. The Big Dipper hanging upside-down, or was it right-side-up? If I'd been navigating by the stars I'd have toppled over.

Two hours by boat from Labuan Bajo, we sailed along Komodo's daunting coast. Its volcanic folds rose high above the water in shades of green, a patchwork of forest and open grass. This island and its fearsome inhabitants were legendarily perilous and famously remote, a speck of land in the Indian Ocean, on the other side of the planet, home to nightmare monsters. Of course I had always wanted to come here! Who wouldn't?

The boat found a small bay where the land was lower and a crooked pier extended well out into the water. We had found the entrance.

At the end of the very long walkway from the pier a sign greeted us -- "Welcome to Komodo National Park", two stone Komodo dragons perched atop it. Just beyond, another sign warned "watch out komodo crossing". Fifty feet beyond that sat the ranger station in a patch of shade.

My little group had almost reached the ranger station when a huge dragon came plodding along the beach, crossing the path we had just been walking, obediently obeying the Komodo crossing sign, and continuing down the beach. We turned like a pack of paparazzi and followed it.

The only good reason for a group of people to follow a Komodo dragon is if they each think they're not the slowest member of the group. Actually, this particular eight-footer wasn't interested in us at all and just kept slowly trudging through the sand, looking for a shady spot, so we got our photos and videos and headed over to the ranger station.

It was time to begin our two-hour hike through the woods and clearings of Komodo, our fearless Ranger leading the way with a weapon deemed sure to keep us all safe in case of attack – a forked stick. Another ranger brought up the rear with his own stick. We encountered another dragon just yards from the station. It reluctantly went away after a few jabs of the stick. I was thinking I could use a stick like that when walking around Albany. A little further along through a wooded area we came to a clearing where another dragon dozed in the shade. His teeth looked like daggers and his claws like can openers. He never moved, just opened one eye. We left him and walked on.

The Komodo dragon grows up to ten feet long and one hundred and fifty pounds, making them the world's largest lizards. If that weren't enough, they're venomous, too.

Komodo dragons will eat just about anything they can find, including young dragons. The first thing a baby Komodo dragon does upon hatching is climb up the nearest tree to get away from mama. The young ones typically need to stay in the trees for their first several years, living on insects and small lizards. The dragons can be found only on Komodo and three or four neighboring islands.

As we continued to hike through Komodo's

woods I wouldn't have been surprised to encounter a T. Rex. It was easily the most prehistoric, primeval place I've ever been. The shadows were sinister, the quiet disquieting. We caught fleeting glimpses of wild boars and colorful butterflies. The path snaked through thickets of gnarled trees, flowering bushes, and wobbly palm trees, some fallen over, their knobby roots having come loose in the sandy soil. We saw several deer, a favorite food of the dragons, and eventually came full circle back to a building near the ranger station where food was being prepared. Eight or ten dragons lazed outside, drawn by the smell of cooking, or garbage, or both. One of them took an interest in my group, and me in particular, walking toward me at a steady pace. The rangers waved me back toward the beach as I shakily filmed my pursuer while I retreated. But I was under the protection of the Forked Stick and therefore immune from harm. I put my camera away and retreated to the back of the group.

There was an open-walled wooden building up ahead, some men inside selling a variety of Komodo souvenirs. And it was there that I found the most mythical beast of all, a creature I had scoured the dark corners of Indonesia looking for, the rarest thing to be found on all of these wild islands – a t-shirt that fit me.

On average, Indonesians are some of the smallest people in the world and I am, in a word, not. As a collector of t-shirts, I had been quite frustrated by how small even the largest ones available were. I mean, come on, plenty of Australian tourists visit Indonesia, too, and they can grow pretty big. We were clearly being discriminated against, me and the Aussies.

As soon as I stepped up into their domain the vendors were upon me. But I fended them off, letting them know I was interested in one thing only, a suitably large shirt. That would be a guaranteed sale, I told them. And even at that, only one of them was able to come up with anything big enough, and he had only one of *those*. A rare beast indeed. And it was a nice shirt. I liked it. I bought it.

The boat took us on a short trip to another part of Komodo where we would be having a picnic lunch on a pink sand beach. We were told the dragons didn't come over this way very often and we had a long view of any that might approach. So I sat in the shade and ate my lunch, which consisted of a ham and cheese sandwich, a bag of cassava chips, and a can of Coke.

The white sand on the beach here had mixed with the tiny, ground-up red shells of small marine creatures that continuously washed ashore, forming a pink mixture that can only be found on a handful of beaches worldwide. The pink color grew and faded in intensity as waves washed up and back down the beach. My footsteps left a pink trail behind me until they filled in with seawater and faded to white again. I tried to wade out into the warm water but the sea bottom was covered with broken pieces of dead coral, unpleasant to step on. I mostly lolled around in the shade and watched the beach turn from white to pink and back to white again, over and over. The horizon, far across a deep blue sea, was dotted with the green humps of other volcanic islands. Our boat bobbed in the waves just offshore, waiting to take us back to the 21st century.

Two hours later we were back in Labuan Bajo and I was soon rinsing off Komodo's grit in the hotel pool, which I had all to myself.

I was standing by the elevator on the hotel's fifth floor when I noticed something amazing out the floor-to-ceiling window. Right there, a few feet away on the other side of the glass, there was a huge beehive clinging to one of the hotel's outer support beams. It looked like a large, flat, spiky cactus leaf, but the spikes were actually a mass of bees that completely hid the hive beneath them. More nests clung to the other struts all the way along the side of the building, forming a sort of hall-of-mirrors perspective.

The glass elevator box arrived and I stepped in, watching my view of the ocean disappear as I was lowered to ground level. It was time for another sunset, and then dinner in town.

We were on our own for dinner that night and the next and Jumena and our local guide were heading into town to eat. Would any of us like to join them? Three from my group, including me, decided to go along.

Right along the harbor in Labuan Bajo are a number of stalls selling and cooking fish freshly caught that day. Each stall consists of a display of colorful fish, a small kitchen space, and a grill with flames shooting out. A row of picnic tables runs along the low harbor wall, boats bobbing up and down just a few feet away. Our guides led us to one of the stalls where we perused the fish and made our selections (white snapper for me). We told them how we wanted our fish prepared (for me it was heads and tails off, filleted, and grilled), crossed the street to buy drinks at a small grocery store, and seated ourselves at a table to wait. A few minutes later our fish was served, along with a steaming bowl of white rice and some mixed veggies. Our guides had requested a soup be made from our discarded heads and tails. The broth was tasty and, although I avoided the heads, I did fish out a tail to try. There's not much meat in there but if you dig it out with a fork it's one of the best parts, soft and buttery. The harbor lights attracted no insects (do they even have insects in Indonesia? I know they do but I never saw any, except for the Trunyan village spiders and the hotel's bees). It was a wonderful dining experience and I returned with our guides the next night for red snapper.

The next day was spent on Flores, first

visiting a tribal village up in the hills called Cecer, where the chief crops were coffee, vanilla, cacao, and various kinds of nuts. They performed some tribal dances that seemed to be a mixture of hopscotch and whip-fighting. Though up in the hills, we still weren't far from the coast; the blue of the ocean could just be seen in the distance.

Next we visited a cave not far from Labuan Bajo. Wearing hard hats with headlamps, we duck-walked under low ceilings to get into the cave. It was an awkward and strenuous descent. I was grateful for my hardhat every time it banged into the rough rock above my head.

Down inside there were the usual things you might associate with a cave – strange rock formations and bats, bats, bats. At least they were all clinging to the walls and ceiling and not flying around us. Entering one large chamber, we all switched off our headlamps to get the full effect of utter and absolute darkness. It was an eerie and uncomfortable feeling. We humans are not used to such darkness – even in the blackest night the stars shine above us. It was hot and incredibly humid in the cave so we quickly turned our lights back on and climbed back out.

The hotel pool was once again the solution to heat and humidity, and I made sure to return there again in time for another sunset before going back into Labuan Bajo for another harborside dinner.

Rinca (pronounced Rin-cha) is Komodo's much less famous sister island and was our destination on our last day on Flores. About half as big as Komodo, and lying a bit closer to Flores, it has a dryer, more desert-y feel than Komodo. Hiking in from the dock we passed some water buffalo wallowing in a shady pond. The land was all open and scrubby until we reached the ranger station, where several small dragons prowled near the buildings. Beyond that lay a tangle of dry forest, home to dragons, cobras, wild boar, deer, and macaques. The hike felt different than our walk around Komodo, a bit hotter but less humid, more open and less dense with vegetation. The only dragons we saw were the ones hanging out by the kitchen garbage, but there were about twenty of them.

On our way back from Rinca we stopped at a small island called Kelor, which was pretty much just a very steep hill with a sandy beach at its base. It was a nice place for a nap – small ankle-biting fish near shore kept me mostly out of the water. We had the small beach to ourselves – another small boat had arrived, but its passengers all seemed intent on climbing the hill for the view. It looked like hot and sweaty work, with a good chance of taking a nasty tumble, so I just sat in the sand and watched the waves roll in until it was time to sail back to Labuan Bajo one last time.

Before flying back to Bali the next day, we had a chance to take a walk through a small village called Nanga Nae. Located near where a river empties into the ocean, the town flooded regularly, so all of the houses were built on stilts. Cows roamed front yards and a massive tree grew out of the center of the town's main road, forcing the motorbikes to ride around it. We stopped to taste the meatballs an old woman was cooking and selling by the side of the road. They tasted pretty good, if a bit gummy.

My time in Indonesia was almost at an end. We would fly back to Denpasar and spend our final night in the nightclub-and-shopping-mall laden Kuta Beach, where a notorious terrorist bombing at a nightclub in 2002 had killed 202 people.

Someone asked me if I was looking forward to going home. At the end of almost every trip I've taken, the answer to that question has been "yes". It has simply felt like time to go home to the old familiar things. This time I thought about tropical weather, swimming pools, chicken satay, new sights, smells, and sounds coming fast and furious every day.

"Hell, no!", I said.

The shopping mall in Kuta had a huge area devoted just to craftsy-looking souvenirs of dubious authenticity and questionable taste, from wooden ashtrays to bottle openers shaped like penises. It was the perfect time to pick up a few items for the folks back home.

The walk from the mall back to the hotel was a long stroll up Kuta Beach's brown sand, past deck chairs and rope swings, bag of souvenirs in hand. I had one last dinner to look forward to, and then, in the morning, the grueling series of flights that would take me home. As I walked up the beach I saw a large airplane coming in low over the water, about to land in nearby Denpasar. That was a fitting sign that it was time for us to go, making room for the new arrivals whose heads would soon be spinning from their first glimpse of magnificent Bali.

I flew from Denpasar back to Taipei, and then on to Los Angeles. This time it would be a little different. Instead of sitting at the airport for eight hours waiting for the next flight, I would be spending the night at a hotel near LAX. My flight arrived in LA around ten that night; I would depart for Chicago, then Albany, in the morning.

The shuttle dropped me off at my hotel for the night, the Four Points by Sheraton Los Angeles. I was tired and thirsty and looking forward to just four simple things, all of which I knew the hotel would be able to provide in short order – a bottle of soda from a vending machine, a quick look at the news and weather on TV, a shower, and a good night's sleep.

The spacious and ferociously carpeted ground floor held numerous meeting rooms, banquet rooms, and conference rooms. It seemed that many of the hotel's clients probably never stayed a night there, just flew into Los Angeles from around the country, or the world, to attend business meetings, with a quick trip back to the airport when they were finished. One look at the rooms on the floors above confirmed the wisdom of that approach.

My cramped third-floor room was halfway down a dimly lit hallway, the room's shower had two temperature settings, icy and scalding, and two directions, straight up and straight down, and every floor had its own vending room, complete with out-of-order soda machines and holes in the floor where the ice machines should have been. I knew there should have been ice machines because one floor actually did have one. It was out of order.

I watched TV for a while, noting, with more than a little surprise and horror, that it had snowed in Albany on this the fourteenth day of May. I was to be greeted by a cold rain when I arrived in Albany. Tropical paradise lay far behind me now. I drank half a glass of warm tap water, set my alarm for the crack of dawn, and fell uneasily asleep.

The next morning I gathered my things and caught the shuttle back to the airport at first light, a good two hours earlier than I needed to. An LAX gate area offered more hope of comfort and style, more chance of rest and refreshment, than the Four Points. Besides, it felt good just to be on my way home again. Chicago next. Then Albany. Forty-two degrees and raining. I hadn't brought a coat, hadn't thought I'd need one. I was missing Indonesia already. But soon it would be time for new Plans, new places. And until then, well, springtime in Albany is not that bad, even when it doesn't start until the middle of May.

Postscript

My travels are all snapshots in time. Some of the places I've been exist almost apart from time. They are simply *there*, solid, unchanging, their presence a constant since time before memory, like Stonehenge or the Himalayas. But even those change – Stonehenge has a new visitors' center and the Himalayas continue to grow higher, millimeter by millimeter.

Some of the countries in which I've traveled would have been much riskier to visit in the years before or the years since I was there. Peru would have been off-limits in the 80s and 90s, though it remains a somewhat risky destination even today. Vietnam in the 60s and 70s would have been a no-go, unless I'd been drafted. Indonesia and Argentina went through their own terrible times. Since my visit to Kenya, that country has become much less safe. Lhasa and Hong Kong have been convulsed by riots. And I'm not sure if I would want to visit Turkey these days, given its increasingly dictatorial leader. Then again, some places, like Cuba and Albania, are just re-opening to the world and look inviting.

Some of the places I've been have changed or disappeared. London has a big Wheel now. The Lake Baringo Club is underwater. The Dutch Guilder has given way to the Euro.

Isaac would be about thirty years old now. The hiking trails to the summit of Poas are closed. The *Orlova* is lost in the North Atlantic. After forty-two years of continual eruption, Arenal has gone dormant since 2010. And the entire landscape of southern Iceland has been altered by massive floods.

New Plans will be made in the future. Perhaps those next trips will form the first chapters of another book. If so, I'd better get going. I have a lot of traveling to do!

Post – Postscript

It's all well and good to have Plans, but we are always subject to the whims of Fortune. As I prepare this book for publication it is April 2020 and the world is at a standstill from the coronavirus pandemic. I will not be going anywhere for awhile. And when the world is open again for tourists and travelers alike there is no telling what may have been altered or lost in the interim. Then again, perhaps, for just a short time at least, the air may be clearer, the beaches cleaner, the wildlife more abundant. It's a new world every time you venture out into it. And while I may be homebound for now, one thing remains true – I still have a lot of traveling to do!

There and Back Again
(Flight Routing)

Chapter One: New York (Kennedy) to London (Gatwick)
               London (Heathrow) to New York (Kennedy)

Chapter Two: New York (Kennedy) to London (Heathrow)
               Shannon to New York (Kennedy)

Chapter Three: New York (Kennedy) to Amsterdam
               Amsterdam to Nairobi
               Nairobi to Amsterdam
               Amsterdam to New York (Kennedy)

Chapter Four: New York (Kennedy) to Keflavik
               Keflavik to New York (Kennedy)

Chapter Five: New York (Kennedy) to Casablanca
               Casablanca to New York (Kennedy)

Chapter Six: Albany to New York (Kennedy)
               New York (Kennedy) to Vancouver

	Vancouver to Hong Kong
	Hong Kong to Hanoi
	Hanoi to Danang
	Hue to Saigon
	Saigon to Hong Kong
	Hong Kong to Vancouver
	Vancouver to New York (Kennedy)
	New York (Kennedy) to Albany
Chapter Seven:	Albany to Philadelphia
	Philadelphia to Miami
	Miami to Quito
	Quito to Baltra
	Baltra to Lima
	Lima to Cusco
	Cusco to Lima
	Lima to Miami
	Miami to Charlotte
	Charlotte to Albany
Chapter Eight:	Albany to Chicago (O'Hare)
	Chicago (O'Hare) to Miami
	Miami to San Jose
	San Jose to Miami
	Miami to Chicago (O'Hare)
	Chicago (O'Hare) to Albany
Chapter Nine:	Albany to Washington (Dulles)
	Washington (Dulles) to Buenos Aires (Ezeiza)
	Buenos Aires (Newbery) to Ushuaia
	Ushuaia to Buenos Aires (Ezeiza)
	Buenos Aires (Ezeiza) to Washington (Dulles)
	Washington (Dulles) to Albany

Chapter Ten: Albany to Chicago (O'Hare)
                    Chicago (O'Hare) to Beijing
                    Xian to Wuhan
                    Chengdu to Lhasa
                    Lhasa to Chengdu
                    Chengdu to Hong Kong
                    Hong Kong to Chicago (O'Hare)
                    Chicago (O'Hare) to Albany

Chapter Eleven: Albany to Washington (National)
                    Washington (National) to New York (Kennedy)
                    New York (Kennedy) to Istanbul
                    Istanbul to Kayseri
                    Izmir to Istanbul
                    Istanbul to New York (Kennedy)
                    New York (Kennedy) to Washington (National)
                    Washington (National) to Albany

Chapter Twelve: Albany to Newark
                    Newark to Los Angeles
                    Los Angeles to Taipei
                    Taipei to Jakarta
                    Jakarta to Yogyakarta
                    Yogyakarta to Denpasar
                    Denpasar to Labuan Bajo
                    Labuan Bajo to Denpasar
                    Denpasar to Taipei
                    Taipei to Los Angeles
                    Los Angeles to Chicago (O'Hare)
                    Chicago (O'Hare) to Albany

How Many Miles Away?
(Distances from Albany, New York)

Place	Miles Away
San Jose, Costa Rica	2346
Reykjavik, Iceland	2494
Quito, Ecuador	2977
Dublin, Ireland	3084
Edinburgh, Scotland	3158
Baltra, Galapagos Islands	3168
London, England	3369
Amsterdam, Netherlands	3546
Casablanca, Morocco	3557
Marrakech, Morocco	3609
Fes, Morocco	3671
Lima, Peru	3786
Cusco, Peru	3882
Istanbul, Turkey	4919
Kayseri, Turkey	5280
Buenos Aires, Argentina	5426
Beijing, China	6696
Ushuaia, Argentina	6740

Xian, China	7115
Nairobi, Kenya	7316
Deception Island, South Shetlands	7338
Lhasa, Tibet	7350
Neko Harbor, Antarctica	7610
Vernadsky Base, Antarctica	7674
Hong Kong, China	7922
Hanoi, Vietnam	8037
Saigon, Vietnam	8745
Jakarta, Indonesia	9916
Labuan Bajo, Indonesia	9934
Yogyakarta, Indonesia	10016
Denpasar, Indonesia	10027
Uluwatu Cliffside Temple, Indonesia (farthest from home I've ever been)	10035

Made in United States
North Haven, CT
02 May 2024